Below Me, the Clouds

Ron Collard

Onwards and Upwards Publications, Berkeley House,
11 Nightingale Crescent, West Horsley, Surrey KT24 6PD

www.onwardsandupwards.org

ISBN: 978-1-907509-31-5
Cover design: Leah-Maarit

Printed in the UK

Dedication

This book is dedicated to my wonderful family: my wife Elizabeth, who has been my loving and faithful co-pilot as we have climbed through life's clouds and sunshine together over the past fifty four years; our four children and their spouses; our fourteen grandchildren; and our three great-grandchildren... so far!

Author's Note

All royalties from this book will be donated to 'Caring for Life' at Crag House Farm, Cookridge, Leeds LS16 7NH. This charity (UK registration 519138) shows the love of Christ in practical terms to vulnerable citizens of our society, many of whom are literally cared for throughout their lives.

Photographs

Most of the photographs originate from me or my family. Others of a military nature were taken prior to 1st January 1961 and are no longer bound by Crown Copyright. Those of individual service personnel, taken after that date and still living, have been included with their kind permission.

Acknowledgements

I am indebted to all those individuals who have contributed in some measure to the publication of this book.

I pay tribute to the Rev. Jim Baker, a prefect with me at the Purley County Grammar School who, fifty three years later, proved to be the final prod in my putting pen to paper.

Initial drafts were dutifully perused by my wife Elizabeth, my sister Mrs. Betty Smith and my brother the Rev. Canon Harold Collard who, between them, corrected some of the family and domestic details. Later drafts were read by Brigadier Ian Dobbie, Squadron Leader Bob Abbott MBE and Mrs. Doris McCartney who together contributed many helpful comments.

I am most grateful to a number of individuals who granted their permission to be identified and for their correction of some details regarding the narrative involving them - in particular Squadron Leader Dick Bell, Mrs. Pippa Bullock, the Rev. Kevin Gruer, Squadron Leader Peter de Bourcier and Robin Oake QPM.

The advice and guidance of the Publications Clearance Branch and the Crown Copyright Unit of the Ministry of Defence was much appreciated.

I acknowledge Edgar A. Guest (1881-1959) with the poem 'I'd rather see a sermon...' and the late Miss L. R. Burden with 'Wings', the original of which she gave me in her own handwriting. The poem 'Monday Mornings' has an anonymous author, and I have been unable to trace its source of publication. I also acknowledge A. B. Simpson (1843-1919) as the author of the chorus 'Yesterday, today, forever...'

My particular thanks go to General the Lord Dannatt GCB, CBE, MC, DL for writing the foreword and to my publishers who displayed such patience with a first time author!

Figures

Contents

BELOW ME, THE CLOUDS

Preface

"Why don't you write a book?"

This question has been put to me on many occasions over the years, particularly after giving illustrated talks to various groups under the title 'A Pilot's Story', or in general conversation with people who have kindly enquired about my life and work.

In consultation with diaries, personal letters and documents, my pilot's log books and various isolated articles written previously, I began to forge a more detailed record of my life experience. What title should I give it?

Climbing through solid cloud and breaking into a new world of sunshine and dazzling blue sky has been my delightful experience on numerous occasions. My life has been like that: living through clouds of war, fear, illness, disappointment, heart-ache, anxiety, failure and despair. I have, however, been lifted through them and above them - not by my own native wit, intelligence or wisdom but by a Power outside of my limited being, yet discernable in history and in the rough-and-tumble of modern everyday life.

I have written 'Below Me, the Clouds' in the hope of encouraging my readers to climb higher and view the clouds of their lives from a different perspective and, in so doing, to be introduced to the most wonderful Friend who can bring them "out of darkness into His marvellous light".

Ron Collard
Ripon
July 2011

Foreword by General the Lord Dannatt

The exhilarating sensation of being above the clouds can only really be appreciated fully by those who have had the privilege of flying. As the aircraft at which one is on the controls bursts through the upper layers of cloud and into the bright sunshine above, the lifting of one's heart and the thrill of the blue sky above and the white clouds below knows no comparison. The claustrophobic uncertainty of flying through cloud always produces a nagging anxiety, but the explosion into the sunshine and blue sky above instantly transforms everything. Ron Collard has experienced these sensations on countless occasions and shares his clouds and his blue skies with his readers on every page of this enchanting book. For Ron, flying was never an end in itself. It was a means to an end, bringing others into the Kingdom of God - that loving God who is the creator of the sky and the clouds that Ron so loves moving amongst.

The twenty three chapters of this book tell the story of Ron Collard from schoolboy to trainee pilot, through a career in the Royal Air Force to a second career with Mission Aviation Fellowship and on to further challenges beyond. The story is open, honest and most engaging. Once begun, it is hard to put down, but it is not just the narrative that holds the attention. From the story in the prologue about his father in no mans' land on the Western Front, through successive chapters, there is constant reference to the word 'constraint'. Just as Ron's father was constrained not to move early from his observation post in the mud of Flanders, a move that might have cost him his life, so Ron and his wife, Elizabeth, were constrained on many occasions to do or not to do something. At the time many of these constraints seemed inexplicable, but a loving Heavenly Father had a plan for the couple that kept them walking in His way and doing His will, both above and below the clouds. In reading these pages, it is clear that Ron both believed and trusted in the promises of God and, like a pilot flying on instruments through cloud, he knew that the outcome would be good. He quotes Romans 8, verse 28 from conviction: "For we know that all things work together for good to those who love God."

It is, however, some of the small incidents that make this book so arresting. A failed Maths exam meant an extension to basic training which enabled Ron and Elizabeth to develop their relationship into marriage. An old-fashioned filmstrip fired Ron's curiosity and took him into his second career with Mission Aviation Fellowship. An inexplicable chemical imbalance in his head produced crushing depression just months into a period of church ministry. These are all episodes that illustrate that a life spent seeking and following the will of God, without knowing the outcome but believing and trusting in Him, is a life lived with purpose and conviction.

After rising through the clouds and enjoying the vast expanse of the open skies, a pilot must eventually bring his aircraft back to earth. Even for the most experienced pilot that moment of touch down is another moment of anxiety, then followed by relief that all is well. What shines through the pages of this book is the absolute certainty held by Ron – a certainty that he wishes to share with so many more – that a life lived in the service of our Lord Jesus Christ will one day be greeted 'above the clouds' with the words of welcome: "Well done, good and faithful servant." (Matthew 25, verse 21). Read on, if you want to fully understand that certainty, and take the opportunity to share in it, if you do not share in it already.

> *"Those who hope in the Lord will renew their strength.*
> *They will soar on wings like eagles;*
> *They will run and not grow weary,*
> *They will walk and not be faint."*
> (Isaiah 40, verse 31, NIV)

General the Lord Dannatt GCB CBE MC DL
President, Soldiers' and Airmen's Scripture Readers Association,
Colonel Commandant, Army Air Corps 2004-2009

Figure 1: My Dad: Trooper F W K Collard, 16th/5th Lancers, on "Bones"
before going to France.

Prologue

The human slaughter of the Great War was raging in Belgium and France. Among the many men called to the colours in those days of 1914-1918 was a young man, small in stature, sporting a waxed moustache (fashionable in those days) and wearing the khaki uniform and brown riding boots of a cavalryman.

His cap and collar badges marked him as a trooper of the 16th/5th Lancers. Around his left upper arm was stitched a blue and white horizontal band identifying him as a signaller. Riding a horse called 'Bones', with a lance in his hand and a rifle sheathed on the saddle, he was a forerunner of the World War Two dispatch rider, responsible for taking messages between headquarters and the front line. On his right cuff he sported the brass crossed rifles of an army marksman.

Sometimes, on his frequent visits to the front line, he was ordered to remain overnight and fulfil the duties of an infantryman in the trenches. Thus it was on this particular night.

He was tasked to watch the enemy positions. This was achieved by crawling over the top and out into no man's land where he would find a suitable foxhole, about half way between his own and the enemy trenches, to listen for any movement that might suggest the enemy's preparations for a night attack. In such an event he was to fire an illuminating flare into the sky to light up the enemy trenches and simultaneously alert the friendly forces behind him. He was under orders to stay at his post until the first streaks of dawn appeared in the eastern sky. He would then be free to forsake his foxhole and crawl back to the comparative safety of the British trenches.

Increasingly cold, tired and hungry, he remained watching the empty blackness throughout the night, fingering the trigger guard on his flare pistol. Alongside him was his loaded rifle. Absolute silence, alertness and keen observation were essential.

Eventually the lightening eastern sky heralded another uncertain day and the soldier considered it time to vacate his post and crawl muddily home. Hardly had the thought passed through his mind than he was aware of an almost physical constraint upon him to remain a little longer.

Seconds later he was aware of two shadows rising from the ground only a few yards in front of his position. They materialised into the unmistakable silhouettes of two *coal-scuttle* helmets – the headgear worn by the German infantry. The British soldier reached quietly for his rifle. He could easily get shots at both and, at that range, could hardly miss!

Poised to fire, a further constraint came upon him: "Those chaps and I have been doing the same job. We've been within a few yards of each other all night. If I'd moved off first, I'd doubtless be dead by now. No - my life has been spared and I shall spare theirs."

Having seen his shadowy adversaries melt into the remaining darkness, the grateful soldier, shaking a little from the shock of the incident, quietly crawled back to the British trenches. The soldier was my father, Frederick William Kellond Collard, and without that almost physical constraint placed upon him that night, this book would never have been written. I was to become acquainted with that constraint myself in years to come. What was it and whence did it come?

A Boy's War

The chilling wail of the air-raid sirens yet again filled the warm August air. Mum grabbed a few essentials that were always kept ready at hand for such occasions, and we hastened to the shelter at the bottom of our back garden. Hardly had we arrived before we heard the distinctive desynchronised drone of the Luftwaffe bombers as they approached their target. Was it to be one of the nearby airfields at Kenley, Biggin Hill, Redhill or Croydon?

The local anti-aircraft batteries boomed their challenge to the bombers which steadily drew nearer until a faint whistling could be heard which rapidly grew louder. Mum pulled me to the ground and covered me with her own body. She placed her hands over my ears in a brave attempt to stifle the frightening scream of the falling bombs. A series of nearby explosions followed - then the silence. Only the receding drone of the invaders could be heard along with the continuing salvoes from the anti-aircraft guns.

Mum was breathing heavily and her voice quivered as she assured me all was well. The steady note of the sirens eventually sounded again, this time heralding the 'all clear'. The danger of death had passed once again, but how had the rest of the family fared - Dad, selling furniture in the centre of Croydon, my sister working on the periphery of Croydon airfield and my two brothers at school in Coulsdon? Mum and I would have to wait until they came home, if they came home at all, as there was no means of checking on their welfare. I was five years old.

I was born on the 20th July 1935 and was christened at All Saints' Church in Sanderstead on the 15th September. In half a decade that date would become one of the greatest dates in the history of human conflict but not because of my christening!

I was named 'Ronald' after my godfather, Ronald Allison, who had been an engineer officer in the Royal Flying Corps. I was the 'tail-end Charlie' of the family. My sister Betty was fifteen years my senior; my eldest brother Fred had a ten year start on me and Harold, eight. Apparently my parents had asked Harold if he would like a puppy or a baby as a birthday gift and he, having a mental aberration, had chosen the latter!

My earliest recollections are of lying in my cot, alongside my mother's side of the bed, at No. 6, Brancaster Lane, Purley (in the county of Surrey). I soon became conscious of the steam trains puffing and clanking over the bridge which spanned nearby Riddlesdown Road and, as soon as I was able to utter a few words, was frequently yelling for Mum to take me to the window to view this remarkable feat of locomotion, but as Southern Rail prospered and the timetable became more extensive, Mum soon tired!

Our house was a typically middle-class suburban detached house, painted chocolate and cream, with a garden front and back and a garage for Dad's Morris 8 which was soon to become a victim to the Luftwaffe's incendiary bombs. 'Uncle' Allison and his wife Judy, together with their young daughter Barbara, were frequent visitors, being my parents' closest friends at the time.

On one of our visits to the Allisons', we spent the whole evening making confetti for Barbara's forthcoming marriage to a sergeant in the RAF. We were each presented with a paper punch and sheets of old newspapers. The resulting little circles were carefully collected into paper bags in readiness for the great day. Such was the ingenuity required during the war when confetti and other trivial luxuries were not available.

Dad and Uncle Allison frequently played bowls on the back lawn (Uncle bowled for Surrey) and spent many evenings and weekends as a foursome with their wives, drinking wine, smoking cigarettes and playing whist.

Uncle Allison was an estate agent, a very tall, imposing man with a deep, loud and resonant voice. On one occasion he greeted me by grabbing me under the armpits and hoisting me, arm's length, above his head as men are wont to do with toddlers. For me it was like going to the moon – I 'screamed blue murder'! Being also a kindly man, Uncle immediately returned me to earth with a puzzled frown on his face, and I retreated upstairs to my cot at the double, shaking with fear and bawling my head off! It took a long time for Mum to pacify me, and I wonder if my life-long acrophobia stemmed from that experience!

Figure 2: "The two Ronnies" with me on the right! The other chap is Lieut. Ron Allison RFC (Ret'd), my Godfather.

Mum frequently had her friends call round on an afternoon, and I heard many a 'blow by blow' account of operations undergone, illnesses suffered, all the local gossip and the details of how Hitler had most recently imposed himself upon their lives.

Home was not always a happy place. I remember the raised voices, slammed doors, periods of sulky silence and the frequent exhortation levelled at me: "Don't start!" (I never quite fathomed what it was that I was to refrain from starting.)

In those days it seemed to me that my seven deadly sins in the sight of my adult family took the following form:

1. ...was never washing,
2. ...was being late,
3. ...was leaving something good uneaten on my plate,
4. ...was dodging bedtime,
5. ...was 'up all night',
6. ...was always being wrong, and
7. ...always right!

All of which I found thoroughly confusing!

Being in the days before the National Health Service, falling ill cost money as did inoculations and vaccinations. Visits to the doctor were therefore rare but occasionally a home visit was required. Such was the case when all three of us boys went down with chicken pox and had to sleep in the dining room to ease Mum's nursing mileage.

My dominant recollection of a home visit was not, however, from a doctor but from a dentist! I was ill in bed at the time, unable to attend the dentist's surgery, so he came to me. Fittingly his name was Mr. Drewitt – an old man, as most of the younger dentists were in the armed forces. He had to extract a couple of my teeth and he did so as I lay on my bed! I cannot remember if he used a cocaine injection as an anaesthetic, which was the common method in those days, or gas from a portable cylinder. I believe it was the latter. Not a pleasant experience either way!

Some early memories were good and formed certain creativity in me for which I have been eternally grateful. Being the youngest by eight years, I generally had to find my own entertainment as 'the boys' (my brothers) were involved in homework, 'rugger' and the army cadet corps which were all way above me. My sister was out working her way in the world at Trojans near Croydon airfield.

Each week took on a certain pattern, in spite of Hitler's frequent and malevolent interruptions which had begun a couple of months after my fourth birthday. Afternoons were usually spent going to see someone, having someone come to see us, cowering from the bombs in the air-raid shelter or listening to the *wireless* while Mum sewed, knitted, stitched or darned.

Monday was primarily wash-day when mother, as usual, clothed in her cross-over apron and 'sensible' shoes would boil up buckets full of water on the gas stove. She would immerse a small proportion of the dirty clothing, being careful to separate whites from coloureds; drop in a *blue bag* which, wonder of wonders, made the clothing extra white; then fish each steaming item out with a wooden stick before immersing it again into a sink-full of hot water in order to rinse it. All this took a long time as each section of the laundry was put through the procedure and the water frequently changed.

Once retrieved from the hot water, each item was then wrung out and prepared for the *mangle*, which was a contraption consisting of two horizontal rollers, mounted one above the other, and held together by powerful springs. Mum turned a hand wheel with her right hand, which operated the contra-rotating rollers, and with her left she steered the item of clothing through the small gap between them. Thus the excess water was squeezed out to run down a spout into a bucket, which frequently had to be emptied. Many a button was crushed, which added to Mum's household tasks as each had subsequently to be replaced. Like the buttons, Mum's fingers were often in conflict with the rollers!

The mangling done, the clothes were then, on bad weather days, systematically arrayed on the *airer*, which was a framework of horizontal wooden laths supported in a metal frame at each end and hauled up by ropes and pulleys into the warmer air immediately below the ceiling of the kitchen. In the better weather the clothes would be pegged on a line suspended in the back garden with a *clothes prop* positioned half way along to prevent it drooping and dragging the clothes on the ground. Occasionally the line would break and all Mum's conscientious work spoiled, requiring an abridged action replay of the morning's chores.

Tuesday was ironing-day. Each item of clothing was lovingly stretched out on the dining room table, suitably covered to replace the ironing board we never possessed and, after the heavy irons (and they *were* heavy) had been heated on the gas stove, everything was pressed until creaseless: underclothes, shirts, blouses, trousers, shorts, skirts, towels, flannels, tea towels, handkerchiefs, socks, slips, 'woollies', pyjamas, night dresses, etc. All went under the iron which had to be re-heated after virtually every item. Mum stood to do this, and it frequently took her all day, interspersed with peeling potatoes, shelling peas, baking, roasting and generally preparing the family's daily meals from the meagre rations available in war-time.

A particular bonus to me was when Mum took the cover off her *Singer* sewing machine before going about her repair jobs. I would invert it, sit in it and perform such manoeuvres which I now associate with a primal aircraft simulator. As I shifted my weight, it rolled beautifully from side to side, yawed both left and right as I heaved on a nearby table leg, and even pitched back into a climb if I transferred my weight aft. All this with do-it-yourself sound effects! Many an imaginary Hun was shot down in flames as a result of meeting up with me in my single-seater Singer.

Wednesday afternoon was Dad's half-day off, so Mum's morning was usually spent sewing on buttons, darning socks, and generally repairing our clothing on the often quoted principle 'a stitch in time saves nine'. After a cooked lunch, Dad would help Mum with the washing up and then turn his hand to gardening, carrying out repairs to parts of the house which had suffered damage from the bombing, making the air-raid shelter more comfortable or, occasionally, sit reading a book or playing a game of billiards on the half-size snooker table in the front room. This, of course, was assuming that he had not been up half the previous night on duty as an Air Raid Warden prior to going to work next morning. Whatever he was doing, he would invariably be puffing at his *Saint Bruno*-filled pipe. Sometimes he just slept in his favourite armchair.

Dad was also an accomplished cabinet-maker by trade and spent much of his off-duty time in the garage with his awesome array of tools, wood and pungent-smelling glue which boiled, bubbling in a pot over a small, hissing gas-ring. In this way he provided us, among other things, with a hall stand made of rose wood complete with mirror, shelves, cupboards, umbrella stands and carved pillars and facades. Back in 1909, when he was an apprentice cabinet-maker, he had constructed a beautifully carved cabinet which housed all our 78 records and the snooker and billiard sets. Still in good condition, it is now in the possession of my eldest son. Dad also took the time to make me a toy rifle which I promptly broke. Dad mended it - bless him - again and again!

Thursday was shopping day, when I would accompany Mum on the bus or tram to Croydon, where we would drag around endless shops surveying materials, woollies, and utility bargains which all seemed to my boyish understanding to cost 'nine and eleven' plus coupons.

The outing would include a visit to Mr. Lane the Chemist. He stood miles high and always spoke with his eyes closed or with eyelids fluttering. A quietly cheerful, corpulent man with a slow and purposeful gait, he would unhurriedly accommodate Mum's requirements and engage her in extra-mural conversation until his next customer appeared - which was usually after a very long time!

We would also visit the grocer, unfortunately named Mr. Mould. Here I would enjoy seeing him slicing the hams with his rotary cutter, pulling the wire through the cheeses to produce just the weight that our ration books allowed. My particular delight was to see Mum's money put into a small can and shot across the shop on a spring-loaded aerial pulley system to the cashier's cubicle. Here a receipt would be issued, change placed in the can and shot back to Mr. Mould. Great to watch!

Then we were off to the butchers! Here one walked on sawdust which was designed to soak up spilt blood and watched a man in a blue-and-white striped apron and straw hat aggressively hacking at lumps of meat as the customer demanded and the ration books permitted. Looking at the state of the butcher's fingers it was obvious that he had occasionally missed the target! Frequently one heard the statement "Sorry Mrs. Collard. You can only have two chops this week and your ration book will only give you a small leg of mutton. I could give you a couple of kidneys if you want them." Such were the limits to our wartime diet.

Rationing came into being on 8th January 1940 due to the increasing success of the German U-boats sinking supplies in the Atlantic, and continued until 4th July 1954. Each person's weekly ration was: one egg per week, 50 grams of cheese, 50 grams of butter, 57 grams of dripping, 100 grams of margarine, 100 grams of bacon/ham, 225 grams of sugar, 50 grams of tea, 1200-1800 ml. of milk, and meat to the value of today's 6p. In addition one was allowed one dried egg and 350 grams of sweets per month and 450 grams of jam per two months.

Food was frequently supplemented with local rabbits, chickens, home-grown vegetables and home-made bread. Posters on the hoardings, in public transport and shops, constantly reminded us of the human cost of our food. One poster in particular remains vividly in my memory. It depicted cigarette ends stubbed out in a plate of half eaten food. In the background was a sinking ship. The caption read: "This food cost sailors' lives!" I still become inwardly angry when I see wasted food today - not only because of the cost of getting it to our plates but also the cost of human life lost through famine and malnutrition in under-developed and war-torn countries where starving people would give anything to eat our waste!

On 1st June 1941 *clothing coupons* were introduced and were in force until 15th March 1949. To give some idea of the restrictions, a mackintosh used up 16 coupons out of one's annual allocation of 66.

Very occasionally, on our shopping sprees, I was allowed to spend time looking around the toy shop, but rarely was anything actually bought. The highlight of the safari was to go upstairs at Wilson's café and have a cup of tea, or coffee if it was available. Often it was *Camp Coffee* made of chicory. I well remember the quaint chocolate and cream milk jugs with their white floral décor in relief; the high-backed wooden 'pews' which formed the open cubicles in which four people sat; and the waitresses in their black dresses, white aprons and caps.

On the way home we would call in at the newsagent which delivered our *Daily Express* newspaper, and Mum would pay for the papers, get the weekly Saint Bruno tobacco for Dad's pipe, a supply of *Craven A* cigarettes, (or *Player's* if available) and, joy of joys, my comic *The Champion*!

Friday was an exciting day as the weekend was upon us and, although Dad would be working all day on Saturday, the boys would not be at school so, if I was lucky, I might be played with in some shape or form. However...

Saturday was sports day for the boys but not before they had dug some of the vegetable garden (which, before the war, had been all lawn), mown what remained of the lawn, cut the edges, swept the paths, washed all the windows on the outside and done any other chore which Mum and Dad deemed necessary. Then it was back to school (would you believe!) either to play in, or support, the school rugger team. Often they took me with them, sometimes accompanied by my sister. The touchline was always crowded with school supporters who cheered their team and generally demoralized the opposition.

Every year the school held a *Hobbies Saturday* when all the pupils would spend the morning setting up their various leisure pursuits in the main hall: toy soldiers, woodcraft, art, sculpture, models, *Meccano*, metalwork, train lay-outs and much more. In the afternoon the parents, friends, masters and pupils would tour the school and enjoy seeing all the exhibited hobbies. In the gymnasium the flying model aircraft were displayed, or outside on the playing fields if the weather was fair. The cadet corps would also parade.

Sunday was the one day of the week when the family were all together, except when my Dad or sister were on duty as local air-raid wardens. Sometimes the boys had to be away at night on fire-watching duty at the school. Generally, Sunday was a day of rest. We would go to church in the morning and enjoy a super Sunday lunch that was the culmination of Mum's progressive preparation over the previous week. On the day itself my sister would help Mum with all the last minute necessities. There was the usual 'culinary council' after the first few mouthfuls: "Are the potatoes done?" "I think the Brussels could have done with a bit more salt." "The mutton could have been in longer." Who cared about the finesse; it was food!

Lunch over and it was time for the family to be involved with washing up, drying up and putting away all the dinner paraphernalia. My job was to brush the tablecloth, remove it from the table, fold it and put it in the drawer, and wipe the place mats with a dishcloth.

Chores completed, Dad would relax in his armchair and either sleep, read a book or both in turn! Mum would follow suit. The boys would walk to their *Crusaders* Bible Class for three o'clock, and my sister and I would walk even further to Sunday school at the Kenley Methodist Church where she was a teacher. On Sunday evenings we invariably listened to the wireless or played family games around the table until it was my bed-time, which I delayed as much as possible.

Assuming Hitler did not have other ideas, I would wake up the following morning to live another week on the same pattern until I too would be known as one of the boys! Unfortunately, by the time I reached that lofty perch, the boys were young men and I was still in short trousers!

Christmas time was always special. The whole family would be together for at least two days and sometimes three. During the previous week the decorations would be brought down from the loft, dusted and strung up. They comprised red and green streamers radiating from the central light in the ceiling and draped with tinsel at regular intervals. Silver bells also featured.

The front room came into its own at this season. The snooker table was turned through ninety degrees and pushed back against the wall where it served as a table for drinks, including Mum's home-made ginger wine and a few special Christmas goodies. The settee and armchairs were drawn around the coal fire and the gramophone played all the old carols. Usually snow fell, giving one the atmosphere of mystery and majesty. A real kid's Christmas in spite of the war!

Although I did not believe there was a real Father Christmas, I always hung a woollen sock up on Christmas Eve and was delighted to find it bulging in the morning! Contents would include sweets such as were available in the war years, an orange if I was really lucky, pencils or crayons, perhaps a small ball, something 'necessary' such as a vest, pair of pants or some handkerchiefs. My presents on Christmas Day would hardly excite a modern young boy but each was precious. My favourite came from my parents: the *Boys' Book of Soccer*. Other gifts might include a model aircraft and usually something aimed to improve my education, my attire or my health. (Rose-hip syrup was not infrequent.)

Christmas Eve was the day I always went shopping with the remnant of my pocket money (I was given 3 pennies per week, approximating to 1.25 pence in today's currency) to buy presents for the rest of the family. It was amazing what useful things you could purchase in *Woolworth's* at the last minute! In those days it was known as *The Six Penny Store* where nothing cost more than sixpence (2½p)

On Christmas Day we would all go to church in the morning, enjoy a chicken for dinner and listen to the King's broadcast in the afternoon. As the national anthem was played we would all stand. Games were played, drinks were drunk, and goodies were consumed. Neighbours and friends would call in at some time including, invariably, the Allison family. There would be much laughter and chatter, games played, food and drink consumed and cigarettes smoked.

The décor and furniture of our home was functionally simple. Sepia and monochrome photographs hung on the walls, including one of Dad in uniform on his horse; one of each of my grandparents; my parents' wedding photo; and one of my sister in her *Guides* uniform, which was colour tinted. There was also a 'head and shoulders' portrait in crayon of me when aged about twelve months. The picture that stands out most in my memory is that of *The Taking of the Guns* which monopolised one wall in the boys' bedroom. It depicted lancers, at full gallop, attacking a German field-gun battery: guns versus lances and the lances won! On the reverse side of that picture was one portraying Christ amid several animals, and the quote from Isaiah chapter 11, verse 6: "The wolf also shall dwell with the lamb, the leopard shall lie down with the young goat, the calf and the young lion and the fatling together; and a little Child shall lead them."

I was unaware of this picture until my brother Harold told me of it just four years ago. He made the comment that this typified the family's outlook at that time: warfare and conflict predominant, the Word of God present but hidden in the background.

Below the picture was a large ink blot on the wall paper which stood as a permanent witness to the fact that the boys were not always as angelic as they seemed! Due to the restrictions of war and the fact that, in those days, the house might not be there tomorrow, let alone the wall, the blot and the wallpaper remained until after I had joined the Royal Air Force in 1954!

Around our home were various mottos etched in wood with a hot poker. Among the collection I specifically remember was "The great thing in life is not to win the game but to play a bad hand well!" Another: "Some men are trying; others are very!" – It took me all my adolescent life to work that one out!

A particular treat was when Dad and the boys set up the toy soldiers. Between them they had some 400 lead models, all individually painted in detail and in pristine condition. There was the massed band of the Coldstream Guards (complete with goat mascot!), cavalry both in khaki and in full dress, infantry, artillery with field guns and a howitzer which actually fired shells, aircraft, pilots, guardsmen in grey greatcoats, sailors hauling a gun, and many different khaki figures in various firing postures in addition to the marching hoards - some with flat caps and some with steel helmets. When the whole collection was sold, many years later, most of the models were still in their original boxes and cotton wool padding.

Dad, with his usual creativity and imagination, had made some very realistic trenches from wood and old rags, suitably painted. They had intricate trench systems, dug-outs, firing positions, sandbags and barbed wire entanglements. Even realistic shell-holes featured. They were kept in the loft and needed extensive dusting before use. Once the whole show was displayed on the table tennis tops surmounting the snooker table and the aircraft strung up from the ceiling, the Great War was graphically evident. With marches played on the gramophone, parades were held and battles fought – all in our front room!

Subsequently, when the boys were away in the army, that same snooker table and the table tennis tops became the foundation of my football ground. Two long floor mats were placed side by side on the tops, a green sheet carefully draped over them and pressed with an iron. With French chalk I marked out a soccer pitch, to the scale of the *Subbuteo* players, complete with corner and half-way flags. The goals, again built to scale, comprised wire enclosed in white, tubular, woven material used by Dad to clean his pipe. The net supports were made of wire bent to shape and glued to the pipe cleaner at the top of the posts. The nets, shaped and cut as required, once held Mum's hair in place.

Out of cardboard and plywood I built a scale grandstand which stretched almost the length of the pitch, complete with a players' tunnel, turnstiles and tiers of seating made from corrugated cardboard. Two dug-outs were also made and positioned either side of the players' tunnel and even two buckets, borrowed from our model farm, served as the receptacles for the trainers' *magic sponges!*

I had been an early customer of Mr. P. A. Adolph, of Langton Green, Tunbridge Wells, who, from his home, created the famous game of Subbuteo Table Soccer. Each cardboard figure was inserted into a plastic hemispherical base which was flicked by the finger to propel it. The footballer was thus able to dribble, shoot, body swerve, yet remain upright most of the time. As the production progressed, the cardboard figures gave way to plastic, and more and more different teams became available in their true colours. Goalkeepers were also mounted on their hemispherical bases, but each had a detachable rod, some four inches long, slotted into a hole in the rear of the base to facilitate the goalie's manipulation by hand from behind the goal. Thus he was able to block shots and, detached from his rod, take the goal kicks.

I spent many happy hours playing all on my own, running league fixtures, cup ties and internationals, but it was a bonus when I found that one or two other lads in the district also had the game. Now it became really serious! Teams travelled 'away' and had to adapt to other grounds. The competition was intense!

Looking back on these days, I thank God for them. I find it pathetic to hear modern kids complaining that there is nothing to do - hanging around and getting into trouble because nobody is giving them facilities for 'having a good time'. Where is their creativity? Where is their initiative?

Modelling aircraft out of wooden kits was another favourite hobby, and I even built a few from balsa wood and tissue paper that actually flew, but perhaps the happiest memory of my earlier days was when Dad had the time to play table tennis with me and taught me billiards and snooker.

During the earlier days of the war I had few friends, as parents were understandably reluctant to part with their offspring for fear of an air-raid but, very occasionally, I was able to 'pop round' to a near neighbour and play with their children, and they would sometimes reciprocate.

Towards the end of the war, when raids were limited to the *V1 flying bombs* and a few *V2 rockets* (which could not be heard coming and for which no warning could be given), I was allowed to accompany the milkman, Mr. Baldwin, on the part of his round which kept me close to home.

I would run down to the United Dairies depot on the Brighton Road and meet up with him as he was getting his brown and white skewbald horse, Sheila, from her stable. He would lead her to the already laden cart, the shafts of which were folded up against the cabin, drop the shafts and reverse Sheila into position between them. He then deftly attached the leather harness, placed the bit in her mouth and extended the reins to the cabin. We would climb up on to the seat and Mr. Baldwin would release the hand brake. A gentle *thwack* with the reins on the horses' flanks and we were off.

A foot brake restrained Sheila as we approached a crossroads or when we were going downhill, and a cheerful "Getchup!" was all that was needed for Sheila to accelerate. Although a whip was provided in the cabin, I never saw it used. At each stop I would be given quart, pint or half-pint bottles to deliver to the various doorsteps, and sometimes a bottle of yoghurt. Half way around the delivery we would put the nose-bag on Sheila so she could have some refreshment.

I thoroughly enjoyed working with Mr. Baldwin, not least because he used to be a professional footballer with Portsmouth and often related his experiences to me. Once he even came into our house to view my home-made football ground which received his praises, much to my delight.

One particular incident stands out in my memory of those days on the milk-round. Hitler decided to send over a spare *Doodle-Bug* (flying bomb) precisely at the time when I was at the furthest point of my permitted radius of action…

I was under orders from Mum and Dad that, in the event of the air-raid siren sounding its baleful wail, I was to don my tin hat and run like crazy back home, the idea being that I should make it before any action actually took place. Today the warning was late! I found myself running for England, hotly pursued by a hungry flying bomb. I was sure Hitler had aimed it directly at me, but it passed over and I did not hear the distant explosion for some minutes. However, I was to have an even closer encounter with one of these deadly devices at a later date.

Sometimes during those years of war we would 'get away from it all' by taking a short summer holiday in Devonshire, usually at Devonshire Farm, Upottery, on the junction of the Chard and Honiton roads where today the A303 and A30 meet.

Having listed everything each person should take, we packed our suitcases, labelled them and set off for the steam train from Purley. After many changes and long waits, we eventually arrived at Honiton. It was here that my father's cousin, Uncle Charles, ran his famous Honiton pottery.

Days on the farm were generally enjoyable and carefree, but we were often reminded of the war, especially in 1944 when the place was seething with American military might. Convoys were frequently passing the farm and often stopped right outside. I received my first ever piece of chewing gum from a passing GI, and the experience put me off that confectionary for the rest of my life. One night an American lorry tried to climb up a telephone pole outside the farm, the driver having gone to sleep at the wheel. Overhead the *C47 Dakotas* and other aircraft droned in and out of nearby Upottery and Dunkeswell airfields.

One evening, after a rather wet and windy day, I was allowed to stay up longer than usual (we worked double British Summer Time in those days) and was watching the farmer, Mr. Drew, and other workers about their labours, when I became aware of an ominous thundering sound which gradually grew louder The work in the field stopped and all eyes were on the sky which was rapidly filling with aircraft. Wave upon wave of Dakotas passed overhead and we noted that each aircraft had black and white stripes painted around the mid-fuselage and wings. We also saw the side doors of the aircraft were open. The date was the 5th June and I now know that I was witnessing elements of the 101st US Airborne Division being airlifted from Upottery to their dropping zones on the Contentin Peninsula in France, where at midnight they would be the vanguard of the D-Day landings, securing the right flank of the invasion.

A day or two later, with the skies eerily quiet of air activity and few American soldiers on the streets, I was in a field where my father and sister were helping the farm labourers, when we saw a single aircraft coming towards us from seaward, trailing a white plume.

"Look at that contrail!" I yelled. I had seen such aircraft contrails high in the sky over our home in Purley, during the Battle of Britain.

"That's no contrail," Dad replied. "He's too low... He's on fire!"

Hardly had the words left my father's mouth than the aircraft turned on its back and a small black dot dropped away from it. Seconds later the dot was encircled by a white disc. We watched as the disc became more obviously a fully developed parachute.

My sister, father and a couple of the labourers set off at a run towards the falling parachutist, and I was taken back to the farm plying my patient chaperone with a thousand questions. Later I was to learn that the survivor was a young Squadron Leader whose Spitfire had been shot up over France but had managed to get back to England before the fire became severe enough to enforce his bailing out. He was having a cup of tea at a farmhouse when my father and sister found him. A few days later we passed the spot where the charred remains of the aircraft still smouldered. At least this guy got away with his life. Such was not the case of the pilot featured in this poem given me by the authoress in her own handwriting some years later, which she had written on 19th September 1941, depicting an incident she witnessed. It was simply called 'Wings':

Over the town you took your flight,
Pedestrians watched and admired the sight:
A silver bird in a sky of blue –
Some there were who envied you!

You went your way on a display,
It was 'War Weapons Week'
And they had done their bit
And done it well.
What happened? Alas! None could tell.

Crumpling up you fell like a stone –
No personal message for your own.
An ambulance reached the burning pyre;
Columns of smoke rose higher and higher.

As you took off into the blue
Came there any thought to you
Of the Pilot to Eternal Things
And that, today, you would get your 'wings'?

A green field strewn with wreckage:
A gaping crowd and a message
For those who had ears to hear
Whispers from out of a Higher Sphere.

Altar! Incense! and Sacrifice!
Some of us thought not once, not twice
But many times 'ere we went to sleep
Of the Rendezvous we all must keep.

L. R. Burden was an elderly lady in whose home in Twywell, Northamptonshire, I used to lead Bible studies whilst stationed at Wyton in the early 1960s. She was house-bound but spent hours in prayer for so many servants of Christ around the world. I was privileged to be on her list, and she gave me the poem on a card entitled 'Remembrance' - so that I would always remember she was praying for my safety as I flew. I have that same card before me as I write.

I was approaching the tender age of nine years when I witnessed the D-Day Dakotas. After this, and the isolated case of the burning Spitfire, the war seemed to stop until we returned to Purley.

I was allowed to experience a little of farm life including milking a cow, turning the sheaves, leading the horses 'Jolly' and 'Smart' when we took them to the Upottery blacksmith for shoeing, and riding on the empty hay cart. I was even given my first driving lesson! Ron, the farmer's son, eight years my senior, sat me on the tractor which he had carefully pointed at an open gateway, and told me to release the brake. He then directed me to gently place my foot on the accelerator. Being so short in stature, I had to dismount from the seat in order to reach it and promptly stood upon it, resulting in the tractor bounding through the gateway like a wild stallion, taking one of the gate posts with it. Happily, I instinctively took my foot off the accelerator, and the vehicle came to a halt. Ron took a sadistic delight in getting me into trouble, or frightening the life out of me!

One evening he talked me into going with him to catch rabbits. Armed with dog, nets and ferrets we sallied forth into the deepening darkness. He would locate a set of rabbit holes and peg nets over each one prior to sending the ferrets down. Soon the luckless rabbits rushed from their burrows into the nets and the dog pinned them down until Ron knocked them into oblivion by a blow behind their necks with the edge of his hand.

I was given two dead rabbits to carry as Ron looked for his next site. There he told me to wait for him until he returned. The wait went on and on. I called him repeatedly but there was no answer. An owl hooted and the odd bat flew by, but otherwise there was an eerie silence. I began to feel very afraid and wondered if anything dreadful had happened to him.

Eventually, I took to my heels and ran back the way we had come whilst there was still a glimmer of light in the western sky. I tripped and fell many times and often got entangled in briars and hedgerows. After what seemed to be hours, I came across a road which I recognised and ran like mad through the darkness with no sound other than my thumping heart and rasping breath. Suddenly, there was an ear-splitting scream from behind the hedgerow on my left. I froze in horror and began sobbing. Ron appeared in the road! Stuttering and stumbling over my words, I asked him through my sobs where he had been and why he had screamed. His explanation was that he had caught two more rabbits, and the scream was because he had fallen over whilst trying to catch me up.

"Why didn't you answer me when I called you?" I pleaded.

"Didn't want to frighten the rabbits!" he replied nonchalantly. "By the way," he added, "where are the other two?"

In my panic, the last thing I had considered was my cargo, which was somewhere out there in the darkness. Ron was not pleased, but I noticed a twinkle in his eye and a smirk on his face when we at last entered the welcome glow of the farm kitchen. He had obviously enjoyed frightening the life out of me yet again, even though it had cost him a couple of rabbits.

Another experience which I believe marked me for life was that of watching Mrs. Drew, or her daughter, Grace, kill the chickens and ducks. The routine in those days was to string the bird up by its legs and cut a blood vessel in its mouth. The poor creature struggled to get at the twine snaring its feet but gradually ran out of strength until it hung limply in death, dripping rich red blood onto the feather-strewn cobbles below. Apparently, pumping the blood out in this way made the flesh whiter and more succulent. I had a frightening encounter with a chicken when I innocently approached a little chick to stroke it but suddenly became aware of its mother advancing not a yard away, spreading her wings and squawking threateningly.

Even to this day I have an aversion to being close up to birds, dead or alive. My fear was probably exacerbated by the starlings that frequently came down the chimney into my bedroom at Purley. I would pull the bedclothes up over my head and yell for help. Feeling the birds walking over my body (especially my face) was one of the worst experiences of my childhood.

Those times on the farm were, in spite of the frights, a welcome break from the days and nights of bombing and latterly the Doodle-Bugs, but once back home, even with only a year to go before the war ended, the threat of death and destruction was never far away. Although the Doodle-Bug menace decreased as our invading armies over-ran the launching sites in France and the Low Countries, the V2 rocket still posed a real threat. It was, in today's parlance, an inter-continental ballistic missile which could be launched from Germany itself. With this weapon there was no warning and no means of defence. One lived from moment to moment. Nerves were taut. The nearest we came to collecting a V2 was when one drove itself into the Sanderstead golf course. The bang was immense and the damage widespread but happily nobody was killed.

As Dad daily plotted the progress of the allied forces on a map of Europe hanging in the dining room, life gradually became more routine and predictable, but for me the clouds of confusion, fear and under-confidence still encircled me.

Hitler's Motorbike

D ad was too old to serve in the military during the Second World War but he and my sister joined up as wardens in the ARP (Air Raid Precautions) and were located at *Post 54*, a dug-out positioned off a side-walk joining nearby Purley Bury Avenue with the upper reaches of Brancaster Lane.

I shall never forget the morning of the 14th June 1944. My father returned home for breakfast after his night watch and with a tremor in his voice announced, "Hitler's started sending over pilot-less planes!" This phrase struck terror into my nine-year-old heart. I could not envisage a plane without a pilot and wondered what fiendish mind and perverted science could bring such a thing into being! I was soon to find out its effect!

Our diminutive milkman, Mr. Baldwin, was making his daily delivery. He had taken mother's order for the following week, cut out our ration coupons, picked up his crate of empties and was making for the gate bidding her a cheery "G'day Ma'am" when we heard it... the unmistakable pulsating throb of a *Vergeltungswaffe Eins* (better known as the V1 or the Doodle-Bug) graphically described by one of our cockney acquaintances as "'Itler comin' on 'is mo'obike."

Mr. Baldwin stopped in his tracks and we joined him on the garden path searching the azure sky. There it was... the small, lethal invention from Hitler's Germany coming to bring death and destruction to those unfortunate enough to be under it when its engine cut. Would it pass over us or...? Abruptly the noise ceased and an eerie silence followed.

Suddenly, Mr. Baldwin was galvanized into action.

"Quick Ma'am! Take cover! It's coming our way!"

In our front room was Dad's solidly built, slate-based billiard table. Mum rushed into the house ushering me in front of her and dived under it, hotly pursued by Mr. Baldwin as he abandoned his hand crate on the doorstep. The table was not an ideal shelter from a flying bomb, but at least it was sturdy enough to afford some protection from a collapsing upper floor.

We knelt down and curled up into a ball with our arms over our heads and our faces in our knees – the posture prescribed by the Government for such occasions! The silence of that summer morning in 1944 was electric. The next few seconds would be decisive. Suddenly there was an almighty explosion and the blast hit us. The front windows disintegrated and we were enveloped in dust as parts of the ceiling fell in.

The silence returned. The dust settled. Our ears were singing but we were still alive. Suddenly Mr. Baldwin remembered his horse and cart tethered to a lamp post in the street.

"Sheila!" he yelled and scrambled from under the table.

Mum and I followed as he scuttled off on his bandy legs to see what had become of his beloved brown and white horse and his cartful of quarts, pints, half-pints and yoghurts.

It was his practice during those war years to tether Sheila whilst he made his calls, in case the explosion of a bomb or crack of an anti-aircraft gun, the roar of a low-flying aircraft or the wail of the air-raid siren, caused her to bolt. On this occasion however, Sheila, though pawing the ground and snorting in agitation, was still in one piece as was the cart, but much precious milk was flowing freely down the gutter. Some broken bottles and empty crates spoilt the pavement.

The flying bomb, forerunner of today's cruise missile, had landed some 300 yards from us, just the other side of the junction between Riddlesdown Road and Purley Downs Road. Fortunately it was after 9 o'clock in the morning and most people were away at work. One person had been injured but, in spite of the devastation which we later viewed for ourselves, it was a miracle that no lives had been lost.

I was beginning to take Hitler's malevolence somewhat personally. He had, once again, come near to taking our lives. Just how near became evident when we took stock of the damaged house.

The glass in most of the front windows had gone, as had some tiles on the roof. Lumps of ceiling had fallen onto the parquet floor in piles of twisted paper and powder. I looked under the table where we had sheltered and there, in a neat straight line on the floor, lay the shards of glass which had come to rest no further than six inches from where I had been kneeling. Why were those shards so neatly aligned?

Dad insisted that the heavy green baize cloth covering the billiard table must always be replaced after a game. The cloth overhung the table by some two feet. As I surveyed it, I noticed that the overhang facing the windows was cut to shreds. The flying glass had been decelerated to some degree by the weight of the cloth and deposited in that neat straight line. I wonder what my physical appearance might be today if that cloth had not been in place!

For the past five years my life had been a confusion of fear, panic, noise and uncertainty of life. My boyish world was a cacophony of screaming bombs, spine-chilling air-raid sirens, booming anti-aircraft guns and the sinister de-synchronized drone of enemy aircraft engines by day and night.

I would frequently be abruptly awakened in the middle of the night by my parents, sister or brothers and, to the accompanying wail of the air-raid siren, would tuck the bottom of my pyjama trousers into my socks, don my dressing gown and sandals, and be hustled into the cold night air to take refuge in our deep shelter at the bottom of the garden. As we scurried along the garden path, I would be conscious of the booming of the anti-aircraft guns and the hollow popping of the shells as they exploded in the darkness thousands of feet above. Colourful lines of tracer majestically arced their way into the night sky from a nearby anti-aircraft battery as it sought the demise of some unseen enemy high in the starry sky, and eerie searchlight beams slowly traversed the heavens

Once down the twelve brick steps of the shelter, one was greeted by a musty earthy smell accompanied by the warm and comforting glow of a small electric fire. We would 'bed down' in our bunks - three suspended from the concrete ceiling and three beneath them at floor level. At the far end of the shelter was a small opening secured by an armour-plated door: the escape hatch for use in the event of bomb damage obstructing the stairway. In the nights of the *blitz* we did not bother to go to bed in the house; we just went to the shelter every night, taking victuals and valuables with us in case we had no home in the morning.

Such an existence left me with shattered nerves. As a result I was, in the parlance of the day, 'tied to mother's apron strings' which seemed then to be my only security. Often I suffered hallucinations, seeing her being removed in a coffin from our bomb-wrecked house. Whenever I ran I frequently fell over for no apparent reason. I was a nervous wreck!

In spite of my unfortunate state, one thing stood out as a lighthouse in my darkness: the serene and peaceful lives of my two older brothers. They would walk sedately down the garden path to the shelter, often pausing to admire a particularly colourful cluster of enemy parachute flares, affectionately known as *chandeliers*. Sometimes they would return to the house and bring back a tray of cocoa and some biscuits, chatting quietly together and often chuckling. The war did not seem to affect them.

Sleeping in the same room, I had noticed that my brothers would spend some time kneeling by their beds and reading a book before they went to bed. They also went to *Crusaders* every Sunday afternoon, but all this meant nothing to me. My sister Betty took me to the Methodist Sunday School in Kenley, but it was another long walk and I did not really enjoy it, especially when the weather was wet. However, one positive memory does stand out: Miss Floyd, my Sunday School teacher. She was invariably smiling and always had a cheerful word to say to me personally. As I sat on one of the tall, high-backed, straw-platted chairs in the large church hall, with my short legs dangling in space, she told Bible stories enthusiastically, as though they were true. The war did not seem to exist for her either.

Church was a bit of a bore, but the tedium was broken when the collection was taken! One of the stewards, Mr. Bleach, was a football referee, and he always gave me a friendly wink as he passed the plate along our pew, as he knew of my newfound love of the game.

One dark, blacked-out evening, early in 1945, when returning from an evening service at Emmanuel Church, South Croydon, I was intrigued to hear my brother Harold quietly speaking to mother about her distress in seeing her eldest son, Fred, go to Malaya as a soldier. Harold himself would soon be joining the army. She was naturally afraid that she might lose both sons in the war. He spoke to her gently of death as a gateway into "the Lord's presence" and not the end of life.

All this reminded me of what Fred himself had said to me the day before he left for Malaya. I had been sobbing about his imminent departure and was halfway up the stairs to have a good cry on my bed when I met him coming down. He sat me down on the stairway, put his arm around me and told me about Jesus and the difference He made to living and dying. I cannot honestly say that Fred's comforting words meant anything to me at the time but Harold's subsequent chat with Mum prompted my memory and made me think.

When I went to bed that night I prayed that, if God could be so real to my brothers, would He please make Himself real to me in a way that I could understand.

Some three or four weeks passed and, typical of a nine-year-old boy, I forgot all about my prayer until one day I was surprised to find I was no longer fearful of the air raids! My hallucinations about Mum's 'death' had gone and I was able to run without falling over. Coincidence, or had God answered my boyish prayer?

Figure 3: Fred, Dad, Mum, Betty, Self, Harold. 1951.

On 8th May 1945 the war in Europe came to its end and the whole country rejoiced. Our family contributed our own celebrations to the night of Victory by leaning out of the front bedroom windows (glass now intact) and blowing 'V' in the Morse Code on Wardens' whistles! We also began the *ceremony of the colours* by hoisting a Union Jack above our porch every day and 'striking' it every evening.

No more air raids! No more rushing for the shelter! No more fear of being bombed! Life was incredible! Day and night followed day and night without death's shadow hovering over us. We were able to sleep all night, every night, in our own beds! We were free!

However, the war in Japan was still raging and Fred was out there in Malaya. He was away from home for four years. Then, on 15th August 1945, Japan surrendered following the dropping of the atomic bombs on Hiroshima and Nagasaki. Fred's only task now was to guard Japanese prisoners. Soon Fred was on his way home. Harold had to report for military service on the day Japan surrendered. His was the only squad to turn up, so it was commended for having done so and promptly given two weeks' leave!

The clouds of war, fear and death had passed, but other clouds would be encountered in the life that was before me. Would I be able to get above them, like my brothers had got above the war, or would I find them dark, forbidding and full of fear like the one I had just passed through? A source of light, warmth and cheer had pervaded my life which was to brighten in intensity over my future years: the Lord Jesus Christ had revealed Himself to me in a way that I could understand. I now knew for myself the source of my brothers' peace and serenity. Could it be the same source of protection and constraint experienced by my father in his foxhole?

"The Happiest Days of Your Life"

The words of a popular song, made famous by Cardew Robinson, eventually proved true for me: "School days are the happiest days, the happiest days of your life..." As most of my primary schooling had been conducted in or near air-raid shelters, scampering to and from school in a state of fear and dread, the end of the war brought a release from the pre-occupation of staying alive and gave the opportunity to think of other things. It must be remembered that my war-time education at primary and junior school was paid for by my not so well off parents. It would be some years before the *Education Act* came into being with free education for all.

My first ever teacher was Miss Blomfield, who held her little school upstairs in her own house in Grasmere Road, Purley. I took an unbuttered scone to eat at break-time; a cup of cold milk was provided at a price. She charged tuition fees by the week, and I have before me, as I write, three receipts recording the payment for three weeks of primary education over the period 24th June to 19th July 1940. Each is for four shillings (twenty pence in today's currency!)

In the summer of 1941 I was devastated to learn that my Miss Blomfield was to leave teaching in order to marry a soldier. I felt that my world had fallen apart. Where would I go to school? How far would I have to travel? Would I be bullied because I was so small? – So many questions loomed in my troubled heart to add to the general trauma of war-time fear and uncertainty.

My next educational 'port of call' was the Sanderstead Kindergarten and Junior School, situated in Purley Oaks Road. Fortunately it had a substantial air-raid shelter in the back garden which was our frequent venue for lessons.

Each day I would run to school, meeting up with a couple of friends on the way, one of whom was Pamela Murray. Her sister Christine was destined eventually to marry Robin Oake who would become a fellow Bible Class buddy of mine in just a couple of years' time. He joined the police force, ending his career as the Chief Constable of the Isle of Man. Sadly, he and Christine were also destined to endure the heartache of having their son Stephen, a Special Branch Officer, murdered by an illegal Algerian immigrant on Tuesday 14th January 2003. Robin, interviewed on TV following the attack, spoke of forgiving the one who had perpetrated the crime and praying for him. The whole family was a testimony to the grace, serenity and peace that only the Lord Jesus can give, and his subsequent book, 'Father Forgive... the Forgotten F Word', was to become a written testimony of the victory of God's grace in lives devastated by tragedy. Christine's and Pamela's brother, John Murray, was also to feature in my later life both at Grammar School and in my days with Mission Aviation Fellowship.

My report at the end of the summer term of 1945 was summarised by my head teacher as follows: "Ronnie's work has been very satisfactory this term. He always tries hard and often does quite well. We wish him success in his new school. He should have an almost certain pass next year if he continues to work well."

The "almost certain pass" was referring to my second attempt to get into a Grammar School. I had failed the 11+ examination held at the Purley County Grammar School, but I would try again later, this time for Whitgift School in Croydon.

My day at Purley County School, sitting the first 11+ attempt, was marked by an unforgettable incident. Having taken my seat in the allotted classroom, the invigilating master called the register.

On reaching my name he stopped, looked up and asked, "Are you related to Fred and Harold Collard who were at this school a few years ago?" On owning up to the fact that I was their younger brother, he rose from his desk, came over to me and offered his hand. "I wish you every success lad. If you are anything like your brothers you will be most welcome at this school."

Thus the testimony of my dear brothers had not been limited to the home but had also shone in their workplace. As they say, "How do you follow that?" It served, however, to teach me at a very early age the importance of what is called *the Christian work ethic*, something that I was to prove again in my very last week at school before joining the Royal Air Force. More anon!

I had outgrown my time at Sanderstead Junior School, so a move was necessary, but to where? My parents faced a problem: I was too old for junior school but not good enough for secondary education. To the everlasting credit of my longsuffering Mum and Dad, they again coughed up from their meagre income so that I could attend the Gregg School at Broad Green, in West Croydon. This was basically a commercial college, training typists, secretaries, etc (thus *Gregg shorthand* which vied with Pitman's for some years) but also provided a general education curriculum.

My time at Gregg's School was not the happiest. However, at breaktimes I used to enthusiastically kick a tennis ball around with the senior pupils in the very dirty back yard devoid of grass. At first the majority of my fellow footballers resented the intrusion of this little pest, but I was soon competing with the best of them and accepted by them.

Every Wednesday afternoon was set aside for sports. All pupils had to make their own way at their own expense (God bless Mum and Dad again!) by bus or tram to the recreation grounds at Addiscombe, Waddon or Winterbourne Park in Thornton Heath. There we would don our meagre kit, select sides and positions, and embark upon a game of football without referee, linesmen or any adult supervision whatsoever!

Traces of the old wartime fear became evident whenever I had to attempt something new such as the first few journeys to these sporting venues, but once on the football pitch I was in my element - so much so that often the opposing team would complain that I should not be playing with seniors! My own team stood up for me, insisting that if I could play to senior standards then I should be allowed to continue. I got a lot of knocks for my participation and not a little bullying during and after the game, but it helped me to hold my own, stand up for myself, and not be intimidated. Unfortunately, my time at Gregg School was marred by some bad events.

Firstly, my Maths master was an undesirable character with a hot temper. He would frequently teach with his cane! Although he never actually hit me, he often threatened me with it and this caused my already addled mind to seize up completely. Fear was again beginning to impinge upon my life. I began to hate Maths although somehow my reports did not reflect my inner struggles. The subject in general, and Geometry in particular, was to become a real burden in my school life and only began to make sense a decade later when I was learning to fly in the Royal Air Force. Maths and Geometry became sensible in the guise of navigation!

Secondly, when walking home from the bus or tram stop at the Royal Oak, I would often be ambushed by a gang of boys who delighted in throwing stones at me. On one occasion I was hit on the head and blood flowed freely. It happened to be a Wednesday afternoon so Dad was at home. Having cut my hair away from around the wound, he stopped the bleeding by applying a lint impregnated with iodine. It did the job and doubtless dealt with any infection, but it stung almost as much as the stone's initial impact! Coming home from school each day was a fear I had to overcome in my own way. I prayed for strength to walk through the ambush and not run. It worked! The gang lost interest in me!

In August 1946 my father received the following letter from the headmaster of Gregg School.

Dear Mr. Collard,

I heard on Saturday morning from Kingston [the local education authority] the results of the scholarship examination and that Ronald has failed. On the subject of Ronald sitting again, I am told that there is a strong possibility that he will be allowed to sit next year...

Thus I failed the entrance examination for Whitgift School in addition to failing the entrance examination for Purley County Grammar. At least I was being consistent! Special Maths coaching, again at my parents' expense, together with my sister's almost daily attempts to appease my frustration with the homework, failed to improve my abilities, but I was happier – I found a new experience in sport! Now I could run and kick a ball without constantly falling over. Seeing the ground speeding beneath my feet was exhilarating, so I ran everywhere. I kicked any ball of any size that came my way and, being frequently bullied at school because of my lack of stature, I found I could stick up for myself by punching the bullies in their bellies (I could not reach their chins!) – I was becoming a delightful child!

By now I had left Gregg School and was catching the number 197 bus which took me in the opposite direction. No longer into the crowded metropolis of Croydon with its noise, bustle and (in those days) smoke, but into the green and peaceful countryside of Caterham Valley where the air seemed clear and pure. This was a liberating experience in every way.

The school was an airy, bright, purpose-built school, unlike Gregg's which was a stately house with dark staircases and claustrophobic rooms, where morning assemblies took place on the staircase, the only location that could accommodate all the pupils.

My new school had large tarmac playgrounds (separate for boys and girls), a well-equipped hall which doubled as a gymnasium, specialized labs for Physics, Chemistry and Woodwork and, above all, a sports field just a five minute walk from the school along a country path. This was heaven!

I thoroughly enjoyed this new experience and was able to indulge myself in all the sporting activities. I eventually represented the school at football, cross-country running, athletics (where I excelled at the long jump and hurdles) and boxing. This later addition to my sporting repertoire was probably the watershed of my character-building. Up to then, although much of my fear and confusion from the war had been dealt with by the grace of God, I was still quite timid and reserved. Boxing did me a service.

The school was tough. The Welsh headmaster and his staff caned when necessary and stood no nonsense in regard to discipline, but they were all very fair and encouraging. Should a couple of lads be caught fighting in the playground, the combatants' names were noted by the supervisory teacher and referred to the headmaster. At the following morning's assembly the names would be announced and a time given when the two would meet in the boxing ring which would be erected in the hall. The sports master would referee as the combatants exchanged their differences within the bounds of Lord Queensbury's Rules.

Only on one occasion was I caught in conflict with another pupil in this manner. A chap took exception to me regularly attending the Purley Crusader Bible Class. Not having reached any significant level of spiritual maturity at that age, I thumped him! We were duly appointed a date and time to face each other in the square ring. In spite of his cronies' verbal assaults prior to the contest and my opponent's alleged boxing prowess, I beat him handsomely and experienced, for the very first time, my gloved hand being raised in victory! My combatant and I subsequently became good friends and played alongside each other in the school first eleven soccer team.

We boys were trained in boxing, as we were trained in all the other major sports. Inter-house games were a regular feature of our sporting curriculum and my house master put my name down to box in the forthcoming tournament to be held one winter's evening in front of pupils, staff, parents and friends. During a woodwork lesson that same day, he came in to announce our opponents for the evening. The very name of my programmed adversary struck terror into my soul – Victor Loasby! He had a reputation as a promising boxer. I went into the small room which housed all the wood cut-offs and physically shook. It took some minutes for me to regain my composure.

Come that evening, my faithful Dad accompanied me to school to witness my first public bout. After waiting for what seemed an eternity, I was eventually called from the cloakroom, where I had been physically sick and had paid numerous visits to the toilet, to duck under the ropes where I was 'gloved-up'. Our sports master, an ex-major in the Army Physical Training Corps, was the referee. He called us into the centre of the ring and gave the usual warnings and instructions. I retreated to the green corner and awaited the bell.

The first two of the three rounds went remarkably well. I managed to make some good strikes, one of which brought an "ooh!" from the spectators (amateur bouts were fought in silence in those days!) However, just before the end of the second round I made contact again and felt a very nasty pain in my left hand. On retiring to my corner at the bell, I pulled off my glove and was horrified to see the little finger no longer parallel with the knuckle but displaced grotesquely above it!

My *seconds* (fellow pupils) called the referee over and showed him the damage.

"It looks as though you've dislocated your finger, Collard. Do you want to retire and have it fixed, or will you box on?" As I said, it was a tough school! He then added, "If you retire, Loasby will be the winner by default." I decided to box on, replacing my glove just as the bell sounded for the third and final round. Loasby must have seen the activity in my corner and knew I was injured. He had obviously decided to finish me off but I managed to parry most of his blows with my left forearm. The pain was acute whenever he caught me on the left glove but I held on and got some good jabs in with my right hand.

Still unconvinced that I was winning, I changed to *southpaw* (leading with the right hand rather than the left). This enabled me to 'rest' the left hand more and attack with the right even though my defence was now more vulnerable. The sudden change seemed to confuse Loasby and I was able to get in a series of stinging right jabs to his face. He backed away and I went after him. In the heat of the moment, I forgot about my injury and landed a telling left hook to his ribs. It made me wince as the punch landed but Loasby winced even more and folded. For the remainder of the round I was all over him and, when the bell sounded, my hand was lifted in victory.

Back in the cloakroom, my injury was examined by the sports mistress, whose father happened to be the trainer (physiotherapist in, today's terminology) at Chelsea Football Club. She doubled as the school nurse. She took hold of my hand and turned so that her back was towards me and my hand was in front of her. (Not all pupils could boast that they had had their arm around the sports mistress!) I felt her tracing her finger over the dislocation. Suddenly her colleague let out the most blood-curdling yell as he fell backwards into a desk. In that instant, when my attention was diverted, she pulled my finger forward and slammed it back into place. I gave a yelp of pain but it was all over in a flash. She bound it with a bandage to give it support overnight and it has never troubled me since!

The following morning at assembly, Victor Loasby filed in just ahead of me. He turned and pointed to a closed and swollen black eye. I held up my bandaged hand.

"Well done!" he said.

"You too," I replied.

A solid friendship was forged.

Although people were being killed in our locality during the war, I had never known any of them personally. Now the war was over, and I was enjoying my liberated young life so fully at the Caterham Valley County Secondary School that death was not even a thought until one day it hit the school.

We were all enjoying the *heats* in preparation for the impending sports day. The girls of the form below mine were off to a cracking start in their hundred yards sprint. Suddenly one girl fell and did not move. Teachers rushed to her with the sports mistress leading the way. The rest of us were kept at a distance. One male teacher was seen to race from the scene towards the school - no mobile phones in those days! Soon an ambulance arrived and the little girl was gently lifted onto a stretcher.

The heats continued. Lunchtime came and went. The early afternoon programme of lessons was completed. We had a football fixture at home against Roke School at the end of the day, so I was soon in position on the left wing, clothed in my smart kit of white shirt, green shorts with white vertical stripe down each side, and green and white ringed socks. At half time the headmaster, accompanied by other members of staff, came on to the field and called us around them. We could see something was seriously wrong. We were informed that the little girl had died in hospital and were asked to dedicate the rest of the game to her memory. We played our hearts out with tears in our eyes.

The following morning at assembly, the school was told the sad news officially and the headmaster led us in a time of prayer for her parents and family. Then it was back to lessons - no counselling in those days!

Newspaper reporters were hot on the trail, but they got short change from the headmaster. They questioned the wisdom of having "little girls involved in competitive sports" but they were sent packing with their tails between their legs and the school continued to grow in its sporting stature.

On Wednesday 21st May 1948, the Annual Sports Day of the Caterham, Purley and Coulsdon District Sports Association was held at the Guards Depot in Caterham. Nine secondary schools and ten primary schools competed. I was selected to represent the school in the long jump, the mile and the hurdles. After winning the latter two races comfortably, I was approached by a *scout* from the London Harriers who informed me that I had the potential to 'go places' in the athletics world. He invited me to attend Motspur Park on the following Sunday for interviews and some initial training and assessment. Without a moment's hesitation I declined the offer, saying that I had more important things to do on a Sunday. He was obviously taken aback but did not press me. Sunday had become a special day for me since my encounter with the Lord Jesus in the last year of the war. It was on the first day of the week that He rose from the dead and each Sunday is a weekly reminder of that historic fact. On Sunday we, as a family, attended church morning and evening, and in the afternoon I walked enthusiastically to my Bible Class which met at the Friends' Meeting House in Downs Court Road. Sunday is special and always will be.

Two years later, in the summer of 1950, I did run at Motspur Park. The occasion was the Crusader South Eastern Sports Day and I came away with a winner's medal for the half mile. Again I was approached by the South London Harriers' scouts who were observing the occasion but my answer was the same.

Easter 1949 marked my last report from the Caterham Valley County Secondary School. It was most encouraging. I was placed first out of a class of forty four pupils - not an uncommon number in those days when teachers were in short supply due to the aftermath of the war. Most were ex-servicemen and women who had done a crash course in teacher training.

On 13th August that same year, my father received a letter from the Chief Education Officer at County Hall, Kingston. It read:

Dear Sir,

I am pleased to inform you that as a result of the recent examination, your son is being considered for an Award tenable from the Autumn Term. The Committee propose, subject to their regulations, to reserve a place for him in the Purley County Boys' School.

It is understood that you will agree for him to remain at the school till the July following his 17th birthday...

Thus it was that I finally made it to the Purley County Grammar School, two years behind schedule, at the age of 13+, but it was not without its trauma; that fear of the unknown raised its ugly head again. I had been so happy at Caterham Valley and had achieved so much, especially in the realm of sport, that I felt I was leaving a loving and trusted friend. Indeed, I considered all the members of staff to be just that: friends that could not be replaced. My dear headmaster, the imposing Mr. R. V. Howell, and my form teachers through the years: the gentle but firm Miss M. L. Barker; the dominant but kindly Mr. C. A. Bassendine (who also showed great patience in trying to teach me Maths); the strict but fair Mr. W. J. Comer, with the delightful sense of humour, who initiated my interest in current affairs and politics through his unforgettable Civics lessons; the erect, smart and crisp sports master, Major W. S. Evans, who gave me so much confidence in myself; and the bashful young Mr. D. Cox who inspired me to greater things in essay writing and English literature.

So attached was I to the school that I re-visited it on a number of occasions during my first term at Purley Grammar School, to help Major Evans mark out the football pitch and inflate footballs! I was also sorry to leave Jean Bruce – my first experience of having a girlfriend! The only identifiable feature for claiming such a relationship was that she cooked me a lunch at school one day as part of her domestic science requirements and accompanied me, on one occasion, to watch Crystal Palace play at Selhurst Park!

Having secured a place at Purley County Grammar School, my parents had to dip into their financial resources yet again to kit me out. Maroon school blazer and cap, grey trousers (short and long), two pairs of grey socks with maroon and yellow ringed tops, white and light blue rugby shirts, navy blue and white shorts, rugby boots, gym shoes, gym vest and gym shorts all had to be purchased.

I think Mum and Dad must have taken stock of their expenditure on me during my short life and decided to spend some of their own money before I exhausted it all – they decided to go on holiday! For reasons that I still do not understand, their choice of dates coincided with my first week at my new school. I was shipped off to stay with a family who lived in Whyteleafe. The son, Roy, had been the goalkeeper at Caterham Valley School and we were good friends.

I found it hard starting my new school from a home other than my own and not seeing my Mum, Dad and sister when I returned at the end of each day. I felt rather resentful, but maybe it was a ploy to get me operating and thinking more independently.

A football was never far away from me. In fact, I took one to my new school on the second day and was immediately challenged by the head prefect, John Asquith. He and his deputy, George McAlpine, accosted me in the lunch-break as I was dribbling the ball around the rugby field. He told me politely but firmly that this was a school that played rugby union football and soccer was banned! I was to take the ball home and never bring it again! Eight years later, George and I briefly served together as pilots on my first operational squadron in the Royal Air Force.

Although my love for football continued, I took to rugby very readily and soon made my mark in the second fifteen in the position of fly-half. Unfortunately, the master in charge of rugby was very anti-soccer and took every opportunity of making a snide comment to me, especially if I adopted a soccer technique in my play. I used to kick the conversions and penalties but, because I kicked the ball with my instep instead of with the toe of my boot (as was the practice in those days) and used a curving run-up rather than the traditional straight approach to the ball, I came in for comments like "Well, that's one way of getting a rugby ball between the posts, I suppose." The fact that my kicking was invariably successful did not seem to change his attitude.

To him the fly-half was just a link from the scrum to the three-quarters. I tried to use innovative moves such as looping into the three-quarters line to make an extra man, having delivered the ball to the wing or centre. This invariably opened a gap in the opposition through which I or the centre could penetrate, but I was told to "behave like a fly-half." I became quite discouraged by his attitude. This, together with an increasing patella problem in my right knee, which gave severe pain whenever I kicked a ball, prompted me to discontinue rugby and take up cross-country running and athletics instead.

The master in charge of this sport was a war veteran who had lost a lung due to a shrapnel wound and had been told to exercise the remaining one as much as possible. He had taken up long distance running and ran marathons frequently. He was an inspiration to me and a man I much admired. He was fluent in, and taught, seven languages.

He had been trying for years to form a cross-country team which would bring home the long-coveted inter-schools trophy but had never been successful even with such fellows as Gordon Pirie in the team.

Gordon went on to win the silver medal for Great Britain, running the 5,000 metres in the 1956 Olympic Games at Melbourne.

Training was hard, with frequent runs after school and even during the lunch hour. The team gradually established itself as a force to be reckoned with among the Surrey schools and even did well in the national championships.

On one notable occasion we ran against a team from the Guards Depot at Caterham. Mr. Baldwin and his schoolboy team arrived at the guardroom and were greeted by a huge and immaculately attired Sergeant Major who seemed to fill the place with his presence. He had his highly-polished pace-stick under his arm and sported a small moustache on his ample face.

"Can I help you sir?" he roared at Mr. Baldwin, who explained who we were and the purpose of our visit.

When the Sergeant Major heard that this motley bunch of school-kids was to run seven miles against his precious Guards, he threw his head back and roared with laughter. Having recovered from his hilarity, he pointed us in the direction of the changing rooms and assured us, still chuckling, of our inevitable defeat.

The cross-country contest was close, but we beat them! As we sauntered past the guardroom on our way to catch the bus home, a subdued Sergeant Major had the decency to come to attention and salute us as we filed past him with our satchels slung over our shoulders and our caps askew on our tousled heads. Mr. Baldwin, with slight embarrassment but with obvious delight, raised his hand limply to his temple in acknowledgement!

Eventually, the big day dawned. We were to run against the rest of the Surrey schools over the *South London Harriers* course in pursuit of the elusive trophy. Mr. Baldwin gave us an inspiring pep-talk in the dressing room and we went to the starting line determined to bring back this silverware, if only for his sake. He had given so much of himself in preparing us for the great event, quite apart from all he had done for the school's cross-country reputation over the years.

We did it! What a moment to savour as Peter Pitt, our captain, received the silver cup and held it aloft. Mr. Baldwin came forward applauding and displayed uncharacteristic emotion as he gathered us around him, slapping us all on the back and repeating, "Well done! Well done my boys! Thank you, thank you!"

Figure 4: The Purley Grammar School Cross-Country team 1950-51.
Author extreme right, front row. [Photo: G & H Bunce. Caterham]

At the assembly on Monday morning, our headmaster, Doctor Birchall, grinning broadly, gave notice of our victory, and Peter Pitt, accompanied by much cheering and clapping, mounted the platform to present the trophy to the head who received it on behalf of the whole school. It was then the team's turn to join Peter and Mr. Baldwin on the platform to receive the school's plaudits. Mission accomplished!

I was subsequently awarded my athletic *colours*. This entitled me to change my red cap for one in navy blue and my red blazer for a blue one, with "A.C. 1951-52" embroidered in gold below the school badge. Earlier in the year I had already been awarded my Surrey Wing Air Training Corps colours for cross-country running and athletics and had broken the Surrey Wing record for the 440 yards in a time of 54 seconds. The years 1950 to 1952 had added athletics and cross-country running to my sporting repertoire, thanks to the encouragement and sound coaching received from the master in charge.

Mr. Baldwin and I often ran together just for the pleasure of it and, as we sweated and puffed our way around the Coulsdon countryside, we frequently discussed the pros and cons of both soccer and rugby. He sportingly suggested that, assuming my patella had healed sufficiently, I might consider returning to rugby for my last couple of years, aiming for my colours in the first fifteen. I responded positively to his advice and, rather tentatively, played inter-house rugby again. I rather doubted if the master-in-charge of rugby would want me, but he obviously liked what he saw in the inter-house competition, despite my soccer techniques, and chose me for the second fifteen again. After a few games, and an injury to the incumbent fly-half, I was promoted to the first team, but I never gained my colours.

Football was still my first love. I wrote to Charlton Athletic regularly, trained with Torquay United whenever I went on holiday to my aunt's home in Paignton, and took every opportunity to improve my skills. I was also on the books at White Hart Lane as a potential junior with Tottenham Hotspur.

Torquay's trainer was Bob John, who had played for Arsenal in the late 1930s. He was a tough Scotsman who took his coaching very seriously. I have him to thank for much of my physical fitness. He also insisted on my using both feet equally well. I am amused to hear today's football commentators, speaking of the modern over-paid prima donnas as having a 'best foot'!

One of his favourite routines was to have us lads pair up according to weight and 'run the terrace'. This involved each of the pairs taking it in turns to pig-a-back the other and run up the terracing opposite the grandstand. It did wonders for the calf and thigh muscles! Not content with that, he would also have us run *down* the terracing which tested one's courage to the full. In retrospect, it was highly dangerous but focussed the mind and sharpened the co-ordination and balance magnificently!

Another of his ruses was to present me with a cricket stump placed between the penalty spot and the goal line, central to the goal. He placed a dozen footballs at the corner of the pitch and expected me to take in-swinging corner kicks with my right foot so that the ball would drop onto the stump from above. When I had exhausted the supply of balls, I would collect them and go to the same corner to kick out-swingers with my left foot. I was then required to follow the same procedure from the opposite corner. I rarely hit the stump, but the training ensured I could generally put the ball unerringly on a centre-forward's head.

Although I was regularly attending the Purley Crusader Bible Class every Sunday afternoon and going to the Purley Congregational Church, morning and evening, my experience of God in 1945 had not seemingly changed my life to any marked degree. I rejoiced in being free from daily fear and relished my new-found confidence. I appreciated all the world could offer me, especially in regard to sport. There was, however, an inward emptiness which was brought into sharp focus one day when my eldest brother Fred, safely home from Malaya, and now seeking his civilian niche in the world, bluntly said to me, "Surely you don't mean to kick a bag of wind around a field for the rest of your life!" I am sure the Lord used Fred to speak to my soul that day, challenging my life priorities!

I could not get his words out of my mind. I had set my heart on becoming a professional footballer and being a Christian one at that! My role model was Bert Johnson who played right half-back for Charlton Athletic and England - a smiling blond-headed young man whose behaviour on and off the pitch was exemplary. He lost his England place when he refused to play on a Sunday - a new practice that had come into international football in the post-war period when continental teams were starting to be engaged in competition.

My inward emptiness and Fred's blunt words continued to goad me. I gave a lot of thought to what had happened back in 1945 when I had asked the Lord to make Himself known to me in a way that I could understand. Things had changed for me, but the emphasis was on the words "for me". What had I done for the Lord? – Nothing! I had just wallowed in all He had given me. Even my attendance at Bible Class and church services had become enjoyable "for me". It all seemed a lot one-sided!

A watershed occurred one evening at an evangelistic rally in London conducted by Tom Rees, the then famous British evangelist. I do not remember what he said but, through him, God spoke to me about sin. At my tender age, I had not committed any outrageous felony, nor had I done much harm to anyone outside the boxing ring, but I saw what pride, jealousy, hate, deceit, anger, bitterness and selfishness had done in getting

Jesus crucified and that my life bore the same sinful characteristics. That night I went to the front of the hall when the invitation to do so was given, and I was counselled by a wise and elderly man who pointed out that Jesus had paid the penalty for my sin when He was crucified and wanted His resurrection life to be real in me. I had been saved to serve.

I committed my life to the Lord and asked that He might use me to His glory for the rest of my days. My counsellor warned me that God would take me at my word and that I was not to express such intentions lightly. He also warned me to be prepared for some surprises. The first of these came only a few weeks later...

That same summer I was again staying with my aunt in Paignton and spending as much time as possible training under Bob John's coaching at Torquay United's ground at Plainmoor. One Saturday morning I received a letter re-directed to me from my home address in Purley. It was from Tottenham Hotspur Football Club inviting me to attend White Hart Lane for a trial that same afternoon at 2 pm! The letter had been written a week before but, what with the slower deliveries of those days and the re-direction from home, it had arrived far too late for me to even acknowledge it. I was devastated!

I took the letter into my room, knelt by my bed, and asked God how I should respond to this disappointment. In just a few moments I found my obsessive love for football had gone and there was a strange sense of peace in my soul. It was my first experience of a personal disappointment becoming 'His appointment'.

I still enjoyed all sports but the worship of the spherical ball was now over. My Bible took its place in my affection, and I studied it avidly alongside helpful Scripture Union notes provided through the Bible Class. From that time on I have studied passages from the Bible every day except when in hospital and too ill to do so. I owe everything to the God of the bible and to His graciousness in showing Himself to me, through the Lord Jesus, and changing my life's direction at an early age. This, however, was not a matter of 'getting religion' as the saying goes. It was life-transforming - a new dimension and a new power and purpose in living, and a rock-like assurance that death was by no means the end but a continuation of life in Christ's actual presence: "Whoever lives and believes in me shall never die."

Soon after my arrival at the Purley Grammar School, I had made contact with four other Christian boys. We met every lunchtime for fifteen minutes in the store cupboard where the French textbooks were kept. It was private and quiet. We prayed that the Lord would teach us to pray in a manner that would glorify Him. We found ourselves praying for individual boys by name, particularly for those with whom we naturally rubbed shoulders during the day. We prayed for those we travelled to school with on the bus, those we sat next to in the various classes, those we ate with at lunch, and so forth. One of those who joined us in the French store cupboard was John Murray: young brother to Christine and Pamela who attended the Sanderstead Kindergarten and Junior School with me. Another was John Balchin - more of him later!

Soon we could not all get into the French store cupboard, so we asked permission to form a School Christian Union and move into a classroom. Subsequently, we grew out of the classroom and took over the school library. In my final year at school we frequently met in the gymnasium in order to accommodate those attending.

I have never seen anything more like a revival. It happened over five years, and there were periods when boys were acknowledging Christ as their Lord and Saviour every day of the week.

On one occasion a Mr. Will Smart visited the Croydon area. He was an evangelist with the National Young Life Campaign and an ex-bomber pilot in the Royal Air Force holding the rank of Squadron Leader. Permission was given for me to invite him to speak to the school squadron of the Air Training Corps. As a result of his talk, a number of cadets asked him very significant questions and requested he be asked to come again. Just a week later he was invited to speak to the Christian Union. I met Mr. Smart off the bus and was walking with him up the path to the school entrance when he abruptly stopped. In a very quiet voice he said, "The Lord is here. He is going to do a mighty work in this school."

I have recently found a typewritten account of those remarkable days in the back of my Pupil's Report Book:

The Christian Union had been praying for Mr. Smart's visit for some time but during the preceding week had met for prayer every dinner hour and for half an hour after school each day.

Figure 5: Some of the new Christians at the School Christian Union party
1953. The cause of all the hilarity?...

Figure 6: The leader and secretary (myself and Kester Carruthers) blindfolded,
feeding each other with sticky rice pudding! Kester became a Lieutenant Colonel
in the Army Chaplains' Departrment. Centre background is John Lewer, a
future physiotherapist in the R.A.F.

On Friday 6th November Mr. Smart spoke at the junior and senior Christian Union meetings at 12.30 and 1 pm. The total number who heard God's message that day were one hundred and forty plus. Mr. Smart visited the school each lunch hour from Tuesday to Friday [during the following week] and addressed both the junior and senior meetings; the combined attendance [on each day] averaging eighty boys. Four masters also attended these meetings and two made professions of faith to Mr. Smart.

With the Mission over, the Christian Union continued its Prayer Meetings at 1 pm on Mondays and for twenty minutes after school each day. Average attendance at the Monday Prayer Meeting had been thirty five.

On the Friday that the mission ended we held our combined meeting with our sisters from Stoneyfield [the Purley Girls' Grammar School] in St John's Church. What a crowd there was and what a thrill to see such a number of lads, some only three hours old as Christians, singing so thoughtfully and thankfully to the One who they now knew as their Saviour!

Now the work of following up each and every individual had begun and so we needed prayers! It was a task fitting up the lads with Bible Classes and Churches, but arrangements were made and all worked out slowly and surely.

Every lad who professed to have accepted Christ as Saviour had been given a 'Next Step' (G.C. Robinson) booklet, a sample of the Scripture Union 'Key Notes' [and the book 'In Understanding Be Men' by T.C. Hammond].

The real results of that mission could be seen in the faces, lives and quality of work of more than fifty boys in our school. To God be the glory; great things He has done!

Over the intervening years I have lost touch with the majority of the boys who were Christian Union members, but I know John Lewer became a physiotherapist in the Royal Air Force with the rank of Chief Technician, Kester Carruthers entered the Church of England ministry and subsequently became an army chaplain of senior rank, as did John Murray following his initial ministry in the Baptist church. John Balchin, after ordination in the Baptist ministry, got his doctorate and became a lecturer at the London Bible College. Prior to retirement he was minister at the Above Bar Church in Southampton and before that at Purley Baptist Church which he had attended as a boy. John Pink became a Wing Commander in the Royal Air Force. Roger Tyler went to Teacher Training College and returned to the staff of the Purley Grammar School where he supervised the Christian Union. David Wortley became a Baptist minister as did Jim Baker who was minister at Stroud and has now retired there. He and his wife Marion visited Elizabeth and me in September 2007 - the first time we had met for some twenty years. It was on that visit that Jim suggested I should write a book. Murray Mash, my closest friend at school and one of the original four in the French store cupboard, was my Best Man when I married Elizabeth and, on 11th September 1982, his eldest daughter became my first daughter-in-law!

Figure 7: Murray Mash, my best friend and later my Best
Man, and I in Grammar School days

Whilst serving with Mission Aviation Fellowship, some twenty five years after leaving school, I received a letter which began "Friends, Romans, countrymen; lend me your ears..." It had come from Graham Docwra, an air cadet at school who had attended those remarkable meetings of the Christian Union but had not committed himself to Christ. He and I had presented a sketch at an air cadet social evening when we enacted the famous lines from Shakespeare's 'Julius Caesar'. He had written to inform me that, some ten years after leaving school, he had committed his life to Christ and wanted me to know because "I knew you chaps in the Christian Union had been praying for me." I subsequently had the great joy of meeting Graham, his wife and two children when I preached at a church in Carshalton many years later!

My desire to tell others of Christ led me to be taken under the wing of the East Surrey Lay Preachers' Fellowship. Mr. Keith Stockbridge and Mr. Ray Burgess were allocated to me as my tutors, and I owe them so much. They channelled my boyish enthusiasm and somewhat elementary understanding of the Bible into a solid, informed ministry.

The first lesson I had to learn was how to read the Bible in public. Keith Stockbridge approached me after a morning service at the Purley Congregational Church and asked, "What are you doing next Sunday evening?"

I replied, "Nothing special - probably be here."

"No, you won't!" he retorted. "You'll be with me at Selhurst Congregational Church reading I Corinthians 13. Practise it, and I'll hear you read it on Tuesday evening."

Once a month, on a Tuesday evening, the East Surrey Lay Preachers' Fellowship met for study, training, and prayer. It took its work seriously. That same evening I read the appointed passage to the assembled gathering of lay preachers who took it in turns to gently but firmly criticise me for the way I had delivered it. I learned a lot from them. Keith then informed me that I was to meet with him at our church on the following Friday evening when he would "put the final touches to the reading". We duly met at the appointed time, and he sat in the rearmost pew whilst I read from the pulpit. It was a big church and there was no sound amplification. I was instructed to slow my delivery, sound the ends of my words and know the passage as much by heart as possible to avoid looking down. Eye contact with the congregation was emphasised. The meaning of the passage was also discussed so that I had a good grasp of what Paul was saying to the church at Corinth. This helped me in putting the correct inflection and emphasis in my delivery. Thus I was equipped to do my first public reading the following Sunday evening which was, again, thoroughly debriefed by Keith.

Subsequently and progressively, Keith and Ray got me to lead a service, lead in prayer, and finally do everything but preach a sermon. This came later after much tutoring on sermon construction and general sermon preparation and, above all, how to know what to say! They emphasised that it was no good just having an idea and preaching it. The preacher had to know it was 'from the Lord'; otherwise he had no right to preach at all! Over the years of my subsequent public ministry I have always been grateful for this advice. Stick to the Bible, allow it to speak for itself, and then a preacher knows it is 'from the Lord'. This is known in the trade as *expository Bible ministry*. The pulpit is no place to project one's own opinions and philosophies!

Keith and Ray gradually weaned me away from their tutorials and I was off solo, taking my first full service on 23rd August 1953 at Walton-on-the-Hill. The bookings began to increase around the Croydon area, and I was soon known locally as "the boy preacher" and was much in demand. Pride began to creep into my life. I was the centre of attention and always got plenty of compliments following the services I conducted. I enjoyed being 'up front' and having people's attention. I even had a fan club of Christian youngsters who accompanied me on my various engagements! To their eternal credit, Keith and Ray recognised the problem and took me out of circulation for a while, gently but firmly reminding me that any gift I had was God-given and not self-constructed. Praise and glory belongs to God alone.

Keith brought me down to earth with a bump when he booked my next preaching appointment. It was to be in a ward of the Mayday Hospital in Croydon and in front of a microphone which would broadcast the service to the whole hospital! Other than telling me the time and place to report, he gave me no briefing but added, "It will be no experience for a proud preacher!"

Having reported to the matron at the appointed time, I was ushered into the ward which contained some thirty bed-bound patients. I was positioned about halfway along in front of a small table on which stood a microphone.

"When you see the green light appear, you're on," said the ward sister. "When you see the amber light you have one minute to finish. The red means you're off the air."

The sister made to leave, and I began to have serious doubts as to my ability to see it through, especially as I saw in the bed immediately opposite me a very old lady who was deathly white and obviously having difficulty breathing.

I drew the sister's attention to her and asked, "Is it okay for me to take a service with this lady in such a bad way?"

The sister replied, "Don't worry about her, young man. She'll be dead by the time you've finished."

I came out of Mayday Hospital convinced that only the Lord had got me through that ordeal and that pride had no place in the ministry of God's precious word.

At the age of 18 years I was formally commissioned as a lay-preacher. Keith Stockbridge and Ray Burgess shook my hand and relinquished their tutorial roles. I have so much for which to thank them.

The time was fast approaching for me to be called up for National Service when all 18-year-olds had to join one of the armed services. Due to my late entry into secondary school I was only just ready for my General Certificate of Education exams (today's equivalent of the GCSE). I managed to pass in six subjects at Ordinary Level (including the dreaded Maths on the second attempt!) but would not have time to complete my Advanced Level subjects in Religious Studies and English. In parallel to my Advanced Level studies I was also studying Physics (which I had failed first time) and Greek at Ordinary Level.

My Headmaster, Dr H. Birchall, wrote many letters to the local Member of Parliament and to the Secretary of State for Education, asking for my entry into National Service to be postponed for one year so that I could complete my Advanced Level courses and exams. In spite of pointing out that I had already been selected for pilot training in the Royal Air Force and that I would be receiving a Short Service Commission as a regular officer, I was refused deferment.

My last week in school, prior to my joining the Royal Air Force, was marked by an unforgettable incident. I was called to the headmaster's study! During my school career I had never been in any major trouble and never been caned. I wondered what I had done to incur the head's wrath in my final week, and I considered it might be prudent to line the seat of my trousers with an exercise book or two!

Entering his study I saw **Dr. Birchall** sitting behind his enormous desk in a relaxed manner, puffing his pipe with his leg propped up on the desk. The leg was artificial due to a flying accident experienced when he was a pilot during the war flying Hampden bombers.

"Look at these!" he invited as he casually waved a hand over the documents spread all over the desk. I duly complied and saw eighteen pieces of paper, one for each class, giving the names of every pupil in order of merit.

"Look at the first three or four names in each of the classes in my school!" instructed the head. I recognised the names but not the significance. To me they were all simply my friends. The head had to enlighten me.

"The top three or four boys in every class in my school are members of that Christian Union you lead, Collard." Then he added in a surprisingly humble tone, "That means more to me, lad, than a thousand sermons."

Many years later, when in Taunton on a deputation tour for Mission Aviation Fellowship, I was able to visit Dr. Birchall at his home. His sight was poor and, as his wife showed me into his presence, he studied me for a while and then said, "I can't remember your name lad (which made my day as I was then 40 plus!) but school Christian Union comes to mind." He was soon to die but I had the joy of telling him of all the boys in his school that had come to know the Saviour and those with whom I still had contact. His eyes filled with tears. I was able to speak to him, for the last time, of the One who died for him on the cross at Calvary in AD 33 and rose again from the dead three days later, the same One who had changed the lives of so many of his own pupils.

School days proved to be some of the happiest and most fruitful days of my life but, above all, they proved to me beyond doubt that the Lord was risen indeed and was at work not only in my own life but in the lives of those around me. School had been a mission field, and there was no reason why the Royal Air Force could not be one as well. God's training for future mission, both at home and overseas, had begun at school, and the importance of the Christian work ethic had been proved, yet again, by my visit to the headmaster's study.

Carnage at Farnborough '52

A friend and I decided we would visit the Farnborough Air Show. It was the 6th September 1952, and I was seventeen years old, mad on aircraft, a Flight Sergeant in the school squadron of the Air Training Corps and having high aspirations of becoming a pilot in the Royal Air Force.

Via bus and train we eventually arrived at Farnborough and made our way to the best vantage point on the airfield: Observation Hill. Here hundreds of people had gathered with their cars and were enjoying picnics prior to the show. In total, 120,000 people were there to witness the flying display.

As soon as the first aircraft taxied out to begin its display, everyone stood up or clambered onto their cars for a better view. Both of us, being short of stature, found we were unable to see a thing, so we decided to vacate the hill and find a less crowded spot. Some way off to our left was an area almost void of people but much lower down. We lost some of the 'grandstand view' but at least had the place virtually to ourselves. We sat on the grass, ate our packed lunch and enjoyed the show.

What a sight to see Avro's test pilot, Roly Falk, actually roll the new Vulcan bomber as he climbed away from a low pass and to see Squadron Leader "Pee-Wee" Judge flying the Supermarine Swift. Sadly he was to lose his life flying a Wallis gyroplane at Farnborough in 1970. Pee-Wee lived near us in Brancaster Lane, and I frequently saw him walking down the road in his uniform with a lady on each arm – his mum and his aunt!

The new thing in aviation was 'the sound barrier' and the De Haviland Aircraft Company had, like most others, been working hard to design an aircraft that could penetrate it. The DH110 and the Hawker Hunter were two such aircraft. Both were billed to break the sound barrier that afternoon at the show.

The public address system boomed out the news that John Derry and his observer Alan Richards had taken off from the De Haviland airfield at Hatfield and were climbing to forty thousand feet to begin their supersonic descent towards Farnborough. Everyone was agog with excitement.

Soon we were told that the aircraft was entering its descent and building up speed towards Mach one, the speed of sound. Suddenly there was a resounding double bang as the barrier was broken; the air around us shook. Almost immediately we heard the high-pitched whine of an aircraft at speed and saw it, way off to the right and still quite high, descending towards us.

John Derry brought his aircraft round in front of the crowd and showed to advantage the aircraft's swept-back wing profile, its double booms and plank-like tail plane. The crowd applauded. What an experience to witness the breaking of the sound barrier! John then turned the aircraft away from the airfield and came in on a low level run towards the crowd at an angle of about forty-five degrees. The public address announcer heralded it as "the DH110's curtain call before returning to Hatfield."

As we watched it approach, the aircraft suddenly pitched up into a climb and items began to fall from it. My first thought was that leaflets were being dropped, as I had seen German aircraft doing this during the war, but then realised the pieces were far too big. Suddenly the public address announcer yelled, "Watch out for those engines!"

I stood horrified as I saw both power units curving earthwards - one to our right and the other heading our way. My friend and I ran for our lives and fell to the ground expecting some sort of explosion, but all we heard was a muffled thump as the engine closest to us hit the ground some distance away.

Shaken, we got to our feet just in time to see the tail plane, still attached to the twin booms, floating gently to earth, like a falling leaf, way over the other side of the airfield. It landed silently in a small cloud of dust. An uncanny silence hung over the scene for a few seconds, then the announcer, with a tremor in his voice, stated, "The ambulances are on their way. Please keep calm and remain where you are." The other engine had landed on Observation Hill and, in the stampede, many spectators had been killed and many more injured.

Soon we saw the ambulances, with bells ringing, roaring to the scene of the carnage, but some were heading for the main spectator enclosure nearer the runway where many of the invited guests had been seated. I did not know the reason for this until a few days later when a magazine printed a double centre page spread of one of the most horrifying pictures I have ever seen. A very brave cameraman had stood his ground and clicked the shutter as the nose and cockpit assembly crashed just a few yards in front of him! Among the mass of flying debris could be seen, unmistakably, a shoe. The chairs were piled high as people had panicked in trying to escape the nose section as it hurtled towards them. In total, 29 people were killed in addition to Derry and Richards, and 60 injured.

The public address system again crackled into life: "The show is to continue. Our next display aircraft is the Hawker Hunter, piloted by Squadron Leader Neville Duke, and he too will attempt to break the sound barrier." This he did successfully.

Winston Churchill, honorary Air Commodore of No. 615 Squadron (Royal Auxiliary Air Force) of which Neville Duke was the Commanding Officer, subsequently wrote a letter of appreciation, congratulating Neville on continuing the show and "banging a salute" to the fallen crew.

At the end of the show, once all the casualties had been removed, the crowd was allowed to leave the airfield. The police were careful to direct us away from the scenes of carnage. I tried to find a telephone box (no mobiles in those days!) to inform my sister that all was well and that I was on my way home, but every box was in use with extensive queues of anxious people trying to phone. In the end I gave up and concentrated my efforts and time in getting home through a traffic system that seemed to have jammed up both buses and trains.

On arriving home I was greeted by a quite angry sister who wanted to know why I had not contacted her. She had heard of the carnage on the radio news. Mum and Dad were away on holiday at the time, so I realised her concern, as she considered herself to be responsible for me. Once she understood the situation she was tearfully pacified.

The cause of the crash was metal fatigue. Apparently there were two DH110s at Hatfield, and the crew had decided to take the reserve aircraft due to a minor fault in the other. Would the circumstances have been different if that minor fault had not occurred? What a tragedy! To add to it, Richards was about to become a father.

Lessons were learned through the accident. Display parameters were changed e.g. aircraft had to keep parallel to the runway and turns had to be made away from the spectators. Regulations were put into place limiting the distance between the crowd and the display line. Loose chairs were also forbidden. Only fixed seating was allowed, and car parking was separated from spectators.

The DH110 did not die at Farnborough. Due to the accident, modifications were made to the airframe, and the aircraft eventually became the trusty Sea Vixen flown by the Navy. My dear friend and colleague who later became the Chief Executive Officer of Mission Aviation Fellowship, Keith Jones, was to pilot the Sea Vixen from the carrier HMS Eagle during his career in the Royal Navy.

John Derry was the first British pilot in a British aircraft to exceed the speed of sound and, to the very day, he died on the fourth anniversary of his achievement. He is remembered by pilots today when they carry out the manoeuvre known as the *Derry Turn* - a combat escape manoeuvre which he introduced. A steep turn one way is changed into a steep turn the opposite way, by rolling the aircraft through the inverted position - a very effective manoeuvre in throwing a chasing aircraft off one's tail. The Sea Vixen is now out of service but the Derry Turn keeps John's memory alive in every budding military pilot.

Swedish Interlude

The Air Training Corps is, and always has been, an excellent organisation. Not only does it promote air-mindedness among youth, it also gives opportunities for youngsters to experience things way beyond those encountered by their peers, at the same time training them in self-discipline, *esprit de corps*, responsibility, accountability and respect.

During my years in the cadet corps, it offered Flying Scholarships, various aspects of adventure training, the firing of various weaponry under strict supervision, attending Easter and Summer camps at Royal Air Force stations, qualifying as a glider pilot up to *Silver C* standard, and overseas exchange visits of which the most keenly contested were those to the United States or Canada.

Figure 8: Receiving the Sydney Black trophy from Air Marshal Fogarty at the school prize-giving, June 1953. Mr Jewitt (Deputy Head) looks on. [Photo: Croydon Times]

I was fortunate enough to be awarded the Sydney Black Cup, presented annually to the 'best cadet' in Surrey Wing. The replica of the cup is before me as I write. It was presented to me at the school prize-giving in July 1953 by Air Marshal Fogarty who was guest of honour. He had been my headmaster's flying instructor in the Royal Air Force. Strangely enough, it was also Air Marshal Fogarty who, fifteen months later, was to be the signatory for the Air Council on the parchment of my Queen's Commission.

Perhaps because of this award, I was recommended as a candidate for an overseas exchange visit. After successfully working my way through various interviews at Wing, Group and Home Command levels, I found myself on a parade at the RAF station at Kenley where the final selections were to be announced.

The procedure seemed endless, and I waited with bated breath to hear my name called, but the parade grew smaller and smaller until there were only six of us left. The final names had been selected for the USA and Canada. I felt rather disappointed but realised I had gained so much from the Air Training Corps that it owed me nothing.

The officer in charge of the parade then announced that there was to be a consolation prize for one of us – an exchange visit to Sweden. My name was called, and I was ordered to report for further briefing. For me this was no second best! My delight was tinged with some apprehension as I had never been out of my home country before.

Together with cadets from the USA, Canada and Northern Ireland, I was to be a guest of the Royal Swedish Air Force for twelve days. Swedish cadets would be exchanged as guests of the Royal Air Force.

At last our big day arrived! On 3rd August we were taken by coach to Northolt, cleared through customs and boarded the *DC3 Dakota* aircraft belonging to the Chief of the Air Staff, Royal Canadian Air Force which was to be our airborne transport throughout the visit.

From Northolt we flew to Stockholm via stops at Amsterdam, Copenhagen and Oslo. Late in the day we disembarked at our final destination, to be met by the Canadian and British air attaches and Senior Swedish Air Force Officers who greeted us warmly. The Swedish press took many photos and interviewed us. Having cleared customs we were taken by several cars to the Örlogshemmet Hotel owned by the Swedish navy and given a fantastic supper at the top table in a curtain-draped alcove. We were treated like VIPs.

Not being *au fait* with Swedish hospitality and cuisine, we scoffed contentedly before realising that another course was being placed before us. A total of four courses appeared in turn, each having about three different dishes! It seemed that each course had a mini-starter served before the main dish, followed by a tail-end chaser. Thus we encountered some twelve dishes that night having at first thought the primary offering was all that was coming!

We literally staggered from the restaurant some two hours later. Our conducting officer wisely took us for a long walk by the river and showed us the lights of Stockholm before we retired to bed bloated, burping and gastronomically wiser.

A fifty mile drive took us from Stockholm to Uppsala air base where we met up with American cadets from the Civil Air Patrol who were to be our companions for the rest of the visit. Uppsala was a flying training school, and we dined with the aspiring Swedish pilots before being taken by coach into the town to visit the castle and the tombs of Viking kings. A tour of the old town ended a most interesting day before returning to base for tea and an evening of entertainment in the presence of the Air Attaches of Canada, America and Great Britain.

The planners obviously recognised the need of young cadets to be constantly re-fuelled. By a fleet of cars we were transported to yet another restaurant in Uppsala, even though it was now late evening. After another ample intake we were given freedom to roam until midnight when the coach collected us. Much singing on the way back to barracks completed the day and saw us into the early hours of the next.

Prior to our leaving Uppsala we were shown over a Saab J29 Fighter, known as *The Flying Barrel,* and one of the Canadian cadets was invited into the cockpit to fire off a short burst from its guns into the harmonization range. The noise was deafening, and the target remained smoking and our ears ringing for five minutes.

One of the Squadron Commanders put on a superb flying display in his J29 which included four very low-level runs across the airfield at speeds approaching Mach 1. Compression waves were clearly seen on the aircraft's surfaces.

After visiting the *Link Trainer* we experienced a Swedish bath where one was gradually heated up in a log cabin to eighty degrees Celsius followed by a wash and scrub all over, a very cold shower and a swim in an even colder lake. It did wonders for our appetites which were duly satisfied with another slap-up lunch prior to re-boarding our DC3 for a flight of two-and-a-half hours to the Kunglig Jämtlands Flygflottilj at Östersund.

Vampire aircraft, known to the Swedes as the J28B, met us in the air and escorted us most of the way. Further press interviews and a photo call followed our arrival at this front-line fighter base. We were warmly welcomed by the Station Commander, Colonel C-O Hugosson, who had the distinction of being both the national ski and chess champion.

My room-mate was Don Holbrook, an American from the Civil Air Patrol. As was my custom I knelt by my bed, read my Bible passage for the day, studied the 'Daily Bread' notes and silently prayed. This led to a very interesting and fruitful discussion with Don into the early hours of the morning.

The next day we were shown over the base and I sat in the cockpit of a Vampire single-seat fighter-bomber. Little did I realise that, just two years later, I would be flying one myself!

One of the highlights of our visit was spending an afternoon and evening with a Swedish family. What hospitality! Don Holbrook and I stayed with Kapten Gunnar Björck, Fru Björck, Froken Björck and four smaller Björcks! The youngest boy had been practising "How do you do?" all the morning.

We were given a wonderful meal comprising of fish and potato pie, mushroom omelette, tomatoes, bread and butter, followed by meat balls rolled in cooked cabbage leaves, lettuce and potatoes, followed by raspberry cake pudding (raspberries in cream on a sugar sponge cake). Kapten Björck was the only member of the family fluent in English, but this did not limit the laughter, fun and overall enjoyment of being in their cosy home. We were sorry to leave them.

Time was spent in the delightful town of Östersund doing some shopping and visiting the local church where Vikings and more modern warriors (pilots) were buried. Later we mounted the hangar roof to see a remarkable flying display by the Vampires. A low-level attack on the airfield was followed by the Squadron Commander's solo display which was unique. He terminated his display by running in very low and fast until over the threshold of the runway, pulling up into a tight loop, selecting his landing gear down when inverted at the top, then completing the loop (presumably by selecting airbrakes and flaps in stages) to land off the final part of the manoeuvre. How he managed to keep below his gear and flap limiting speeds I shall never know!

Figure 9: Arrival at Östersund, Sweden. Our American escort officer being greeted by the station commander, Colonel C-O Hugosson RSAF.
[Photo: Swedish National Newspaper]

The rest of the working day was spent first in visiting some twelfth century log houses, reputed to be the oldest in the world, then preparing for a day and night in the mountains. We were fitted up with all the necessary equipment including mosquito repellent and waterproof tunic and trousers. Later we were taken to a cinema where we saw the film 'It's in the Air' featuring George Formby. Swedish subtitles ensured that the non-English-speaking audience could enjoy the dialogue. The audience was in fits of laughter throughout. I felt quite proud to see the American cadets crying with laughter over a British comedy!

A very early start was made next morning. Having changed into our mountain rig we travelled by coach for two hours to Tännforsen waterfall, then on to Åre where an aerial rope-way took us up the four thousand feet of Åreskutan, the highest mountain in Sweden. Kapten Eric Goliath, who was in overall charge of our visit, led us in a long hike through imposing mountain forests to a log cabin which was the Swedish Air Force Survival School. Kapten Goliath demonstrated map-reading and survival techniques along the way. We also visited a genuine Lapp in his tented home.

On reaching the cabin we chopped wood for a fire before stripping off and diving into a mountain lake to clean up. We prepared a meal cooked over the fire before climbing into our sleeping bags. The sleeping quarters were sparse, each room having two bunk beds only - no other furniture. Again, my 'Quiet Time' with the Lord and His Word resulted in a useful discussion with my Canadian room-mate as we gradually fell asleep after a tiring but enjoyable day climbing through the picturesque mountain scenery.

Having returned to Ostersund, we rejoined our faithful Dakota aircraft, which took us on a flight of nearly three hours to Visby on the Isle of Gotland, escorted by Vampires.

At Visby we were met by representatives of the tourist industry who briefed us on Visby in particular and the Isle in general. Kapten Goliath informed us that a Dakota had been shot down by Russian Mig fighters only a few months earlier and that we were within fifteen minutes' flying time of the Russian border; he said he thought it best to keep this information to himself until we had landed! Kind of him! It also explained the Vampire escort!

We were lodged in an infantry barracks and were given excellent hospitality which included lunch in a local restaurant followed by a tour of Visby's ancient churches and many interesting ruins. We saw some remarkably large and beautiful roses which apparently thrived on fighting the elements. The deeper the winter snow, the better the roses! King Gustav always had Visby roses on the table when he and his family enjoyed their Christmas dinner.

We had been ordered to take all our kit with us to breakfast next morning, as we were to go directly to the aircraft for our flight back to Stockholm. Unfortunately my American colleagues had left their bed-spaces in a dreadful mess: unmade beds, litter everywhere and furniture awry. I decided that this was no way in which to repay our hosts for their generous hospitality so I set to, in order to leave the place neat and tidy.

As I was completing my task I was aware of someone standing quietly in the doorway. I turned to see the Swedish Duty Officer, a Lieutenant, watching me. He had a very kind face which broke out into a warm smile. I stood smartly to attention as he approached me. He withdrew from his pocket a small blue book which I have before me as I write. He handed it to me. On the cover was the word 'Fälatandaktsbok' in red. This meant nothing to me, and I look enquiringly at him. He took the book from me, turned a few pages, and returned it, pointing to a sentence. It read: "Jesus Kristus är densamme I går och I dag, så ock I evighet." As my knowledge of Swedish was limited to the word 'Stockholm' this meant nothing to me except the first two words. I recognised my Saviour's name. I also recognised the text, Hebrews 13:8: "Jesus Christ the same, yesterday, today and forever".

I think my eyes and my smile must have borne witness to the Lieutenant. In his face I recognised a brother, and he must have recognised a brother in me, for we hugged each other and went off down the corridor with our arms around each other, singing; I don't know what he sang, but my chorus was the musical version of the text he had just shown me:

Yesterday, today forever, Jesus is the same:
All may change but Jesus never,
Glory to His name.
Glory to His name.
Glory to His name.
All may change but Jesus never...
Glory to His name.

It was a most remarkable incident which taught me that the 'Jesus people' were in the *entire* world and that the reality of Christ broke through all barriers of race, language, age and rank. The rest of my party was waiting for me, and their faces were a picture as the Lieutenant and I shook hands warmly and said our 'goodbyes' and 'God blesses' in our different languages but in the unity of the Lord.

As the coach took us to the aircraft, one of the Canadians, Al Massey, asked me in amazement, "Did you know that guy?"

"No," I replied, "not until five minutes ago, but he's turned out to be my brother!"

I then had the joy of explaining to the lads exactly what I meant by that and how it had come about. There was a thoughtful silence on the coach all the way to the aircraft except for one quiet comment: "That's amazing!"

Late that night I was woken by the American lads raiding our room in the hotel. The ring-leader approached my bed menacingly but, on recognising me, asked if I wanted to join in the fun or go back to sleep.

I drowsily mumbled "...sleep" to which he replied, "OK, boy!", put my arm between the sheets, and literally tucked me up; the rest of the room was not given any option, with beds overturned and individuals selected for throwing into cold baths! I ended up having very little sleep!

After breakfast we were taken by coach to the central railway station in Stockholm and paraded in a large waiting room. We were kept waiting for some time before Kapten Goliath called us sharply to attention. He then informed us that we were about to be presented to King Gustav VI who was about to join his royal train to go on holiday. What an honour!

When he came to me, he asked where I lived and showed interest in the fact that my home was near Croydon. "Oh, I know Croydon well," he said. "I've often flown to the airport on my visits to your country."

After exchanging a few more pleasant words about our visit to Sweden he was gone, but the memory of that brief encounter will always remain with me. I spoke with a King!

Lunch was taken at the American Embassy where the Air Attaché, Colonel Pew, was our host. The afternoon was spent visiting the Royal Palace and Stockholm city centre before being shown over the AGA plant at Lading.

Our visit to Sweden was drawing to a close. The American cadets left at 05:00 hours on 13th August from Bromma, *en route* to Paris. They left a delayed pyrotechnic on the windowsill which exploded during breakfast. Al Massey was cutting into his sausage at the time, and the look on his face was a sight to behold! Some banger!

A short coach ride brought us back to the Air Ministry, where we were presented to the Commander-in-Chief of the Royal Swedish Air Force. He invited us to be seated in his ample armchairs, and we spoke with him for about half an hour with the press taking photos. The C-in-C's *aide-de-camp*, Kapten Lornberg, presented each of us with a photo of the J29.

Our final day in Sweden was spent on an air-sea rescue launch in the archipelago. It was a beautifully warm day, which invited one into the water. We bathed from the launch, and I was amazed to see one of the Swedish pilots strip off, revealing an artificial leg. He deftly unscrewed it, chucked it into the stern of the boat and dived into the water, swimming like a fish!

A car took us to the Air Ministry to bid farewell to the Commander-in-Chief, who, to all intents and purposes, was our ultimate host. We each made our own short speech of appreciation for all that had been done for us by his staff at the various stages of our visit.

So ended my Swedish interlude! What an experience and what an honour! Even today the visit still stands in my memory as a milestone in my life - not only for all the sights seen, the people met and the sheer adventure of being in a foreign land, but also for having had the opportunity of sharing something of my Saviour with others. Perhaps most remarkable of all was my encounter with the Swedish army officer at Visby barracks - an event brought to my memory every time I look at the little *Fältandaktsbok*, still among the books in my library. This was my first experience of meeting people of a different culture and language who also knew Jesus and could be recognised by His Spirit within them.

The Dakota aircraft touched down smoothly at Northolt, and I bade farewell to my fellow travellers. On the train home to Purley, I re-lived the visit in my mind and read again my scrawled diary that has been the skeleton for this chapter. I was pleased to be home, with the familiar language, sights and sounds around me, but I thanked God for another adventure in life that most of my peers would never experience. The visit could be summarised in the Air Training Corps motto: "Venture Adventure".

Aircrew Selection

As usual on a Tuesday and Thursday, the school squadron of the Air Training Corps paraded at lunch time and after school. Our Commanding Officer was our Physics master, and he lectured the squadron on Airmanship and Rules of the Air. The squadron adjutant taught us Biology but gave the squadron the benefit of his past RAF experience on Weaponry and General Duties Training.

Our lecture programme was further assisted by other ex-service members of staff which included a navigator holding the rank of Squadron Leader, a technical Flight Lieutenant engineer, and a Lieutenant Colonel in the Intelligence Corps who occasionally told the squadron of his experiences interrogating German prisoners of war.

By the time I was in the sixth form I had risen to the rank of Cadet Flight Sergeant and was responsible for taking the parades, organising the training programme and lecturing on the Morse Code and Aircraft Recognition.

As I was about to leave for home on this particular Tuesday, the Commanding Officer called me into his office. I entered, saluted and stood wondering what I might have done wrong! The CO had two habits noted well by his pupils: one was saying "er..." as he was speaking; the other jiggling his right knee up and down when seated. I noticed on this particular occasion that the knee was going 'ten to the dozen' as he looked at some papers on his desk. At last he looked up and said, "How... er... Collard would you like to... er... be put forward for a... er... Flying Scholarship?" Such a scholarship, which was paid for by the government, was awarded to selected air cadets, training them up to Private Pilot's Licence standard.

My mouth opened and shut like a fish. I was speechless. The previous two cadet flight sergeants had been offered the same privilege and had gone on to become Royal Air Force pilots.

My response was, "Do you think I stand a chance, sir?" to which he replied: "Frankly... er... no! Your maths is lousy and your... er... physics is worse. You need both to be a pilot. However, I feel... er... constrained to put your name forward. Are you... er... willing to have a go?"

I stuttered, "Yes sir, please sir!" with my mind in a whirl.

I must admit that I went through the various selection interviews at Surrey Wing and regional level assuming I would be rejected, but in December 1953 I was ordered to attend an *Aircrew Pre-selection Test* at the Royal Air Force station, Hornchurch.

This proved to be a very enjoyable experience. It began with a medical, which proved to be the most thorough I would ever have. Even a small irregular lump in my left ear, obtained either at rugby or boxing, was examined with diligence and concern, but I was eventually passed fully fit and allowed to progress to the next hurdle in the testing procedure which was designed to examine physical / mental co-ordination and intelligence.

It was rather like playing at a fairground. One sat at a desk facing a vertically-mounted contraption containing a drum which rotated horizontally. On it were flat electrical studs, about the size of a drawing pin head, which weaved as the drum rotated. To the right of the drum was a handle mounted on a loose fly-wheel which controlled a single contact that traversed across the face of the drum in the horizontal plane. Thus, by turning the handle by variable amounts and speeds, the operator endeavoured to hit the rotating studs with the single contact.

The *finger dexterity test* resembled an enlarged chess board divided into about one hundred squares. A square peg, vertically coloured half black and half white, sat firmly in a recess in each square. On the word "go", one had to lift each peg out of its slot, turn it through one hundred and eighty degrees and replace it. Thus a board full of white pegs became a board full of black pegs by the end of the exercise, assuming you were able to manipulate all the pegs in the time allowed. There was a chap on our intake who worked in a biscuit factory as a packer. He turned his board from white to black and back again, which caused quite a stir with the invigilating staff as they accused him of not having started!

The final co-ordination test was the nearest some candidates got to flying an aircraft! On a screen similar to the early televisions, one was faced with a small electronic green dot which drifted randomly all over the screen. The operator had a centrally-mounted *joystick* with which he could control the movement of the dot vertically and pedals at his feet to control the dot horizontally. The aim of the exercise was to keep the dot within a half-inch square in the centre of the screen. At the same time one's peripheral vision and physical / mental response was tested by a light set to the top left hand corner of the box in which the screen was mounted. Under one's left hand was a *throttle* lever. If the light appeared red the throttle had to be retarded. If the light showed green the throttle had to be advanced. Great fun - especially as I found it dead easy!

Various papers were introduced which tested one's general intelligence and abilities, including Maths, Interpretation of Pictorial Devices and Graphs, Mechanics, and Logical Progressions. I struggled with the Maths-orientated papers but thought I had done well enough.

Next came the interviews! The one which particularly sticks in my memory was a one-to-one with a rather aloof and stern Squadron Leader. Among the many topics on which he questioned me and sought my opinion was my parents' view of my desire to fly.

I responded by saying, "Well, sir, my dad was a cavalryman in the First World War, and he reckons the back of a horse is high enough for anyone!"

This brought a huge grin to the face of my interviewer, and it obviously scored a point or two! He noticeably softened after that exchange.

As the interview closed he started filling in a form as I answered his questions about my schooling and my Air Training Corps squadron.

"What number is your school squadron?" he asked.

"One six one zero, sir," I replied.

I had been keeping an eye on what he had written in reply to my questions, albeit reading upside down as I faced him across the table, and noticed that on this occasion he wrote, "one zero one six". I immediately called his attention to the error. An almost imperceptible smile of satisfaction wafted over his face, and he looked me full in the eyes and simply said, "Thank you!"

Later in my career I was to fulfil a similar role to his, interviewing student pilots. One of the interviewing techniques was to see if the candidate was monitoring your record of his answers and correcting any mistakes – some made deliberately - the idea being to test the candidate's observation, attention to detail and willingness to speak up.

On the strength of my cadet rank I was exempt thc next day of tests which were designed to examine initiative and leadership, so I was able to return home and await the results of my enjoyable day at Hornchurch.

A letter from the President of the Pre-selection Board, dated the 5th January 1954, arrived in the post a couple of weeks later stating:

This is to certify that you have taken the full selection tests for an Air Training Corps Flying Scholarship. The results of your tests will be forwarded to Headquarters Home Command who are responsible for the final selection.

Whether or not you are successful in obtaining a vacancy for a Flying Scholarship, the selection tests are also valid for flying duties in the Royal Air Force. If at a later date you wish to take advantage of the pre-assessment scheme for aircrew service in the Royal Air Force, you should apply to the Aircrew Transit Officer at this centre.

This I did and received the following letter from the Aircrew Transit Officer dated the 20th February 1954:

Further to our letter of even reference dated 20th ult. Now that the flying scholarships have been awarded, we can inform you that you were found suitable as a pre-assessment candidate for the Royal Air Force in the aircrew categories of Pilot and Air Signaller...

The medical examination that you undertook at Hornchurch is valid for six months only, therefore if you do not enter the Royal Air Force by the end of June 1954 it will be necessary for you to be medically re-boarded before you can be considered for aircrew training.

I was ecstatic with joy! I had been found acceptable in the pilot category! I noted with interest that I had *not* been accepted as a possible navigator – my maths had let me down again! If I failed as a pilot, at least I might stand another chance of flying as an Air Signaller. My Morse Code was pretty hot from its regular use in the cadets, so I had no fears of failure on that score.

A few weeks later I found myself at Kenley airfield, standing in front of a senior officer from Home Command who said, "Congratulations, Collard! You have been awarded an Air Training Corps Flying Scholarship, and you will begin your training to Private Pilot's Licence standard at the commencement of your Easter school holidays.

"You will report to the Chief Flying Instructor of the Airways Aero Club at Croydon Airport on the first day of that holiday. Meanwhile, at a time convenient to yourself, you are to take this authorization [he handed me a paper] to the equipment section where you will be fitted out with your flying kit. Well done!"

What a thrill it was to present that piece of paper to the airman in the equipment section and draw from him a "helmet leather flying one with Gosport tube", "goggles mark eight one", "suit flying one", "gloves satin inner one pair", "gauntlets leather one pair", "boots flying lamb's wool one pair", and finally a "holdall aircrew" in which to carry everything.

In stature I was a diminutive five feet four inches, the majority of my height deficiency being in my short legs; thus my holdall scraped the ground as I carried it away from Kenley - but I felt ten feet tall! Croydon Airport, here I come!

A Fledgling at Croydon Airport

At last the Easter holidays arrived. On the 4th April 1954 I reported to the Chief Flying Instructor of the Airways Aero Club at Croydon Airport who introduced me to my instructor Ted Boggis: himself an ex-RAF pilot. As he showed me over the silver Tiger Moth and introduced me to the instrument panel and controls, I felt over-awed. How would I ever cope with all this? Then, into my mind came the words "My grace is sufficient for you, for my strength is made perfect in weakness" and "Your mercy, O Lord, is in the heavens and your faithfulness reaches to the clouds." (Quotes from 2 Corinthians 12:9 and Psalm 36:5.)

I remembered the words of my wise old counsellor who told me to expect some surprises and changes if I wanted God to take me seriously when I surrendered my life to His service. Could God be in this? Did He really want me to fly rather than "kick a bag of wind around a field for the rest of [my] life"? What was the purpose in it? How could it glorify Him?

Figure 10: G-ANEW. The aircraft in which I received my first dual instructional flight on 4th April 1954.

Ted Boggis took me up for my familiarisation flight on that same day. I was told to sit in the rear cockpit and enjoy the ride. I cannot say I did!

To me it was a bit frightening, albeit thrilling. The thumping and whipping of the airflow in the open cockpit, tearing at face and clothing, was both noisy and imposing. Looking over the side and seeing the ground a thousand feet below was not the same as seeing it from the closed snug cockpit of the Chipmunk aircraft in which we had, as cadets, been flown on our *air experience* flights.

Ted Boggis pointed out various things to me on that familiarisation sortie but gave no overt instruction. He conversed with me through the *Gosport Tube* - a simple device comprising a flexible, small calibre tube fixed to each earpiece in the helmet, becoming a single tube at chest level. The end was plugged into a conduit in the rear cockpit, terminating in a mouthpiece in the front cockpit. An identical system enabled the rear occupant to speak to the front cockpit.

I cannot adequately describe my emotions that night as I re-lived my first flight and contemplated the real work that was to begin on the morrow. There was no sitting back and enjoying the ride from now on. My confidence, character, mental and physical abilities (and my maths!) were on the line - as was my faith in the One who had brought me thus far.

Soon a routine took shape! Cycling from my home in Purley, I would daily enter that famous forecourt at Croydon airport, park my bicycle at the side entrance, climb the stairs above the refreshment room, and make my way along the corridor to the Airways Aero Club lounge overlooking the main apron on which many and varied aircraft were constantly arriving and departing.

My instructor's first major objective was to get me to fly solo, but for this I needed to show consistency in my take-offs and landings. I had little trouble with the take-off, but I found the landing very difficult, either hitting the ground at too great a speed and bouncing into the air again, or holding off too high and at too low a speed, inviting a stall and threatening to write off the wheels! Ted Boggis, together with two other instructors, patiently explained the technique on the ground and demonstrated it in the air, but I could not reproduce it to their satisfaction. My landings were plain awful!

Whenever I felt defeated and upset, I used to walk up to Riddlesdown and lie in the grass to contemplate my lot. It was a quiet place of open country, backed by woods, overlooking the Kenley and Whyteleafe valley. On this particular day the sky was blue and the sun warm. Without shutting my eyes I began to share my problem with the Lord, asking Him to somehow intervene and either give me the ability that I was sadly lacking or help me to accept that I would never become a pilot after all.

It was some minutes later that I was aware of a bird circling above me. I watched it with ever-increasing interest. It veered off to my right and then flew a steady approach, landing a few feet in front of me. After hopping and pecking at the ground for a while it took off, circled above me again and repeated the previous performance. I was now sitting up and observing the creature attentively. To my amazement the bird flew yet another circuit, landing on the same spot.

As I studied its approach, I noticed how it 'held off' just above the ground as the angle of its wings increased with decreasing speed. Suddenly, all the instruction I had received seem to click into place and I eagerly anticipated my next flight. I left Riddlesdown elated!

Ted Boggis looked unusually bored as he climbed into the front seat.

"Let's have another go, young Collard. I don't think I can tell you any more than I have already, and I've shown you how to land this thing umpteen times! Take off, fly a circuit and try a landing. If you don't like the approach give it full power and go round again and have another crack at it but *please* try not to frighten me anymore!"

As I made my first approach, I tried to replicate what the bird had done. Rather than immediately trying to match the aircraft's rate of descent with an increasing wing angle, I 'held off' in level flight just above the ground and waited for the aircraft to begin sinking. Only then did I ease the joystick progressively back into my stomach. The wheels bounced once, very gently, and I was down.

There was no immediate comment from my instructor, but as I was about to ask him what he wanted me to do next, he quietly said, "Do that again - another circuit!"

Off I went and this time landed without a bounce.

"One more!" demanded Ted.

The third landing was equally successful.

I shall never forget that moment when, at the far corner of the airfield away from the control tower, on the north-facing grass strip (which now approximates to the present Lindberg Road), Ted Boggis climbed out of the front cockpit of G-ANDE (affectionately known as "Mahatma" for obvious reasons), secured the front seat harness, grinned at me behind his flailing white scarf and shouted at me over the noise of the idling engine and slipstream, "Off you go! One circuit and landing, then pick me up here!" The date was the 24th April 1954.

The Tiger Moth was flown solo from the rear cockpit, so the absence of that familiar leather-helmeted head in front of me caused momentary apprehension which immediately dissolved into concentration as I carried out my *Vital Actions* prior to take-off. Pointing the nose towards the Stafford Road end, I slowly opened the throttle, corrected the swing with rudder, eased the joystick forward to lift the tail, a touch more rudder, then lift-off – I was airborne on my own!

Figure 11: After first solo in Tiger Moth G-ANDE at Croydon airport. 24 April 1954.

As I clambered away I was rather disturbed to see another aircraft, not 200 yards to my right, also climbing on a parallel heading. He overtook me and cut across my bows - a little off-putting on one's first solo, but it taught me right from the start to keep a good lookout, and I was saved on many occasions in my future flying career by the principle learned from that initial scare!

It is difficult for a pilot to describe the feelings experienced on his very first solo. For me there would be many more first solos on twenty seven different aircraft types or marks but this was, and always will be, something special to me. Alone in the sky with only one's own ability and judgement to get back down again; the cheerful chattering of the Gypsy Major engine; the ready response of the machine in three dimensions to one's finger-tip touch; the whistle of the air through the landing and flying wires and the thumping of the slipstream as it eddied into and around the open cockpit buffeting goggles, face and clothing; each was something special to savour entirely alone. What a privilege to experience, so early in life, something that most mortals would never know: to be alone in the sky!

The flight seemed to last only a few seconds, such was my concentration. With engine throttled right back and reduced to a gentle, pulsating throb, I eased "Mahatma" G-ANDE towards the grass. Exhilaration was replaced with total mental focus.

"Wait until you can see the daisies, then ease back on the stick - right back into your stomach - and stall her on." Ted's words rang again in my ears as though he was still in that front cockpit. A gentle bump and we were down! Again Ted's voice roared at me in my mind: "Keep straight! Use your rudders until she stops! Don't relax just because you're down!" I kept the nose steady and felt the aircraft slow to a halt. I had done it! I had flown an aeroplane all on my own and brought it safely back to earth again – and it would be another four years before I got my licence to drive a car!

Ted slapped me on the shoulder as he climbed back into the front cockpit with a brief "Well done!" He taxied the machine back to the apron "to give me a rest", and over a coffee in the lounge he debriefed me on the flight.

"What should you do just before lining up for takeoff?" he asked quietly.

The answer came easily in the lounge - so easily that my stupidity at the take-off point came back at me like a kick in the teeth! I had forgotten the cardinal rule of looking at the control tower for a green light before lining up to take off! The reason that I had shared my first solo take-off with another aircraft was because he had a radio and had been cleared to go, whilst I had failed to see the red light telling me to hold my position!

I must say I considered it a little unjust that the radio aircraft had been given clearance to go when it was obvious that I, without the advantage of radio contact, had been given a red. The controller would have known I was about to embark upon my first solo and could have given me priority. However, another valuable lesson had been learned early in my flying experience.

Thus, after some thirteen hours and forty five minutes of outstanding bravery and saintly patience on the part of my longsuffering instructors, and much unseen aerodynamic wincing on the part of the forgiving Tiger Moths G-ANEW and G-ANDE, I finally but tentatively became a fledgling!

Being so short in stature, mainly due to my lack of lower leg length, I had to have the rudder pedals adjusted to the minimum setting, two cushions behind my back and two underneath! Even then I sat very low in the cockpit and peered, rather than looked, over the cockpit coaming.

During the latter part of the course, Ted Boggis took me up to three thousand feet to demonstrate a spin. Having completed his pre-spinning checks, he closed the throttle and allowed the aircraft to lose speed. Just above the stall he applied full left rudder and heaved the joystick fully back. The Tiger Moth rotated around its horizontal axis prior to dropping its nose steeply towards the ground, continuing to rotate at what appeared to be an alarming speed. I crouched down in the cockpit and held on to the front of my seat.

Ted recovered from the spin, explaining everything he was doing, until we were once again in straight and level flight. I then heard a sudden cry of alarm from the front cockpit: "Collard! Collard, where are you?"

"I'm here sir," I replied, lifting my head. In the mirror I caught sight of Ted's white face and wide eyes staring at me through his goggles.

"Oh thank heaven for that," he exclaimed. "I thought you'd fallen out!"

Croydon Airport holds many other memories for me. There was the time when, before being taught cross-wind landings, the wind changed dramatically whilst I was away on a solo map-reading exercise and I tried to land on the same strip from which I had departed! The strip in question was south-westerly which meant approaching over the cooling towers, Duppas Hill recreation ground, the open air swimming pool on Purley Way, then past the control tower at virtually window height just before touchdown. My approach was, to say the least, erratic, but I managed to put the aircraft down in a series of bumps, swings and lurches without damaging anything more than my nerves. I think it would have been even more disastrous if I had known that Ted Boggis and the other three cadets on my course were watching the episode and biting their fingernails to the elbows! After climbing out of the aircraft I was given an unforgettable exhortation by Ted Boggis to always land into wind on a grass airfield, irrespective of the landing strip in use when one took off!

It was also at Croydon Airport that I faced my first emergency in the air. The date was the 12th May 1954 and my log book entry reads:

Tiger Moth, G-ANDE, Solo Circuits and Bumps, 45 minutes, lost rearward sparking plug at 600 feet.

Having just taken off in a westerly direction on the strip at the southern end of the airfield and parallel to Hillcrest Road, my engine began running very roughly. At the time, I was climbing over the built up area of Carshalton-on-the-Hill and the thought flashed through my mind: "What happens if it stops?!" I elected to turn downwind immediately and complete a very curtailed, low level circuit pattern which terminated in my stopping the Tiger Moth only a hundred yards from the western boundary fence.

Typical of a novice, I taxied the aircraft back to the hangars instead of closing the engine down and walking! The mechanic who waved me on to the chocks threw the engine cowling up as soon as the propeller had stopped rotating and, after a moment's inspection, turned a rather pale face towards me and blurted out in Cockney, "Cor! No wonder it sounded like Wa'erloo station! One o' yer spark plugs is gorn and yer ignition lead was sparkin' on yer fuel pipe! You're a lucky bloke! Could have 'ad a fire!"

Other memories of Croydon go back to my earlier childhood, remembering the Spitfires and Hurricanes warming up every morning and frequently seeing them roar over the Purley valley to engage the encroaching enemy bombers and, latterly, the dreaded Doodle-Bugs.

Croydon Airport came in for the enemy's malevolent attention on many occasions, and at Brancaster Lane we had a good view. We were often more than mere spectators. In addition to my encounter with "'Itler's mo'obike", one night a retreating low level bomber had the audacity to strafe our house (no other building in the vicinity was touched!) severing the telephone and power lines and shattering those front room windows again! The German gunner also left part of a cannon shell deeply embedded in our front door. I remember Dad filling in the hole and painting over it.

Douglas Bader, the legless fighter pilot, was every boy's idol in those days. Nine years after the war, whilst waiting in the Airways Aero Club lounge for my next flight, I would often see a twin-engined Gemini aircraft roar into the Croydon circuit and taxi (rather fast!) to the apron below. I would see the hood fly up, a briefcase thrown out closely pursued by a raincoat, both expertly fielded by an attendant mechanic. Two stiff legs would then emerge from the cockpit as the pilot eased himself onto the wing. Sitting himself on the wing root he would slide earthwards until his artificial feet touched the ground. Standing erect and squaring his shoulders, he would reclaim his briefcase and coat from the mechanic, brusquely jam his pipe into his mouth and stomp off with his characteristic gait, giving the mechanic a curt but not unfriendly nod of his head. Group Captain Douglas Bader DSO DFC RAF (Retired) had arrived! What a man! The CBE was later added to his decorations for his work for the disabled.

More memories linger in my mind like the lumbering DC3 Dakotas waddling from the apron in front of the control tower to the far south-eastern corner of the airfield, turning into wind, taking advantage of the short metalled surface of the north-westerly strip which gave them a little more acceleration before experiencing the greater drag from the grass. They would swing their tails close up to the boundary fence on Purley Way, thunder their engines against the brakes, then roar off, trundling and rocking their way towards the Stafford Road and Sandy Lane corner, clawing themselves into the air.

I remember the work's hooter sounding off at midday, announcing the lunch break for the workers in the factories that skirted the Purley Way perimeter. I remember the majestic and unique control tower, below which each flight was booked out; and the walk across the apron to where the Tiger Moths were lined up into wind, silver in the sunlight with the blue flash along the length of the fuselage; and that never-to-be-forgotten smell in the cockpit of warm leather, oil, dope and fuel.

My last flight from Croydon was on the 22nd May 1954 when I flew my Private Pilot's Licence test, again in G-ANDE. My Tiger Moth was parked on the same spot as was a Gemini aircraft just six years previous, about to fly to Sudan. It belonged to the newly-formed Missionary Aviation Fellowship[1] and left Croydon Airport on the 13th January 1948 to examine the feasibility of using aircraft in the support of missions working in remote and isolated parts of the world.

Squadron Leader Jack Hemmings AFC, RAF (Ret'd) and Flight Lieutenant Stuart Sendall-King RAF (Ret'd) were the pioneer crew. In another twenty one years' time I would have the privilege of being part of this great work which, in 1948, was just a vision in the minds of a few as the Gemini aircraft rolled from that same position on the apron at Croydon Airport from which my chocks were waved away in 1954.

Unknown to me at the time, God did have a purpose in getting rid of football in my life and getting me airborne!

Croydon Airport was a happy and challenging experience frequently tinged with healthy apprehension and the occasional full-blooded fright! It was the birthplace of my flying career and the bedrock of many good disciplines and habits which were to further develop over the years and ensure my safety on so many occasions.

On the 3rd December 1997 I was watching the TV programme 'Police, Camera, Action' in which the opening scene was of Alistair Stewart commentating from a Tiger Moth carrying out a traffic survey for the police. I could not believe my eyes, for the registration of the Tiger was G-ANDE!

Through writing to the programme producer I was able to identify the current owner, with whom I carried out further correspondence. He very kindly invited me to be reunited with G-ANDE the next time it was loaned to the flying club at nearby Sherburn-in-Elmet, but as yet our paths have not crossed. I hope they will! What an occasion it would be to fly

---

[1] Later renamed as the 'Mission Aviation Fellowship'.

again in that faithful aircraft which launched me into a flying career that lasted thirty five years!

Into the Blue

I t was with a sense of adventure and excitement that I boarded a bus at the Royal Oak in Brighton Road, Purley, to go on the first stage of my journey into the Royal Air Force. My first port of call was the recruiting office alongside West Croydon railway station.

A very friendly sergeant welcomed me and introduced me to four other young lads who were on the same venture. Because of my experience in the Air Training Corps, I was put in charge of our small party and given custody of the railway warrant which authorised British Rail to transport us to Bedford. There a lorry collected us from the station, together with other new arrivals, and took us to the Initial Reception Centre at Cardington where we were shown into a barrack room which was to be our home for the next three days.

Having made our mutual introductions, we realised just what a motley crew we were - all shapes and sizes from a variety of backgrounds! At least I knew what living in a barrack room was like from my five years as a cadet. I had been on many Air Force stations, was conversant with the various ranks of the Royal Air Force, had handled weapons and live ammunition, and had a Private Pilot's Licence in my baggage! I also knew what the food was like and the potent NAAFI tea!

The first destination for most of my newfound friends was the Medical Centre where they had to undergo their initial medical examinations. I was exempt this visit due to my having already passed the Aircrew Selection Board. Our next port of call was a large room where an officer swore us in as members of Her Majesty's Royal Air Force and we signed copies of the Official Secrets Act. We were then presented with the *Queen's Shilling* which was soon spent in the NAAFI.

We were 'kitted out' and had to sign as having received a *best blue* uniform, *working blue* uniform, beret, service hat, webbing, fatigue overalls, gas capes, knife, fork, spoon and enamel mug, socks, shirts, collars, ties, vests, pants, flannel pyjamas and all other necessities for making a recent sixth-former into an Aircraftsman Class Two (AC2) commonly referred to as "the lowest form of creeping life". We were also issued with a large kit bag in which to place our newly acquired assets.

Once back in the barrack room we examined our collection of goodies but were interrupted by the door being flung open and the crash of a studded boot on the highly polished floor. There, framed in the doorway, was a corporal immaculately attired from head to toe, his boots shining like mirrors. He stood rigidly to attention with a silver knobbed cane, parallel to the ground, tucked under his left arm, with his left hand supporting the knob.

"Gen'lemen!" he bawled. "I am your conducting corporal for the next three days. The rest of today is your own, but tomorrow at 06:00 hours I will collect you for breakfast after which I will teach you the fundamentals of formation flying!"

He performed a smart about-turn, crashing his left foot on the ground, and disappeared.

What was he talking about? – How was he going to teach us anything about formation flying? He wasn't a pilot, and there were no aircraft at Cardington - only barrage balloons! We put it down to a warped sense of humour and enjoyed the rest of the evening in the camp cinema followed by a visit to the NAAFI where we supplemented the cooked tea taken a few hours earlier, with further eggs, bacon, beans, fried potato and fried bread washed down with a large enamel mug or two of strong tea. Some opted for the even stronger beverages and subsequently had difficulty in navigating their way back to the barrack room.

As one might expect with a group of some thirty senior teenagers, laughter, yelled conversation and horse-play went on for some hours before the room became quiet enough for sleep; and there was not much of it before the re-appearance of our guardian corporal at 06:00, announced once again by the door swinging noisily open and the crash of the studded boot on the polished floor.

"Gen'lemen!" he bawled. "You are to carry out your ablutions pronto, dress in your working blues with berets, belts and boots and fall in outside by 06:30 latest. Anyone falling in after that time will be given fatigues this evening. Mooove!"

The barrack room became a hive of noisy industry and discovery. Some chaps had never worn a collar and tie before so those of us conversant with the skill of studding a collar and tying a tie had to help out - but have you ever tried tying someone else's tie from the front?!

By some miracle we all managed to present ourselves by 06:30 albeit in a state of doubtful uniformity. For most of the group this was their first time in a uniform, and it was surprising how many variations and permutations could be made out of the same items of clothing and headgear.

The corporal looked suitably unimpressed and informed us of his opinion of our efforts in no uncertain manner. However, he got us into some resemblance of a squad and marched us to breakfast with our mugs, knives, forks and spoons held firmly in our left hands, swinging only our right arms. Some of the less knowledgeable among us were informed by the corporal, to the discomfort of their eardrums, that it was not the 'done thing' to swing the left arm when something was being held at its extremity. Hey ho! What a lot to learn!

Breakfast was consumed speedily, noisily and ravenously before dunking our knives, forks, spoons and enamel mugs into a steaming tank of increasingly greasy hot water as we left the airmen's mess to march back to the barrack room. We were instructed to leave our utensils on our beds and assemble immediately on the parade square.

Well over an hour later, with our ears ringing with the corporal's commands, counter-commands, exhortations and censures, we collapsed exhausted on our beds with feet steaming, arms aching and backs sagging. As we were attending to our blisters and aching limbs, the corporal again framed himself in the doorway, immaculate and cool as ever, announcing in a matter-of-fact voice, "Gen'lemen! You 'ave just 'ad your first lesson in formation flying!"

It was only later in my career, when I was flying in formation with other aircraft, that I realised how true the corporal's words had been. What chaos and death could be caused to a whole formation by a pilot turning right instead of left! On the parade ground one is in formation with many other guys. Each has to concentrate, understand what is said, obey the commands immediately and without question, and be aware that one's individual mistake could have embarrassing results for the whole squad, not just oneself. The fundamentals of formation flying were indeed learned on the parade ground!

The corporal later shared another pearl of wisdom with us: "Now, gen'lemen, you will be taught the importance of observing detail."

He then proceeded to demonstrate how we were to make up our beds every morning and how to lay out our kit for inspections. The bed first had to be stripped down to the three 'biscuits' that formed the mattress, then the blankets and two sheets folded in such a way that, on completion, they looked like a large sandwich (blanket, sheet, blanket, sheet, blanket). The fourth blanket, folded along its length, encased the sandwich and the lot was placed centrally at the head of the bed with the pillow on top.

The towel was then draped across the bed amidships and the enamel mug placed, inverted, at the centre with its handle parallel to the sides of the bed, facing the front. The knife was positioned vertically to the right, fork vertically to the left and spoon horizontally above the mug.

All webbing equipment was laid out around the towel in a particular order, with all footwear, again in a prescribed pattern, on the floor at the foot of the bed. One's wardrobe had its own precise display of hanging clothes and hats, and other items such as shirts, physical training gear, shoe cleaning kit etc similarly laid out in one's bedside locker. Anything out of place on subsequent inspections brought fire and brimstone down upon the offender with the sentence of more fatigues.

Again, I was to learn in later years that such attention to detail, both in the air and on the ground, was a matter of life or death. The Royal Air Force taught well, and I am eternally grateful for its instruction.

Thus hard lessons were learned in those first few days with the colours, and many more were to come my way as the days wore on. Looking back, some fifty-six years later, I thank God for that corporal and for the likes of him that inflicted themselves upon me in the early years of my life 'in the blue'. Without them I would not be alive today! Whatever branch of the Armed Forces one might join, the basics taught at recruiting depots are essential for the survival of oneself and of one's colleagues when it comes to the operational crunch.

For many, the discipline was too much and hard to handle, but I found it challenging, invigorating, enjoyable and, subsequently, life-saving. "Per ardua ad astra" ("Through Difficulties to the Stars") was more than just the Royal Air Force motto; it was a fact! However, there was a lot more "ardua" to come before we got anywhere near the "astra"!

Initial Training

Leaving Cardington as No. 3518711 Aircraftsmen Class 2 Collard R, I joined our small band of a dozen potential Officer Cadets to catch the train which would take us on to the next stage of our venture. To us it was an unknown destination. At least we knew the name of it, as it was printed on our rail warrant, but none of us had ever heard of it before: Kirton-in-Lindsey. Here, at the No. 1 Initial Training School, we were to be re-classified as Officer Cadets and hopefully graduate as Acting Pilot Officers before moving on to a Flying Training School which may have been in the UK or Canada.

We travelled in our full kit, including back packs, water bottles, ammunition pouches (stuffed with goodies for the journey), greatcoats and kit bags. We felt like pack-asses! Running for our connection at Retford we realised how unfit we were and collapsed breathlessly into our carriage just as the train steamed out.

Kirton-in-Lindsey duly turned up and we disembarked. What had we come to? - A small and insignificant station in an apparently barren land, no built-up area to be seen, no hills and certainly no population – just an elderly ticket-collector who was obviously used to seeing boys in blue cluttering up his station.

We boarded the three ton truck that had been sent to collect us and we were welcomed on board by a sergeant wearing the brevet of an air signaller over his left breast pocket. We began to pay him due respect until he introduced himself: "Don't get the wrong idea chaps! I'm just one of you. I've been posted on to your course, so we're all equals." Bob became a good friend to us and initiated us into the finer points of being in the Royal Air Force. He was also wise to all the dodges!

As the truck was passing a few houses on its way to our destination, one of the lads asked Bob where the bright lights of the town might be.

"We've just passed through it," he said. "Didn't you see it? That was Kirton Lindsey! Lincoln's the nearest place for nights out and that's seventeen miles away!" A groan echoed around the truck.

Little did I realise at the time that I was passing within a few yards of the house in which lived the girl who would become my wife and the church which would be the scene of our wedding in just three years time! It is amazing what God has up His sleeve!

Bob further informed us that we would be working every Saturday morning until mid-day and that Wednesday afternoons would be devoted to compulsory sports unless otherwise engaged on training. Another groan circulated through the truck. "Colditz!" someone remarked.

On arrival at the camp, where we were joined by seven other fellows, a corporal informed us that we now comprised the new intake in the *Aircrew Cadet Transit Unit* (ACTU) where our initiations began. Our first barrack room was small with two-tier bunks, wardrobes and bedside lockers.

Within a few days we were allocated to our training squadrons and our first domestic job was to sew the white tabs on to the collar lapels of our best blue tunics and working dress blouses, thus marking us as Officer Cadets. As we had been assigned to No. 3 Squadron in Red Wing, we had a small red stripe running longitudinally down each tab and a red epaulette with a '3' surmounted on each shoulder flap of our working blue (No. 2 Dress). We also fixed a white circular plastic disc behind the RAF badge on our berets. Blue webbing belts and rifle slings were issued to wear with working dress and white belts and slings to wear with best blue (No. 1 Dress) which included a white band around our service dress hats.

Kit lay-outs and inspections were carried out daily and the training proved interesting and enjoyable with a good balance between activities and academics. Usually the mornings, after a session of Physical Training, were spent in foot and rifle drill followed by lectures on Service Writing, Etiquette, Air Force Law, Leadership, Aeronautical Maths, Aeronautical Science, Air Force History, First Aid, Service Administration and Organization, Ground Combat Training and other such subjects deemed necessary for budding officers.

The afternoons were devoted to initiative, leadership and map-reading exercises, weapons practice on the firing range, gas and respirator drills, dinghy drill and swimming at the Scunthorpe public baths and various visits to places of interest to improve our general knowledge of military and civic matters.

During our training as Officer Cadets we had to keep a daily diary to record not only our activities and experiences but also some of the current events of the day. This was to ensure we read the newspapers and kept abreast of national and international affairs. In addition to fulfilling its required function, my diary also traces my deepening relationship with a young lady from the local Methodist Church. Our first meeting is worthy of mention...

In the Royal Air Force of those days, one was either 'C of E' (Church of England), RC (Roman Catholic), Jewish or OD (Other Denominations). The latter included Baptist, Congregational, Methodist, Church of Scotland, Free Church, etc etc.

One's religious denomination was annotated, together with rank, number and name, on a label surmounting one's wardrobe in the barrack room. Mine bore the inscription "3518711 Officer Cadet Collard R. OD"

Being the only OD on the Course, and not wishing to be left out of the Church Parade, I fell-in with the 'C of E's on the Sunday morning. The corporal in charge inspected us before we marched to the station church. He came to me, looked me up and down, then said, "Collard, I thought you were OD. What you doing 'ere among the 'C of E's?"

I informed him that I was the only OD on the course but wanted to attend a church service and so had fallen in with the C of E contingent. He seemed a bit surprised that I actually wanted to attend a church parade and replied, "Fall out! Go and 'ave a church parade on yer own! You'll find a Methodist Church in the village."

So I found myself walking into the village entirely on my own, feeling somewhat self-conscious wearing my best blue and whites for the very first time. Even the cows in the fields seemed to view me as a curiosity as I passed them by.

I found the Methodist Church and was handed a hymnbook by the steward who greeted me with the words "Good to see you! You're obviously a new boy!" I took a seat a third of the way into the church on the right hand side and accustomed myself to my new surroundings. The pulpit was very high up and the choir stalls were even higher behind it. Higher still was the organ.

Eventually the choir began to file in from the right and the first three were young ladies. As the third young lady came into view something very remarkable happened. I simply found myself bowing my head and praying, "Lord, if that girl is *not* to be my wife, please make it clear to me."

As the members of the choir took their seats I noticed 'my girl' and her two friends either side of her scanning the congregation quite disinterestedly. I suppose they were simply seeing who was there and who was missing this week. I could not take my eyes off 'my girl'. She leaned against her colleague and said something to her as she briefly looked in my direction. Years later I was to discover that she had said, "Look at that one – a proper Mummy's darling!"

After the service there was the usual talking outside as the congregation gradually dispersed and I found myself alongside 'my girl' and one of her choir friends who turned to me and enquired, "Do you play tennis?" Perhaps an appropriate game, for the courting started there! That was the beginning of a relationship which blossomed into romance and eventually marriage in that same church on 23rd March 1957. However, in the interim much was to happen.

One of the chaps joining our course at Kirton Lindsey was Peter Galyer who had been a fellow pupil at the Purley Grammar School and a sergeant with me in the Air Training Corps. He was always cheerful and saw the funny side of everything. I appreciated his companionship greatly.

At least once a week there was a major inspection and parade. The previous night was spent cleaning the barrack room, the ablutions, the reading room and our individual kit, leaving only the sweeping and final polishing of the floor with the *bumper* to be done on the morrow.

Kit had to be displayed in a particular manner, as per our initial experience at Cardington, but the bedside locker and wardrobe lay-outs were additional. For example, on the top shelf of the locker a yellow shoe-polishing duster had to be folded lengthwise with its folded edge in line with the front of the shelf. On it was centrally placed a *Kiwi* black boot polish tin with both boot brushes either side. The tin had to be stood on its edge with the Kiwi horizontal! The brushes had to be equidistant from the tin and positioned bristles downwards at 45 degrees to the front edge of the shelf.

On one particular inspection a cadet was given seven days "confined to camp" for having his Kiwi in a dive rather than horizontal! Being confined to camp meant exactly that, but in addition it entailed wearing one's best blue after working hours when everyone else could wear casual clothes and having to march oneself down to the officers' mess and personally report to the Station Duty Officer every hour until 22:00 hours (10 pm). The NAAFI and cinema were out of bounds, all other privileges forfeited, and one had to march wherever one had to go. I myself experienced the humiliation of this sentence on one occasion...

One of my pre-inspection tasks was to ensure that all the brasses in the reading room were cleaned and polished - door knobs, window latches and stays, cupboard door handles, etc. Imagine my horror when the inspecting officer, coming into my barrack room bawled, "Who's responsible for the reading room brasses?"

"I am, sir," I replied.

"Look at this!" he shouted in my face, showing me the middle finger of his white-gloved hand. It had a large black imprint on it! I had put the polish on this particular brass fitting (which was behind a curtain) and failed to polish it off! Lack of attention to detail!

Seven days confined to camp was my lot, with all that entailed, but for me it included the loss of seeing Elizabeth for a week. To add insult to injury, I was marching on my own down to the officers' mess to report to the Station Duty Officer when who should pass me in the local bus but Elizabeth and her friends from the church, grinning at me and waving from the back seat; I could not even wave back but continued stoically marching with eyes to the front!

Being in the days of National Service there were many aspiring pilots even though the Air Force would only have operational use out of them for about six months, as it took eighteen months training to *Wings* standard. Failure at any point on the course inevitably meant suspension from aircrew training and re-mustering into one of the ground branches.

Thus it was with a heavy heart that I learned of my failure in Aeronautical Maths. I now had to face the Suspension Board (appropriately nicknamed "the Chop Board") made up of the Station Commander, the two Wing Commanders, the Chief Ground Instructor and my Squadron Commander.

As I left the barrack room in my best blues, my colleagues, who had all passed their exams and were in the process of getting fitted for their officers' uniforms, shook my hand and 'wished me luck'. I was touched by their concern for me - especially Peter Galyer, who had also won a Flying

Scholarship as an air cadet and knew how I must be feeling to see my flying career in the Air Force about to end before it had begun.

Entering the room and saluting the Board smartly, I awaited their decision with bated breath. The members of the Board had obviously discussed my case prior to my arrival as the Station Commander, in his capacity as President of the Board, briefly scanned the papers in front of him before looking me straight in the eye.

"Why the trouble with Maths then, Collard?" he asked. I had to admit that it had been my weakest point in my education, even from primary school days. I briefly related the difficulty I had experienced learning from the maths master at Gregg School who taught with his cane and the fact that I had failed the 11+ on two occasions, both through poor Maths results.

He again looked down at my documents and then sideways to each of the Wing Commanders in turn. I noticed a brief nod pass between the three of them; then he turned to me again. "You failed the Maths exam with distinction and should be suspended from further officer training; however, we as a Board feel constrained to give you one more chance. You will be re-coursed to the new intake but will study only Maths. You will take the exam again in six weeks' time and, assuming you pass, you will join the senior course for graduation. If you fail, you will be suspended from officer training and re-allocated to a ground trade. Do you have any questions?"

I found it difficult to answer. I was so grateful for another chance to prove myself. I stammered a very sincere, "No, sir. Thank you, sir!", saluted and retired from the room with my heart thumping. I felt like a man reprieved who had been facing execution!

As I marched back to the barrack room I saw all my colleagues hanging out of the windows calling to me. "How did it go?" "Have they chopped you?" "Are you still with us?" I simply held my two thumbs aloft and grinned. A great cheer echoed from the barrack room and a round of applause. My chances of wearing that coveted thin blue ring around my sleeve, the insignia of a Pilot Officer, were still alive.

Whilst having my Quiet Time that evening, I mused upon the events of the day and recalled what the Station Commander had said to me. It suddenly dawned upon me that he had used the phrase "feel constrained"

– the same phrase that my CO in the Air Cadets had used when he had offered me the chance of a Flying Scholarship. Had the Board, without knowing it, been subject to a Power outside themselves in making this exceptional decision?

Unknown to me and the Board, God was at work. Today I am able to thank Him for allowing me to fail that exam! I am reminded of Paul's words to the Romans in chapter eight and verse twenty eight: "We know that all things work together for good to those who love God, to those who are the called according to His purpose." Could God possibly have a purpose in my failing that exam?

My relationship with Elizabeth had developed from the girlfriend stage into a very real romance. She regularly attended the Methodist Church, was a teacher in the Sunday School and a member of the choir, but it was not until those extra six weeks, imposed upon me by the 'Chop Board', that she began to realize that good works and religious practice in themselves were not enough. She came to recognize her need to know Jesus in a personal way and to identify herself with the truth that "all have sinned and come short of the glory of God". The Bible speaks of salvation from sin not being achieved by a person's good works but by faith in Christ's sacrifice of Himself upon the cross at Calvary on our behalf.

During my extended stay at Kirton-in-Lindsey, God had brought Elizabeth into a deeper understanding of what it means to be a Christian, and she had become even more precious to me as a result.

I re-sat the Maths exam, full of apprehension, realizing that a failure would draw the curtain on a flying career but, would you believe it, I passed with full marks!

God has a way of putting icing on the cakes He makes! Not only had He turned my failure into a triumph and, more importantly, brought Elizabeth into a personal relationship with Himself, He had also done something else...

Due to the numbers of aircrew undergoing training in those days, Flying Training Command was over-stretched. The Empire Training Scheme, devised during the war years, was still operating. Courses graduating from Officer Cadet training alternately remained in the UK or went to Canada or the USA to undergo their flying instruction. Going to North America would have meant separation from Elizabeth for some fourteen months. My original course, including Peter Galyer, went enthusiastically to Canada, but the course with which I finally graduated was destined to stay in the UK for both basic and advanced flying training. Thus Elizabeth and I did not have to endure that lengthy separation, and our relationship with each other, and our joint relationship with the Lord, blossomed.

Following my interview with the 'chop board' a remarkable event occurred on the first night after joining the new course. There were about twenty of us in the barrack room, and the noise level was high. It was a beautiful August evening, and we were preparing for the inspection scheduled for the next morning. I had introduced myself to my new colleagues and, being the 'old lag' among them, had fielded many questions. "What was the CO like?" "How strict is the sergeant?" "What's it like to undergo gas drill?" etc. I gave them all the information they wanted and assured them the course was tough but enjoyable.

I was in the process of polishing my boots and putting that mirror-like shine on the toecaps with spit, polish and plenty of 'elbow grease', when an overwhelming constraint came upon me to have my Quiet Time. It seemed a ridiculous idea. How could I have a Quiet Time with all this noise going on? I dismissed the thought. Still the constraint bore in on me. "I'll have my quiet time when I go to bed," I argued to myself. "Most of the lads will have retired by then, and the place won't be so noisy." Thus resolved, I settled down again to polishing my boots but... I had no peace. Minutes later, recognising that this constraint may be from the Lord, I threw caution and my better judgement to the winds and knelt by my bed. I opened my Bible and my notes and began reading the passage for the day. I noticed a marked decrease in the barrack room noise. As I began my time of prayer I was aware that someone had turned down the loudspeaker which had been assaulting our ears with the latest pop music. Other than some subdued voices and sounds of general moving around, the barrack room was silent.

Having prayed for courage to get onto my knees, I now had to pray for courage to get up again and face the derision and mockery of my colleagues - something I had experienced on occasions as an air cadet. I slowly rose and was about to start my polishing again when I noticed other chaps kneeling by their beds! As each completed his devotions I greeted him warmly and asked to hear his story.

It transpired that all had come from Christian homes but had never been out in the 'wide world' before. Apparently their parents and friends had been praying that God would assure them of His presence with them on their first night as Officer Cadets.

From then on we all met regularly for prayer, Bible study and fellowship. Some of the permanent camp staff also joined us. It was the start of the Officers' Christian Union branch at Kirton-in-Lindsey which continued after I left for basic flying training. This was one of the clearest examples in my whole life of the Lord speaking to me in a way which could not be ignored. The lesson I learned from it was the importance of being obedient to that 'still small voice' that speaks even above the noise and clamour of our immediate circumstances.

At our graduation parade the Station Commander addressed us with words that made a great impact on me and doubtless saved my life on many subsequent occasions. He commented on the strict discipline that had been imposed on us as Officer Cadets and reminded us that this was nothing compared to the self-discipline that we would have to impose upon ourselves when we were flying one of Her Majesty's aircraft. He even quoted the incident of the Kiwi boot polish tin and said that a cadet who was not trained to pay attention to detail in minor matters, such as his bedside locker display, might not, one day, notice a detail in his cockpit which might claim his life.

These words proved to be prophetic for the cadet in question, as will be seen later.

At last I was fitted for my officer's uniform. What a proud moment to view myself in the camp tailor's mirror and see the thin blue ring around both sleeves, the peaked dress cap with the officer's badge surmounted by the Queen's Crown, and the smart brown kid gloves. All that was missing was a pair of wings above my left breast pocket!

Before reporting at Hullavington for basic flying training, Acting Pilot Officer R. Collard was granted seven days leave. It was hard to part from Elizabeth, but it was only right that I should spend time with Mum, Dad and Betty before my new phase of training, so I caught the train for Purley.

In those days a commissioned officer in uniform had to travel first class so the Air Ministry, ever conscious of costs, prohibited officers on leave travelling in uniform. I therefore had to pack my uniform in a suitcase and travel in civilian clothes. Having arrived at Purley station, however, I dived into the 'gents' and gleefully dressed in my new attire.

Walking home through the familiar streets of my childhood and teenage years, clothed in the uniform of those who had fought in the skies above me for the freedom I now enjoyed, caused me to feel ten feet tall! I must admit it was the proudest moment of my life - especially when a passing Coldstream Guardsman, seemingly twice my height, threw up a very crisp salute as we passed in opposite directions. I was so surprised I nearly forgot to return it!

As the front door opened, Mum's eyes nearly popped. She embraced me warmly and immediately called Dad to witness this new phenomenon in the family. Dad spluttered his congratulations through suppressed emotion and wrung my hand. His repeated "Well done, lad! Well done!" meant more to me than I could ever say.

The week flew by, but during that time I was able to meet up again with my friends at church and Crusaders, visit both my schools at Purley and Caterham and spend time with my preaching tutors Keith Stockbridge and Ray Burgess. I also addressed the cadets of my old Air Training Corps squadron. Then it was time to pack away my uniform, jump on a train for Wiltshire and face the next phase of my life: basic flying training. It also meant an increase in salary from £200 per annum as an aircrew Officer Cadet to £382 as an Acting Pilot Officer on probation for six months – no longer the "lowest form of creeping life", just the "lowest form of *commissioned* creeping life"!

Wingless Wonders

No. 2 Basic Flying Training School, situated at the Royal Air Force station Hullavington near Chippenham, was the next port of call in my flying career. I experienced a deep thrill as I walked up the long drive from the bus stop. I was impressed by the brightness and cleanliness of my new home built in beautiful Cotswold Stone and bathed in November sunshine. The whole place seemed to exude an atmosphere of promise and excitement.

I was now a 'pilot under training' in addition to being an Acting Pilot Officer (APO).

As officers, albeit of the lowest form of commissioned life, we had a strict code of dress even out of uniform. One had to wear headgear, be it a cloth cap or a trilby, in order to acknowledge the salutes of other ranks who may recognise a holder of the Queen's Commission even when wearing *civvies*. A suit was the norm (mine was one of Dad's cast-offs!) but a blazer and flannels were also acceptable. Ties were mandatory except when wearing blazers, in which case an open neck with cravat was an option.

I approached the guardroom, loaded up with suitcase and kit bag, dressed in my regulation cravat, blazer, flannels, and cloth cap. I dumped my baggage on the ground and knocked on the glass window, above which was the heading 'Reception'.

The window was opened by a very smart corporal policeman who, recognising me in my 'officer undress' attire, immediately came to attention and addressed me as "Sir". Although this was to be the form from now on, it came as a bit of a surprise, and it took me a few seconds to collect my thoughts. Having identified myself by showing the policeman my Form 1250 (identity card), he confirmed my right to be on the station by consulting a list of expected arrivals, then pointed me in the direction of the students' mess.

The main officers' mess was out of bounds to mere APOs until we became the senior course, but the student's mess was comfortable enough even though it was only a temporary building. Each of us had a separate room containing a bed, chair, bureau, built-in wardrobe and bed-side locker. We also had a *batman* between three of us who kept our rooms tidy, polished our footwear every day and pressed our uniforms. The ablutions block was at the end of a narrow corridor. There was also a lounge containing the comparatively new gimmick known as a TV, and a mess hall where meals were served by airmen stewards.

In order to keep an ever-watchful eye on us, three officers of the permanent staff lived in our mess, albeit in their own separate quarters, and were always present at meals, seated at the top table. In order to give us experience of life in a real officers' mess, the student body was required to elect a Vice President and Mess Committee, under the Presidency of the senior permanent staff officer. Each committee member was responsible for a particular aspect of mess life, under the guidance of the President.

Our course initially numbered some thirty budding pilots, drawn from three main sources: the Initial Training Schools; members of University Air Squadrons who had already been awarded their *provisional wings* and held the rank of Flying Officer; and a few regular officers who had 're-mustered' for pilot training, one of which was a Flying Officer in the RAF Regiment. He spoke with a marked Oxford accent and became the butt of much teasing by the rest of us less educated types. Some of the intake were awaiting the results of scholarships to the Royal Air Force College at Cranwell.

One such gentleman was Dick Bell - an interesting character! Evenings were often spent over a night-cap, informally discussing many topics which included philosophy, religion, marriage etc. I had the opportunity of testifying to the grace of God in my life and how He had changed me from a frightened little boy during the war into my present disposition.

Often Dick would be on the periphery of the conversation for a while, then threw in a couple of verbal hand grenades which usually blew the conversation to bits! However, I frequently challenged his pre-suppositions and threw a few hand grenades back!

On one occasion I challenged Dick to simply hear the Word of God proclaimed, rather than just kicking it around in debate. I invited him to come to the Christian Fellowship meeting which the Christians held every week in the station chapel. Dick became the subject of our prayers. Much to my delight he turned up at the next meeting. I happened to be the speaker on that occasion and took as my subject the passage from John's Gospel chapter nine: the account of Jesus opening the eyes of a blind man.

Dick disappeared from Hullavington almost overnight, as he had successfully gained his place at Cranwell. Some ten years later I saw his photo in the Officers' Christian Union magazine! He had committed his life to Christ whilst at Cranwell! I was not to meet him again for a further eight years - but that is a story in itself, to be recounted later.

Although officers, our commissions were only probationary. We had not finished being trained in officer duties. Much of our General Duties training, started at Kirton-in-Lindsey, was extended and deepened at Hullavington, including our leadership and initiative exercises. These were most enjoyable in addition to being quite a challenge at times.

The easy tasks were, for example, producing a poached egg on toast for our Course Commander in the middle of the afternoon, with the cookhouse out of bounds! Another was to acquire a TV licence - a very rare commodity in those days.

Jimmy, our deputy course leader, was given one of the more difficult assignments: to get the master key from the guardroom! He dressed himself in a workman's overalls and greasy cap, borrowed a well-used briefcase, filled it with various tools, locks, oil cans and rags, and cycled up to the guardroom. Speaking in a rather uncultivated voice, sniffing hard and wiping his nose on his sleeve, Jimmy convinced the RAF policeman that he had been asked to oil all the guardroom doors and check the locks. He presented a carefully manufactured pass and job card, ostensibly signed by the Clerk of Works, to the policeman on duty.

Although the permanent staff at Hullavington knew initiative tests were part of the student pilots' curriculum, the policeman remained blissfully ignorant that he was the fall-guy on this occasion. He obligingly allowed Jimmy into the guardroom and let him go about his work. Jimmy took his time, oiling all the door handles and locks, noting carefully the cabinet in which the master key was kept. After about half an hour he had the cheek to ask the policeman if there might be a "cuppa char" available, as he had started work at seven o'clock that morning. This was duly served up, plus a biscuit!

Jimmy continued his unhurried work in the guardroom, finally getting to the cabinet holding the master key. "Sorry mate! Can't do this one; it's locked. S'pose I'd better just pop a drop of oil in it and 'ope for the best." The policeman, busy with other things, produced the key to the cabinet and handed it to Jimmy without a word! The psychology had paid off!

Once the cabinet was open, the master key was whipped off its peg and secreted down Jimmy's neck. The lock was duly oiled and the cabinet closed and locked. The cabinet key was handed back to the unsuspecting policeman who was asked to sign that the job had been carried out satisfactorily. The master key was duly presented to a somewhat surprised Course Commander who then asked Jimmy to return it to the guardroom immediately and explain the situation to the duty policeman.

You can imagine the chap's embarrassment and horror when Jimmy, now dressed in his officer's uniform, approached the policeman, smiling broadly, dangling the master key between his thumb and forefinger! Explanations were made, no harm done, but the young corporal policeman was a wiser and more attentive sentinel thereafter.

Such initiative tests were designed to make us think widely, achieve required results with minimum resources and 'make things happen' rather than sitting around, like Mr. Macawber in Charles Dickens' 'David Copperfield', saying, "Something is sure to turn up."

Some weeks later, an officer wearing the uniform of a Squadron Leader came to the guardroom - which so happened to be manned by the same young corporal policeman who had been duped by Jimmy. The Squadron Leader asked for the key of the ammunition store, stating he was an inspecting officer from Group Headquarters. He briefly flashed his Form 1250 in front of the policeman's eyes and nonchalantly reached for the visitors' signing-in book to enter his details.

He was rather taken aback when the policeman politely asked "Sir" to step inside the guardroom for a moment. "Sir" was led down a corridor and, before he could say "knife", found himself thrust through the open door of a cell. The door was slammed shut and the lock, working beautifully due to Jimmy's recent visit, slipped its tumblers into the locked position. Yells of indignation, threats and abuse issued from the cell but to no avail. The policeman made his way slowly back to the reception area, picked up the phone and asked the operator to put him through to the

Station Commander. "Sorry to trouble you, sir, but I thought you should be informed that I have in custody a demented Squadron Leader who thinks he is the Archbishop of Canterbury!"

On closer inspection of the Squadron Leader's Form 1250, flashed in front of the policeman, the photograph proved to be authentic but the name was given as "Arch Bishop". All credit to the young policeman who had obviously learned from his encounter with Jimmy and knew his ecclesiastical terminology! The 'Squadron Leader' turned out to be a Royal Air Force policeman of the Special Investigation Branch, authorised by his superiors to carry out a security check. Such checks required the spurious character to have something false about him such as a medal ribbon in the wrong position, an incorrect cap badge, a false button on his uniform or, as in this case, a fictitious entry or photograph on his identity card.

The corporal policeman was commended for his attention to detail by both his Station Commander and the inspecting security officer on his release from the cell!

Our first few weeks were spent purely at ground school, extending our knowledge of all the subjects necessary to be an officer, in addition to learning the systems of the Percival Provost and furthering our understanding of aviation matters. Every subject was, of course, tested with examinations, culminating some seven months later in 'finals' which marked our becoming the senior course and taking up residence in the permanent officers' mess.

It was frustrating to hear from our classroom the throaty roar of the Percival Provosts' engines every frosty winter day and not be flying ourselves, but eventually the day came when we visited *flights* for the first time and were introduced to this delightful aircraft. Thereafter, mornings and afternoons alternated between flights and *ground school*.

If at flights in the morning, we had to report to the ground crew Flight Sergeant at 07:15 hours and manually push all the aircraft out of the hangar, lining them up on the taxiway. We would then march to the parade ground for the hoisting of the ensign. The duty student would be responsible for reporting to the meteorological officer, to copy the synoptic chart with coloured *chinagraph* pencils, in preparation for the weather briefing at 08:00.

It seems incredible now but on occasions when the runway was covered in snow, the whole student population, armed with shovels, would be lined up across the runway's width to make some attempt to clear the worst of the snow so that some flying could take place.

On our initial visit to flights, after a briefing from our Squadron Commander, we were introduced to our instructors. I was allocated to Flight Sergeant Law. The fact that he wore the red and white oblique striped ribbon of the Air Force Medal below his wings made me immediately proud to be his student, and I resolved to do the best I could for him.

The Provost had a radial Leonides engine and a three-bladed metal propeller. It had a long fixed undercarriage and a tail wheel, so the cockpit stood quite high off the ground. Compared to the Tiger Moth it was a 'big' aeroplane.

Figure 12: Climbing aboard a Percival Provost T10 during basic flying training at Hullavington.

Having introduced me to the aircraft in general and to the cockpit in particular, Flight Sergeant Law supervised my strapping in and took me up for my first flight on the 9th December 1954. I felt immediately at home and relished getting to grips with this apparently formidable machine.

Having a Flying Scholarship behind me was a distinct advantage. There were many similarities between the Tiger Moth and the Provost but there were also some new things, such as a closed cockpit, side-by-side seating, oxygen mask, radio, flaps, brakes and variable speed propeller controls.

Doubtless because of my previous flying experience, I had the honour of being the first student on the course to go solo after six hours and forty minutes' instruction. What a thrill it was to fly one of Her Majesty's aircraft as pilot in command and to land it successfully on a tarmac runway! Having completed my after-landing checks I spent a moment musing on my achievement before taxiing back to dispersal. I looked at the RAF roundel painted near the wing tip, gently quivering with the vibration of the idling engine. There was something special about that moment. It was as though *someone* was saying, "This is where I want you... for the present."

Flying around the Cotswold countryside was a pleasure in itself, especially during that winter of 1954/55. Circling a snow-covered Stonehenge at five hundred feet on a day blessed with a blue sky and sunshine, was an unforgettable experience. Flying my first solo navigation flight on a beautiful winter's day across the River Severn to Newport and back is also a delightful memory.

Flight Sergeant Law was a cheery chap with a keen, though often coarse, sense of humour. He held his place well among the officer instructors but was known to be somewhat unorthodox. For example, he always wore his oxygen mask down over his chin. We did not carry oxygen in the Provost as we never got anywhere near ten thousand feet by day, nor above four thousand feet by night. The oxygen mask was worn purely for its built-in microphone, so John saw no reason why he should "suffocate" by having it round his nose!

He also liked to get his hands on the controls and did not believe in being on the ground a moment too long, so checks were sometimes rushed.

On one occasion, as we were taxiing out towards the runway, John shouted, "I have control; I'll do the power check for a change!"

This required the engine to be run-up virtually to full power, then the variable speed propeller exercised, temperatures, pressures and the magnetos individually checked, before returning the engine to idling revs.

Swinging the Provost into wind he opened the throttle briskly. Suddenly the tail lifted! I instinctively pulled back on my control column and grabbed the throttle, but the Flight Sergeant had already slammed it shut on his side and was also heaving backwards on his control column. It was too late, however. The aircraft's nose pitched slowly forward and the propeller came to a dead stop as it gouged into the tarmac cutting the engine abruptly. The torque experienced within the engine would have been immense, necessitating an engine change; doubtless the damaged engine would be sent back to the manufacturers for examination, stripping and rebuilding - an expensive accident!

My instructor's face reddened, and after a momentary silence the air turned blue as he let vent to his feelings! He switched everything off, and we carefully climbed out of the aircraft, sliding down the leading edge of the wing to *terra firma*. With our parachutes draped over our shoulders, we trudged disconsolately away from our broken aircraft standing ignominiously on its nose.

Realising that my instructor would doubtless be severely reprimanded for the accident, I said by way of encouragement, "Don't worry about me, sir. I nearly had it happen to me once, in a Tiger Moth. I never want to fly with any other instructor."

He hesitated momentarily in his stride and muttered, "Thanks, young Collard. I'd like to see you through the course too."

Being only the student and not being in control of the aircraft when the accident occurred, I never knew what happened to Flight Sergeant Law. I had to write a statement for the unit enquiry but was not called to appear before it. Significantly, a few days after the enquiry, an order came out stating that power checks were not to be carried out in front of hangars. The slipstream from an aircraft at nearly full power, rebounding from a structure behind it, could get under an aircraft's tail and lift it, as we had found out to our cost!

Whether or not it was a result of that accident I shall never know, but I was allocated to another instructor, a Flight Lieutenant Douglas - very much a 'no nonsense' man. On our very first flight together, on the 9th

March 1955, he noticed my oxygen mask covering my chin and reprimanded me in no uncertain terms! He added, "If you get used to wearing an oxygen mask like that, one day you'll suffer hypoxia and probably write off a valuable aircraft. Wear it as though you're breathing oxygen; your life will depend upon it later in your career - if you last that long!"

My new instructor was crisp, precise, demanding and a thorough professional. I had enjoyed flying with John Law, but I now had to be far more alert. Flight Lieutenant "Duggie" Douglas was uncompromising. His briefings and debriefings were comprehensive, and he quizzed me endlessly to ensure his instruction was being absorbed.

When I eventually flew my Final Handling Test on 11th July 1955, both Flight Sergeant Law's and Flight Lieutenant Douglas's instruction bore fruit. The testing officer complimented me on my performance. Douglas was in on the debrief and, after the testing officer had vacated the room, he held out his hand and said, "Well done lad – I'm proud of you!" Words like that from Flight Lieutenant Douglas were equivalent to a Knighthood!

It so happened, some eleven years later, that I had the pleasure of meeting up with Duggie again at the Central Flying School. He was on the staff, and I had just graduated as a newly Qualified Flying Instructor (QFI). At the graduation dinner I was seated with him on one side and Flight Lieutenant Thomas, who had taken me successfully through the instructor course, on the other.

In conversation, speaking of our days at Hullavington, Duggie said, "Your fault, Ron, was that you tried too hard. You should have relaxed more!"

I think he had a point, but how can a chap relax with an instructor like him watching every move?!

The basic flying course continued through its ups and downs. One of the major downs for me was instrument flying. To simulate night time, amber screens were placed all around the cockpit windows and the student pilot wore blue-tinted goggles. The combination of blue and amber made black. Unfortunately, the goggles had a habit of steaming up, blurring one's vision. The other 'down' was pilot navigation – maths again!! I really struggled but managed to eventually get to the right places at about the right times, so was passed 'low average' in that discipline.

Elizabeth and I were delighted to be able to see each other regularly, instead of having to be separated by the Atlantic Ocean, as would have happened if I had passed that Maths exam first time at Kirton-in-Lindsey.

We were now geographically displaced by some hundred and seventy miles as the crow flies - but I was no crow! I had no transport of my own and the train service between Chippenham and Kirton was impractical due to the number of changes and waiting times. The only answer was to hitch a lift with another member of the course whose wife lived in Sheffield.

We were not released from duty on a Saturday until noon. Lunch was forgotten and a quick change into civvies was made before clambering into the Humber car, with two other escapees, to roar northwards through the towns of Cirencester, Stratford, Coventry, Nuneaton and Derby to Sheffield (no motorways in those days!) where I was dumped at the central station. I then caught a train to Retford, waited an hour, then leaped on the slow train to Kirton - slow being the operative word! I rarely arrived before early evening. Sometimes I could only get a train to Gainsborough, necessitating a ten mile hitch-hike which sometimes proved to be more hike than hitch! On a few occasions I had to hike the full ten miles due to the lack of hitches offered by the few motorists that passed me.

On one occasion, when my colleague was confined to camp for some misdemeanour, I travelled to Kirton on the pillion of a motorbike, the rider of which delighted in going over every manhole cover he could find, much to my discomfort. Neither did he seem to know the meaning of a red traffic light! Be it by car or motorbike, my time with Elizabeth was very limited, as I had to leave again in the late afternoon of the Sunday in order to be back at Hullavington by the mandatory and bewitching hour of midnight.

One of our return journeys proved to be a disaster. The car broke down! We managed to get to Nuneaton where a relative of one of the passengers lived. We were given some sustenance and left the car for repair. We then set off down the road, thumbing lifts. In this manner we got to Cirencester, but it was in the early hours of Monday morning! Traffic was at a premium, so we jumped up and down on the rubber sensor which changed the traffic lights in those days and ambushed the first vehicle forced to stop. It turned out to be a garbage lorry, but 'beggars cannot be choosers'!

We eventually got to bed at about three in the morning. Our batmen woke us at the usual 06:00 hours for another day's work. The added problem, however, was that this same night we were to begin the night flying part of our course!

I shall never know how we managed to do it, but despite our sleep deprivation my 'chauffeur' and I were the first two to be sent solo that night, though he did blot his copybook somewhat by rolling his wheels across the roof of a passing bus as he made his approach across the main Chippenham to Malmesbury road!

On the Tuesday morning we were called before our Course Commander and reprimanded for being back so late at the weekend and for having travelled beyond the statutory limit of fifty miles from base. We were sentenced to seven days confinement to camp, but I think the Course Commander realised that we would be making exactly the same journey as soon as our punishment had been exacted. He was wise enough to appreciate that, where young love is concerned, anarchy is bound to prevail!

In those days there were, of course, no mobile phones. In fact there were no public phones on the base. Elizabeth was phone-less at home, so when we wanted to speak together we had to wait until I called her from the one and only public phone box in Hullavington village after evening service on a Sunday, when she would be at the Kirton Manse with the Young People's Fellowship. Three minutes was the usual limit due to financial restraints, even though Her Majesty had now seen fit to increase my pay to £419 per annum as I had survived the statutory six months probation as an Acting Pilot Officer.

Times with Elizabeth were very precious, and I am for ever indebted to her mum and dad for the meals and accommodation that were always there for me whenever I happened to turn up. Due to the dearth of phones, advanced warning of my approach was rare, but they always received me and never threw me out!

If my arrival on a Saturday was in the late afternoon or early evening, Elizabeth and I sometimes managed a trip on the bus to a cinema in Lincoln or Scunthorpe, followed by a supper of fish, chips, mushy peas and bread (costing 12.5p in today's currency) before catching the last bus back to Kirton.

On Sunday mornings we would be off to that same local Methodist Church where I had first met Elizabeth and, after lunch, we would both be teaching in the Sunday School. If the weather was fine we sometimes got a short walk together before tea and then it was off to the railway station and the long trail back to Hullavington.

On one occasion we had a whole weekend together and the Saturday afternoon was spent looking in jewellery shops for an engagement ring. A diamond cluster was eventually selected for Elizabeth and a signet ring for me with the initials E. R. engraved upon it. On 25th June 1955, in a field above the local railway tunnel, I had the great joy of placing the diamond cluster on Elizabeth's finger and receiving the signet ring from her. Returning to Hullavington that Sunday evening, my ring felt like a placard on my finger and I wanted to tell everyone, "I'm engaged to be married to the most beautiful girl in the world!"

Our engagement gave me a new attitude towards my flying. Although I had always been a rather cautious and careful chap, ignorance was often bliss with a youthful sense of daring and adventure. Now I was living for someone else and this sharpened my conscientiousness and matured me almost overnight. I faced the realities. Flying could be dangerous. I was training for war. If I was to survive, I had to be a true professional and not accept second best. Learning became a serious business, not only about flying but about life in general. I think I can truly say that this was the point at which I passed from being a youth to a man. I had at last grown up, or so I thought!

Meanwhile the basic flying course progressed and we celebrated the end of our ground school finals by going to the cinema in Chippenham and having a fish and chip supper! The sense of relief at clearing this academic hurdle and becoming the senior course was immense!

We moved into the main officers' mess with its spacious rooms, beautiful décor and valued traditions. We were introduced to the formal dining-in nights which occurred every month. I was to experience many of these in my future career, and I must admit I viewed each one with mixed feelings as there were both enjoyable and undesirable features.

All officers dressed in either mess kit or interim mess kit. Contrary to the belief of most civilians, officers are not given everything free. An officer has to pay for his uniforms, pay for his meals and pay for his accommodation. Not only did we have to pay mess subscriptions, to cover accommodation and victuals, we also had levied a mandatory mess contribution to foot the bill for all the extras.

The mess kit comprised of two options: white waistcoat and blue waistcoat. White was normally the order of the day when civilian or special guests were in attendance. Blue was otherwise the norm. Whichever was worn, it was accompanied by a white shirt, winged collar and black bow-tie, a *bum-freezer* jacket with miniature wings and medals (if appropriate). Rank insignia was in gold braid. Soft black leather shoes completed the kit. The interim mess kit, for national service officers and those not yet in possession of the full mess kit, was simply best blues with a soft white shirt and black bow tie.

A typical dining-in night began half an hour prior to the scheduled time. Officers began to arrive in the ante-room for small talk. On arrival one would first approach the most senior officer present and greet him with, "Good evening, sir." He would acknowledge, and then one was free to join one's mates.

Soon the ante-room was full of noise, but no drinks and no smoking were allowed until after the royal toast had been observed at the end of the meal.

At the scheduled time the senior mess steward would appear at the door announcing, "Gentlemen, dinner is served." Everyone waited until the most senior officer present had left the room, then all followed into the dining room. This was often lit with candles, and the highly polished floor and furniture reflected a homely glow. Sometimes a band, positioned in the gallery, would be playing as we entered.

The tables were arranged either in a 'Π' or 'T' shape, depending on numbers, with the President of the Mess Committee central on the top table, the Station Commander to his right, and the padre to his left. At the bottom end of the table, furthest from the president, "Mr. Vice President" was positioned. He was the most junior officer in the mess and would feature at the end of the meal.

We would stand behind our chairs at our allotted places and the band would cease playing. The President would tap the gavel and ask the padre to "say grace" after which we all sat down and started chatting as we awaited the arrival of the starter.

Soon the noise level was quite high, and one often had to shout to be heard in conversation across the table. One was allowed to discuss any subject other than politics, women and religion, which were forbidden until after the royal toast!

Once the main course and sweet had been devoured, the tables were cleared for the royal toast. Port and Madeira decanters were passed from right to left around the tables from which glasses were filled. Following the progress of the decanters was a steward with a jug of water. The Queen had made it very clear that the drinking of her health was just as acceptable with water as with any wine or spirit. I always passed the decanters by and received water in my glass, but if looks could kill I would have dropped dead many times by the pointed glare of some disapproving senior officers!

With all glasses filled, the president would rise and say, "Mr. Vice: the Queen." We would all stand and "Mr. Vice" would raise his glass and say, "Gentlemen: the Queen." We would echo the toast, drink and take our seats again. Sometimes, when ladies or special guests were present, additional toasts were made and the exhortation from Mr. Vice amended accordingly.

Coffee was then served and smoking was allowed. Sometimes speeches were made, and this, for me, was usually the point at which an enjoyable evening started to go downhill. Some speeches were excellent, but others, sad to say, were hardly worthy of officers and gentlemen. Eventually, with speeches over and the night noisily wearing on, the president would rise and, accompanied by other senior officers, retire to the ante-room. This was the signal for everyone to stand until the entourage had left. Mr. Vice was now in charge and had to remain as 'President' until all other officers vacated their tables.

The hubbub now reverted to the ante-room where games would sometimes be played. A few were quite amusing and enjoyable, but sometimes drunken officers made complete idiots of themselves and things became both stupid and dangerous. During my career I saw some officers end up in Station Sick Quarters or the local hospital due to unnecessary or irresponsible horse-play.

At such a point I usually left. I just could not stand the sight of people who I admired and learned from during the day acting in this manner. Furniture and glasses were broken, uniforms soiled. The delightful ante-room was turned into a rubbish dump with cigarette burns in the carpet and armchairs, cigarette cartons and fag ends littering the floor.

Officially one was expected to wait until the president left before leaving oneself but, with the knowledge that I would be flying in the morning, I invariably slipped away to my room leaving the noise and horse-play behind. Occasionally, however, I stayed until the bitter end and helped some of my drunken colleagues back to their rooms and got them to bed.

Sometimes, especially when on Orderly Officer duties, or later in my career as Station Duty Officer, I would return to the scene in the early hours to give a word of thanks and encouragement to the mess stewards cleaning up after the night before. Here were young airmen and airwomen getting the place back to normal again after some of their officers had let off steam.

The reason given was that "officers need to have their play-time". One cannot argue with that, but surely there are far better ways of doing it that do not bring the officer corps into disrepute with those it leads.

Hullavington had the tradition of holding an annual sports day, open to all ranks. I decided to go in for the steeplechase on this occasion. The water jump comprised a multi-crew dinghy filled with water positioned just beyond a bar mounted three feet up. I adopted the technique of hurdling the bar, landing in the water with one foot, thus keeping the other dry.

My Squadron Commander, standing alongside the jump, shouted to me as I passed, "Jump *on* to the bar, Collard. It's easier than trying to clear it!" Finding that my opponents were all adopting that particular approach, I continued with my choice of technique and found I was saving yards by doing so. I won the event comfortably and, as prizes could be chosen from the appropriate category of first, second and third place, I duly selected a carving set which lasted Elizabeth and I for many years of our married life. The broken-handled knife was used to cut the wallpaper when we decorated our home fifty three years later!

I also represented Hullavington at rugby, soccer, cross-country running, athletics and even hockey on one occasion, but that was certainly not my favourite sport!

Every Sunday morning I would get an early breakfast and walk the six miles into Chippenham to join with the Christians at the Congregational Church for the service at 10:30 hours. The Rev. George Nuttall M.A. was the Minister, and he and his wife invariably invited me to lunch at the Manse. In fact I usually spent the rest of the day with them, staying for the evening service and then walking back to Hullavington. Sometimes, especially when the weather was inclement, George would take me back in his car.

I so much appreciated this generous hospitality and the opportunity to talk in more depth with someone who had studied at a Theological College and was an experienced preacher. I would not have called George evangelical in his theology, but both he and his wife were not only tolerant of my views but prayerfully supported me in my witness among my fellow-student pilots. The Manse became my second home. A reminder of those days is still on my bookshelf: a Greek New Testament that George kindly gave me, which had been presented to him in 1919.

Twenty three of us started the course at Hullavington on the 30th November 1954 and fourteen of us finished successfully on the 26th July 1955. In that time I had flown sixty four hours and fifty minutes under instruction and sixty hours solo. In addition to the general handling sorties I had also flown many navigational flights by day and night and reached the required standard in both instrument and close formation flying. The latter discipline concentrated the mind wonderfully! Keeping station on another aircraft as it climbed, descended, banked and generally cavorted around the sky was to me the ultimate flying experience. It was during the formation flying phase of the course that we flew down to Keevil for a week of living rough.

Keevil itself was an historic airfield. It saw echelons of the D-Day and Arnhem air-lifts takeoff in 1944 and featured the hangar through which a stunt pilot flew for the film 'It's in the Air', starring George Formby, the film I saw as an air cadet in Sweden.

Instructors, students and ground crew all lived under canvas and we flew our various sorties from the now disused runways. Emergency services were supplied from Hullavington on a daily basis as was Air Traffic Control. A small catering staff was also *in situ* but we had to take turns preparing and serving food.

Two particular incidents stand out in my memory of Keevil. The first was the unfortunate experience of one of our instructors. Their toilet facility was a small corrugated iron shed referred to as "the thunder box". It housed an *Elsan* toilet which had to be emptied and re-charged daily. The duty student had this unenviable task. The toilet was re-charged with a type of creosote-like acid - none of the sweet-smelling blue waters we enjoy in our *portaloos* today!

On this particular morning, the duty student was up before the rest of us to go about his various duties, among which was the re-charging of the instructors' toilet. He duly completed the task but failed to read the instructions on the tin; he was therefore unaware that the liquid creosote should have been diluted!

The first instructor aboard the single-seater that morning had his backside liberally peppered with neat acid! The first we knew about it was an anguished yell synchronized with a resounding crash as the instructor was propelled off the seat, hitting his head on the corrugated roof. Needless to say, the duty cadet was duly reprimanded and put on fatigues. The instructor was seen for some days later walking to his aircraft armed with an additional cushion!

The second vivid memory of Keevil was being awakened very early one morning by the roar of many low-flying Provost aircraft attacking our tents. Our sister flight at Hullavington had elected to 'beat us up'. Naturally we all leapt up to see this display, but a shout from one of the instructors ordered us to remain unseen in our tents.

Some days later, the Station Commander at Hullavington received a letter written in a feminine hand, supposedly from a Girl Guide captain, claiming that her girls had been frightened out of their lives by a bunch of aerial hooligans, in the early hours of the morning, beating up their tented camp on a disused airfield at Winsley. (Winsley and Keevil were both twelve miles from Hullavington, but displaced from one another by seven miles.) It was, of course, our Flight Commander who had written the letter!

The offending Flight Commander was duly called before the Station Commander who was in on the plot. Putting on as serious a face as he could muster, he condemned the Flight Commander's poor navigation and his failure to identify the correct airfield! All ended well, as such pranks usually did in the Air Force during those early post-war days. Subsequently both flights, the Flight Commanders and the Station Commander, threw a party – any excuse for a party!

A hog roast ended our stay at Keevil, and we returned to Hullavington in preparation to leave No. 2 Flying Training School for yet another adventure. Our next step would be to No. 4 Flying Training School at the Royal Air Force station, Middleton-St-George in County Durham (now known as the Durham Tees Valley Airport). Here we would undergo the advanced flying course which would secure the coveted pilot's wings. We would be leaving the propeller aircraft behind us and flying jets!

The Jet Set

I t was a beautiful August evening. I stood at the open window of the steam train as it puffed sedately through the green countryside bathed in the lowering summer sun. An airfield came into sight, and I viewed it with interest. This would be my new home for the next eight months where I would get to grips with a jet aircraft and, hopefully, gain my wings.

The train took me alongside the perimeter of the airfield: Middleton-St-George. On the far side I could see the majestic hangars and the squat control tower, but closer to the near perimeter track, single storied huts, some still in their drab wartime camouflage of green and brown, dotted the grassy expanse which was crossed by three intersecting asphalt runways.

Above the chuffing of the engine I could faintly make out the sound of a bagpipe, and it became clearer as the train passed by one of the huts. A lone piper was slowly perambulating, and another was sitting on the grass clearing his chanter. The haunting sound gradually drifted away as the train trundled on.

Arriving at Eaglescliffe station I gathered my belongings and began walking along the road towards the airfield. Hitching a lift to the main gates in a passing car, I arrived at the guardroom and, with some pride, asked the station policeman the way to the officers' mess. Having checked my identity card and ascertained I was a student pilot on No. 106 course, he pointed up the road and indicated a two-storey building some two hundred yards further on.

"Actually it's the sergeants' mess, sir, where all the student officers are accommodated. The main officers' mess accommodation is reserved for permanent staff, but you will eat there."

My room was on the ground floor. It was small but adequate and contained a bed, wardrobe, bedside cabinet, chair and a table above which were a couple of shelves - very much 'student accommodation' with no luxuries such as an easy chair. Its one and only window overlooked the station sick quarters and the mortuary!

After dinner in the officers' mess (today the airport hotel) I made myself at home in my new surroundings and wrote a letter to Elizabeth and my parents giving them my new address. I linked up with the other fellows who had arrived - all graduates from Hullavington. Suddenly we were conscious of a fire tender and ambulance speeding past the building with lights flashing. We thought no more of it, assuming it might be a road accident, until the following morning when the course assembled in the Ground School building.

We were addressed by the usual entourage of senior officers: the Station Commander, the Chief Flying Instructor, the Chief Ground Instructor and our Squadron Commander.

The Station Commander then informed us that the senior course, in the middle of their night flying phase, had just lost a pilot. Apparently he had called "turning inbound at twelve thousand feet" on a controlled descent through cloud but had misread his altimeter. He had in fact turned inbound at two thousand feet and crashed into the Hambleton hills.

On hearing the pilot's name, my blood ran cold. He had been the cadet at Kirton Lindsey whose Kiwi on his boot polish tin had not been horizontal! I recalled the remarks of the Station Commander at our graduation parade. His words had indeed proved sadly prophetic. The incident was a salutary lesson in paying attention to detail.

In those days deaths during flying training were not uncommon but this was very close to home and we as a course were understandably subdued as we hung on to every word our senior officers said in that initial briefing.

The first two weeks were spent in the classroom undergoing intensive ground instruction on subjects already covered at Hullavington but now applied to flying a jet-propelled aircraft. The moment for which we had all been waiting finally arrived on 15th August 1955 when we made our way to the squadron hangar and were introduced to our flying instructors. Flying Officer Larry Allen was unfortunate enough to get me as his first ever student! The poor chap had only just qualified as a flying instructor from the Central Flying School and now had the unenviable task of trying to get me my wings.

He was a young, enthusiastic and rather cavalier fellow who wore his cap at the jaunty angle associated with fighter pilots. He walked almost as fast as I ran and was, to put it mildly, 'bright-eyed and bushy-tailed'. He was not too impressed when he asked me what type of aircraft I wanted to fly operationally. My answer was, "The Canberra on Photographic Reconnaissance, sir." His reaction was typical of a fighter pilot! From then on he tried to convert me, but I found his prodding and cajoling rather irritating and not conducive to a good instructor-student relationship. This is not to say that he was a poor instructor. He taught me a lot and I am forever grateful to him, but I learned a lesson that was to stand me in good stead when, eleven years later, I was to face my first student and ask him the same question; I vowed to remember that every student is an individual. An instructor's job is to teach him to fly and become a good officer, not to coerce him into one's own mould.

Larry's briefing, prior to my first jet flight, included the physiological effects of flying at altitude, especially in regard to the ears and the gut. He exhorted me not to hold back any wind that might accumulate! He sensitively reminded me that we were both breathing oxygen so smell was not a problem and the noise of the engine would drown any thunder from the nether regions of my anatomy! He said, "In any case, I'd rather have a smell and a blow out than the cockpit full of exploded gut, so don't keep it to yourself!"

That same morning we had been subjected to the decompression chamber. Having been checked by the Medical Officer for any signs of colds, blocked ears or noses, six of us at a time clambered into this contraption and took our seats. The chamber was gradually evacuated of air to simulate a climb to fifteen thousand feet for the anoxia demonstration. The MO was constantly checking us and giving us valuable information as we 'climbed'.

Once established at a pressure altitude of fifteen thousand feet we each, in turn, had our oxygen switched off and tasked to write backwards from one hundred. At first the victim seemed to do well but gradually the concentration waned, the writing scrawled and the sequence of numbering lost, head lolled, eyes closed... gone! Immediately the MO switched the subject's oxygen back on and within a few seconds he was back to normal – a graphic example of what could happen if one's oxygen is not checked every one thousand feet in the climb and at regular intervals when at heights above ten thousand feet. I was reminded of "Duggie" Douglas' reprimand and exhortation when he first flew with me at Hullavington and saw me wearing my oxygen mask incorrectly!

Next came the *explosive decompression* when the MO opened the tap, simulating what would happen if the aircraft's cockpit pressurization failed. The altitude shot up to thirty five thousand feet. The temperature dropped instantly and mist filled the chamber. Breathing became more laboured and the gut expanded giving one a bloated feeling with the need to pass wind. Emergency oxygen (full flow) was selected and a rapid descent simulated to eight thousand feet. Pressure in the ears was felt acutely and the need to clear them frequently was emphasised. The final advice from the MO was "never fly with a cold"; otherwise the pressure built up on the eardrums during a descent would likely burst them.

Having fully briefed me about the familiarisation flight on which we were about to embark, Larry grabbed his parachute, bade me do the same, and together we walked out to the flight line on which stood Vampire T11 XE927. I say "walked" - I had to trot to keep up with Larry! He just could not get to the aircraft quick enough!

In those days no ejector seats were fitted to the Vampire T11 and one wore a standard parachute and leather helmet with oxygen mask and goggles as per the Provost. Having shown me the external checks, Larry led the way into the cockpit which was reached by a step ladder drawn alongside the aircraft. When we had strapped in, Larry signalled to the crewman who slammed the Perspex hood down over our heads and locked the handle. We were well and truly in!

The Vampire had side-by-side seating, with the student on the left, so I was able to see all Larry's actions as well as hear his boyish enthusiasm ringing in my ears as he went through the internal and pre-start checks. The object of this first flight was simply for me to absorb the sensation of flying in a jet and to try my hand at a few basic manoeuvres.

Larry was like a child with a new toy! "Now, listen to this," he chuckled as he pressed the starter button for two seconds then, fifteen seconds later, slowly opened the high pressure fuel cock. A gentle whine grew higher in pitch followed by a "whoomph" as the fuel was ignited in the burners. The engine noise increased to a scream and the nose dipped politely forward as the three thousand two hundred pounds of static thrust from the Goblin 3 turbo-jet pushed against the brakes.

Having a nose wheel rather than a tail wheel, the Vampire facilitated an excellent forward view. Taxiing was therefore very easy and the pilot did not have to weave along the taxiway in order to see ahead either side of a high nose as was necessary in the Provost and other tail-wheeled aircraft.

At the take-off point, Larry rattled through the checks before taxiing the aircraft onto the centre line of the runway.

"Follow me through now!" he invited enthusiastically.

I placed my feet lightly on the rudder pedals, my left hand encircled the throttle and my right hand rested on the control column.

"Right, here we go! Get a load of this!"

Smoothly and slowly, I felt the throttle move forward under my left hand and the whine of the engine grew into a scream as we accelerated along the runway.

"No need for rudder, see?" chortled Larry. "No propeller torque to bother you! Just open the tap and fly!"

I also heard the hissing of the pressurisation system as the cockpit was being conditioned to cope with higher altitudes and I felt the gentle increase of pressure on my eardrums.

As we sped along the runway, I saw the speed registering eighty five knots. I sensed Larry pulling the control column gently back to bring the nose wheel off the ground. At one hundred and fifteen knots I felt a further rearward movement under my right hand and we were airborne, with speed increasing. The landing gear clunked up into the belly beneath us and Larry made his appropriate calls to the control tower as we whistled over the Durham countryside climbing into the deepening blue of the sky at two hundred and fifty knots to a height of twenty thousand feet, which we reached in six minutes – the fastest and highest I had ever been!

For me that first jet flight was sensational. After some general handling, Larry gently introduced me to some aerobatics before returning to Middleton St. George to experience my first jet landing. At these higher speeds everything happened much faster and the downwind leg did not seem long enough to complete all the pre-landing checks. Once on the final approach, the runway seemed to loom up at an alarming rate. Larry gently eased the control column back very slightly as the speed read one hundred knots and the two main wheels kissed the tarmac in unison. The nose-wheel followed and we were down - no stalling the aircraft onto the ground as I was used to in the piston aircraft; he just flew it on!

The flight left me with mixed emotions. It had been a thrill to fly so fast and to attain such a height, to experience oxygen, cockpit pressurisation, lack of propeller torque and less use of rudder on the take-off run. However, I seriously wondered if I could cope. There was so much to think about, so much to do, so much to remember and so much to transmit to the tower in such a short space of time. My thought processes had never been very fast and now they would really be put to the test. It would be a quantum leap from the gentle, forgiving and low-speed piston Provost with its fixed landing gear, to the demanding, fast, screaming Vampire.

After six hours and five minutes of instruction, including steep turns, stalls, spins, and many 'touch and go' landings, Larry put his career on the line by sending me solo on 19th August 1955. Unlike my very first solo in the Tiger Moth, I cannot remember a thing about that first jet solo other than that I got down safely and Larry congratulated me rather than bawling me out! I had joined the 'jet set' in my own right!

Another of my airborne 'firsts' was the *High Speed Run*. This was started at forty thousand feet where compressibility effects were experienced as the aircraft reached its maximum speed bordering on, but not entering, the sonic barrier. At .78 Mach the aircraft began rocking laterally and slight buffeting occurred. As speed increased still further to .84 Mach, the ailerons became quite sensitive and considerable forward pressure was required on the control column to stop the nose rising. All good exciting stuff with a tinge of danger thrown in, but the main hurdle for me to overcome was that of having to learn so much, retain it, and apply it at the speed necessary. My mind just had to become sharper!

Thus the course progressed both in the air and on the ground. As usual, I found some of the academics hard, especially Navigation and other subjects involving maths. I did, however, shine at public speaking, and my lectures, given to students and staff as part of our general training, went down well. So did my sport, with athletics and football being my main contributions to Middleton St George's sporting reputation.

As was the custom in the Royal Air Force, Wednesday afternoons were spent in compulsory sport and Saturday mornings were devoted to normal work, during which the permanent staff officers were allowed to wear their civilian clothes so they could get away quickly at the end of the morning. We students had to return to the mess to change. Most of us sacrificed lunch in order to make the most of the free hours available to us before reporting again for duty at 08:00 on the Monday.

As soon as I had changed, I would make a bee-line for the Darlington bus and catch the train to Retford. There I would embark upon the one and only train for Kirton Lindsey in order to spend some time with Elizabeth. Often I would miss the train and have to settle for getting only as far as Gainsborough by rail before walking or hitch-hiking the now familiar ten miles.

On the 8th September 1955 Larry authorised me to go solo in the single-seat Vampire FB5. Although a Vampire, it differed in many ways to the T11 trainer. Again, there was no ejector seat, and the pilot sat on the centre-line of the aircraft. Having a bubble canopy, the view was even better. The starting procedure was more complicated and the five fuel tanks had individual gauges, so they all had to be added up rather than reading from a composite gauge as in the T11 – another strain on my mental mathematics when under pressure!

How does an instructor teach a student pilot to take off and land a single-seat fighter? Easy! Larry got me strapped into the cockpit and had me go through all the various checks and drills which would be required during the flight. All had to be memorised and word perfect. When satisfied, he got a bunch of ground crew lads to push down on the tail plane until he shouted, "Stop!" He then drew my attention to the nose attitude of the aircraft and told me to remember it. This was the angle I had to hold after getting the nose wheel airborne.

He yelled for a bit more pressure from the ground crew and called my attention to the higher nose attitude.

"This is what you want to see as you lift the aircraft off the ground. Remember it! If you get it too high the wings will stall and you will never get airborne!"

Further pressure was exerted on the tail plane until the rubber skids under the booms were on the ground.

"This attitude" emphasised Larry, "is what you must never see! If you ever get near it, touch the nose forward. I don't want to see you scraping your backside along the runway!"

He then carried out a similar exercise to show me the correct landing attitude before dismissing the ground crew and monitoring my starting checks.

Satisfied that I would not kill myself at least until I got to the take-off point, Larry waved me a cheery farewell and retired to the control tower to witness my departure and wait for an agonising thirty five minutes before I entered the circuit pattern for my first attempt to land this lively fighter-bomber. All went well and, as I guided the aircraft back onto its chocks outside the squadron hangar, there was Larry bustling towards me, beaming contentedly. As I clambered from the cockpit and removed my helmet, he placed an arm around my shoulders and said, "Well done! Now you can really start learning to fly!"

Aerobatics, instrument flying, cross-country navigation and high altitude work continued, interspersed with the statutory tests carried out by the Flight Commander, Squadron Commander, and Instrument Rating Examiner, until a new dimension to my jet experience was introduced on 2nd January 1956: jet formation flying.

After three instructional flights with Larry in the T11, I was off on my own in the Vampire FB5, flying as number two in a three-ship formation with Larry leading. By keeping the leader's navigation light aligned with the furthest point of his aircraft's nose, one was able to keep station laterally and maintain the correct spacing in azimuth. By seeing equal amounts of the leader's upper and lower wing, one was able to keep station vertically. Both elements were maintained by very small movements of the throttle and control column. Concentration, rapid appreciation of change and immediate reaction to it, were the tenets of safe formation flying. The leader's aircraft became one's horizon; the natural horizon had to be ignored.

Unlike the piston Provost, where changes of throttle were immediately felt, the jet aircraft lagged behind the throttle movement, so throttle anticipation was a new skill to be mastered. The use of rudder, so necessary with the Jet Provost, was not necessary in the Vampire. One also had to listen to the leader's instructions and obey them correctly, instantly and without question – yes indeed! That young corporal at Cardington knew all about the basics of formation flying. I learned them on the parade square! Thanks, Corporal, for your wisdom and far-sightedness!

I thoroughly enjoyed the formation flying but found the effort and concentration very tiring. In a single-seat aircraft, maintaining station on the lead aircraft is achieved in the same manner whether flying in the number two or number three position - but line astern is very different! Seeing the same amount of the upper and underside of the leader's wings keeps you in station vertically, with the added assistance of the leader's jet wash. If you get too high, the turbulence burbles over your canopy. Keeping station laterally is not so easy. One tends to constantly overcorrect, thus swinging from side to side. This is particularly annoying for the chap behind you. Does he formate on the leader and ignore your oscillations or try to follow you? If he does the latter, line astern becomes an ever-increasing lateral whiplash! Thus a three-ship student formation can be identified from the ground by its snaking progress across the sky. However, practice makes proficient! Watch the Red Arrows for perfection!

The sky above me was bright blue. The brilliant sun, shining down upon the tops of the clouds below me, made a world of dazzling white visible to the furthest horizons - a world somewhat different from the one I had left just fifteen minutes ago. Earthbound mortals, looking up at the clouds, saw only darkness and drizzle, but we who could penetrate the clouds in our 'chariots of fire' had entered an altogether brighter and more beautiful world.

On this particular sortie I was *Red Two* in a formation of three Vampire aircraft which had left the runway at Middleton St George, entered cloud at about two thousand feet and climbed through the murk to break out into this brilliant fairyland some three thousand feet later.

I was enjoying myself but concentrating hard. Flying an aircraft just a few feet from another leaves no room for error, particularly when you are still only a student pilot and in cloud! One is working hard all the time to maintain station on the lead aircraft. In cloud, the leader's aircraft becomes the *only* horizon! Bob Meadows, our Flight Commander, was leading us on this occasion and I saw him turn his head towards me just to check how I was doing. He gave me an approving 'thumbs up' before looking over his left shoulder to check Peter Sharman's performance on his other wing.

In spite of the physical separation from the other two pilots, I felt our unity and comradeship as we were led in a series of manoeuvres first in *vic* formation, then in *line astern*. Finally we were ordered into long line astern for a tail-chase. Aircraft were separated longitudinally by about a hundred and fifty yards, and the idea was to follow the leader. Again, the number three had the hardest job as he reflected the errors of the number two in addition to his own.

All too soon our leader called us to *reform vic* in preparation for our descent through the cloud and our recovery to base. His confident voice crackled in my earphones calling for the Approach Controller to guide us down through the cloud and position us for a visual run-in, but there was no reply. Bob called again a couple of times, but still the ether remained sullenly silent.

"Red Two. You have a go!"

I also called a couple of times unsuccessfully, then Peter tried his luck. Still no response!

The cloud stretched below us unbroken to the horizon. The hills of Durham and Yorkshire waited below to claim any unwary aviator who dared to venture down through cloud without the aid of an Approach Controller and his direction-finding apparatus. In those days radar approach aids with a *talk down* controller were few and far between in the UK, and the nearest one was too far away for us to even consider.

By now our fuel was getting disturbingly low. Both Peter and I had pronounced our *Bingo* calls, indicating to our leader that we had reached our first minimum fuel level. Calls were made again, and on this occasion a rather broken and muffled response was audible. Gradually the transmissions became clearer and the controller gave us the necessary headings and heights to bring us safely down through the clouds.

Peter and I tucked even closer to the leader's wing tips as the puffy white cloud fast approached in our descent. Suddenly the dazzling world of blue and white was transformed into grey fog as the clouds enveloped us. Losing sight of the leader's aircraft now could be fatal for all of us. Concentration and effort to maintain station was of prime importance. The natural inclination to over-correct for small deviations had to be mastered with self-discipline. I seemed to hear Larry Allen's voice shouting at me as he had done on many earlier formation training exercises: *"Don't over-control, Collard!* Concentrate and fly with your fingertips! Keep the aircraft trimmed!"

The crisp directions from the controller and clipped acknowledgements from our leader continued as Peter and I grimly maintained station on the lead aircraft. Sensations had to be ignored. The natural horizon, even if it could be seen, was irrelevant. The only datum in our present world was our leader's aircraft. Surely we must be visual with the ground by now? I mentally anticipated the next order once we were below cloud: "Red Section, echelon starboard, echelon starboard, GO!" But no such call came. I spared a fleeting glance at my fuel gauge and immediately wished I had not! I had never seen it reading so low!

At last... the controller's voice was loud and clear: "Look ahead for the runway and continue visually."

My immediate relief was suddenly shocked back into tension when I heard the leader's reply: "No contact – not even with the ground below."

There was a stunned silence eventually broken by his calm voice spelling out his intentions. He decided to make one more effort, aided by the controller, to get below cloud. If unsuccessful we were to use our last remaining fuel to climb back above the clouds, fly out towards the east coast on a timed run, and bail out when it was estimated we were clear of the built-up areas or when our fuel ran out, whichever happened first.

I felt my heart thumping hard in my chest and my mouth became very dry as I contemplated my first parachute jump. Getting out of a Vampire FB5 was no mean feat as everything had to be done manually. But first things first: concentrate on maintaining formation!

It was not until that moment, as we began our final attempt, that I realised I had completely forgotten the promises my Saviour had made to all those who follow Him: "I am with you always, even to the end of the world." "I will never leave you nor forsake you."

Although I continued to work hard maintaining formation, I now silently prayed that my Saviour would take control of the situation and bring it to a conclusion that would glorify Him. I rather cheekily asked Him to solve the problem by parting or lifting the clouds sufficiently to get us in! I remembered the way He had stilled the storm on the Sea of Galilee: "Even the winds and waves obey Him".

After what seemed an age, the controller's rather anxious voice announced, "Runway dead ahead! Sorry, I can assist you no further."

I spared a very quick glance out of the corner of my eye to the view ahead. My heart sank. There was no sign of the airfield - only the foreboding grey of solid cloud. Then... what was that? Suddenly I became aware of a faint amber glow encroaching into the cloud. It became more persistent and penetrating until - oh boy! - there were the runway approach lights spread out before us, the most beautiful sight in the world!

"Runway dead ahead!" I yelled over the radio, as though the other two chaps needed any telling.

"Roger!" acknowledged our leader in a matter-of-fact voice.

As I landed I was able to see the whole length of the runway stretching out before me, but even as I rolled to walking pace at the far end and taxied back to dispersal in Bob's wake, I saw the hangars on the far side of the airfield disappearing again into fog.

Apparently the deteriorating weather had been a source of concern soon after our departure and unsuccessful attempts had been made to recall us. The visibility had dropped dramatically, the airfield shrouded in fog and the cloud base fallen below the limits allowed for even dual flying.

On questioning the Met Officer it was found that the inexplicable clearance had lasted for less than five minutes. Coincidence or a prayer answered? How would I have felt if the situation had not worked out so happily and we had had to bail out? Would my faith in God have held? Would I have accused Him of not answering prayer because He had not answered it my way?

In chapter 4 of Mark's account of the stilling of the Galilean storm, verse 36 states, "Other little boats were also with Him." Jesus had been asleep in the stern of the boat but had responded to the disciples' anguished cries for help by rebuking the wind and the waves. The "other little boats" on the Sea of Galilee would also have experienced the sudden stilling of the storm even though Jesus was not in them and the crews may not have known Him. Had my prayer been used as a means of saving not only my "little ship" but also the two others with me?

It was another grey day. The cloud base was low and the visibility poor but good enough for the flying state to be declared "Dual only". My fellow students and I were congregated in the crew room reading, studying and quizzing each other on the various subjects with which we had to be conversant prior to our final ground exams. We were all looking forward to the day, just a few weeks ahead, when we would be awarded our wings and would become substantive Pilot Officers in Her Majesty's Royal Air Force... with a pay increase! We would also qualify for additional *Flying Pay*.

Peter Sharman was discussing the characteristics of the Vampire, remarking on the way it dipped its nose when the brakes were tested when moving off the chocks. He laughingly likened it to 'nodding thanks' to the marshaller before turning on to the taxiway. Peter was a delightful chap: tall, swarthy, solidly built, and rather slow of gait. He took his studies seriously and was regarded by the staff instructors as a potentially above-average pilot. Son of a Squadron Leader, Peter was a born service officer and gentleman. Surely he would have a promising career!

The crew room door flew open and Peter's instructor yelled, "Come fly with me, young Sharman! It's too cloudy for the birds but we have some instrument flying to do."

Peter sprang from his seat enthusiastically and disappeared through the door to change into his flying kit, singing the opening bars of 'Off we go into the wide blue yonder..!' I looked out of the window and saw no blue - only low, grey cloud and a light drizzle.

Just a week previous, No. 105 Course had lost a student in a flying accident. He had been flying as number three in a formation of Vampire FB5s, led by his instructor. As the formation was running in at a thousand feet for the usual break and landing, the leader noticed fire issuing from the student's aircraft and shouted a warning over the radio.

By then he was on the downwind leg parallel to runway 24, and to the south of the airfield, and attempted to bail out. The drill was: to disconnect the oxygen tube and radio lead, release the hood, trim the aircraft fully nose down, invert the aircraft and operate the seat harness quick release box. The pilot, on releasing his hold on the control column, would be bunted clear of the aircraft before having to pull his parachute

D-ring manually. All these drills Ken had carried out correctly, but the parachute was still streaming when he hit the ground.

On this same grey day that Peter Sharman and his instructor were climbing into the clouds on their instrument flying sortie, the Station Commander, together with the deceased student's family and course colleagues, were returning from the internment at Darlington cemetery following the funeral in the station chapel.

As the Station Commander's entourage entered the main gate, a service policeman stopped the car and, saluting smartly, informed the Station Commander that another Vampire had just "gone in". Both instructor and student had been killed. The fire tenders and ambulances were already at the scene. The Station Commander, a veteran of the Battle of Britain, quietly wept.

As students, we were among the last to hear the news. A white-faced Flight Commander entered the crew room and haltingly told us that Peter Sharman and his instructor had taken off successfully and had reported to the control tower that they were turning on to the climb-out heading. Nothing else had been heard, but an aircraft crash had been witnessed by a member of the public, not many miles from the airfield. We were told to return to our rooms but to re-assemble in the crew room after two hours. We all went our separate ways with our own private thoughts and lumps in our throats.

I was one of the first to enter our student quarters and I passed the half-open door bearing the label "Mr. P. Sharman, Royal Air Force". I paused before it with a heavy heart. How many times had I, with other fellow students, enjoyed Peter's high-spirited yet mature company in that room as we laughed, joked and studied together?

By the door, standing against the corridor wall, was a pair of black, leather shoes recently polished by the batman - an empty pair of shoes, never to be worn again. Past the open door I saw Peter's dressing table, and on it, facing me, was the photograph of his beautiful fiancée. I had seen the portrait on many occasions with its handwritten greeting angled across the right hand corner: "Don't break anything, darling!" I quietly closed the door and went to my room. It looked out on to the mortuary. Later I saw the ambulance arrive to deliver its tragic load. I closed the curtains but slept little that night.

Peter's funeral was held at the station chapel a few days later. We accompanied the coffin, draped in the Union Jack, to Darlington cemetery where we laid our colleague and friend to rest alongside Ken.

Following the internment, the remainder of our Course was presented to Peter's father, Squadron Leader Sharman, who addressed us briefly.

"Peter was a good lad," he said. "Thank you for being his friends. He thought highly of you all. My wife didn't feel she could come today. It would have been too much for her, but she asked me to say that, if she had come, she would have given each of you a big hug."

He then shook hands with each of us and asked our names. When he came to me he said, "Ah yes, Ron Collard." He looked me long in the eye as he held my hand, smiled and simply said, "Thank you so much!"

I do not know to this day what was meant in that kindly greeting, but I would like to think it was a reference to an incident which took place earlier in our Advanced Flying course...

As part of our ongoing officer training, each student had to give a lecture to the rest of the course and the instructing staff. I cannot remember the title of my talk but I spoke openly of how God had answered my boyish prayer some eleven years earlier and what He had meant to me ever since. I hope it did not sound 'religious' but personal and sincere. I spoke of the peace He had brought to my life and the purpose of doing everything, no matter how mundane, to His Glory... even flying!

As was the requirement, I invited questions at the end of my talk. One came from Peter. He simply asked, "How can one find God as you did?" I replied as simply and briefly as possible, outlining the good news of the Gospel. Had Peter spoken of this lecture in his letters home? Had Peter responded in his heart to the Gospel?

It is interesting to recall that I had also spoken privately with the other student on the night before his death. He and I were discussing various matters in the students' mess and the subject of 'the difference between faith and belief' arose. When we had met up on the way to briefing the following morning, he made the point of drawing alongside me as we entered the briefing room.

"How are you doing then Ken?" I asked.

"Absolutely fine!" he replied with a huge smile on his face. "Absolutely fine!"

They were the last words I ever heard from him. He and I were then separately swallowed up in the mass of students finding seats before the morning briefing began. Ken had only ninety more minutes of life left. Proverbs 27 verse 1 comes to mind: "Do not boast about tomorrow, for you do not know what a day may bring forth."

By the tender age of five, I had seen the death clouds brooding over me and my family through the war years but now, at the age of twenty one, they were encompassing me again in the loss of three friends and colleagues. Each new day became more of a challenge to stay alive and an air of quiet resolve permeated those of us still left on the course.

The 'Grim Reaper' Calls

The stark events experienced over the previous days were etched in our minds. The recent deaths remained very raw, but life had to go on.

With all the ground examinations successfully passed, it only remained to jump the final hurdle which was to convince the Chief Flying Instructor that we were worthy of being presented with our wings.

On 20th April I was authorised for a solo flight in the two-seater Vampire T11, serial number XE857, to complete Exercise Number 68 *(Final Solo Revision)* in preparation for my Final Handling Test. The sortie comprised steep turns, stalling, aerobatics, practice emergencies and a practice forced landing back at Middleton St. George. This was to be followed by various types of circuit patterns and approaches with 'touch-and-go' landings known in those days as *rollers*. (Having touched down, the throttle was immediately opened again and the aircraft lifted off the runway. This saved precious time and fuel by not having to complete the landing run, taxi back to the take-off point and start all over again!)

All went according to plan until I started the circuit flying. I had completed my practice forced landing, touching down on runway 24 and was climbing to one thousand feet, when I found the aircraft would not level off. I pushed the control column as far forward as it would go but the nose of the aircraft continued to rise.

My mind suddenly recalled an article I had recently read in an aviation magazine regarding a similar incident. The pilot had used large angles of bank to drop the nose, so I tried it. Pushing the control column to the left I found that the nose, as well as the left wing, dropped. Great! But as soon as I centralised the control column, the nose lifted again. I then found that the elevator control was jammed. I could not move the control column longitudinally more than an inch from its present position which was fully forward. Whenever I removed the bank and tried to get the aircraft back to level flight, the nose began to rise again of its own accord.

I continued this roller-coasting manoeuvre as I transmitted my predicament to the control tower.

"I have a control problem. I can't prevent the nose from rising and the control column seems to be jammed in the fully forward position."

The local controller's reply made my blood run cold.

"Bail out," he yelled, "bail out!"

I immediately went into the drill (forgetting the bit about unplugging the radio lead) and actually had my fingers around the canopy release handle when a most uncanny event occurred. An almost physical constraint, similar to that experienced by my father in his fox-hole, came upon me. It was as though a presence entered the cockpit and I was no longer flying solo. I glanced at my altimeter. It was reading seven hundred feet. If I had jumped I would have doubtless ended up like Ken. First him, then Peter and his instructor, now it looked like being me! My stomach seemed to come up into my throat, and I broke out in a cold sweat.

I found my hand coming away from the jettison handle and back onto the throttle. I continued to fly the same chaotic pattern around the circuit with the nose rising – applying left bank to drop the nose - bank off - nose rising - left bank applied again, etc. etc. Down to my left I saw the runway controller's red and white chequered caravan pass under my wing twice as close as was required for a good position to turn onto the final approach, but this presence urged me on to bank the aircraft tighter and to lower the landing gear and flaps.

Pilot's Notes for the Vampire T11 state: "At 400 feet the airspeed should not be less than 125 knots." An aircraft's stalling speed increases with an increase in bank angle and I was now pulling a tight turn with only one hundred knots indicated! The aircraft should have stalled, but it kept flying around that tight turn towards the runway, losing precious height all the time as, with the bank applied, the nose of the aircraft was on another downward path.

Another Vampire T11 was standing at the marshalling point, waiting to enter the runway for take-off but had been held by the controller because of my emergency. The two pilots later informed me that they thought their time had come! There they were, unable to move, watching helplessly as my aircraft became ever bigger in their windscreen as it curved towards them.

My left wheel hit the grass shoulder of the runway and my left wing tip scraped the grass, but I managed to straighten the aircraft as it headed off at a shallow angle across the tarmac. I was down in one piece!

Much to my consternation I found the control column was now completely free and had full movement! I called the tower: "I'm OK. The control column seems to be free now."

As I taxied the aircraft towards the dispersal pan, I saw the reception committee: the Station Commander, the Chief Instructor, my Squadron Commander, Flight Commander, all the staff instructors and all my colleagues on the course, together with a crowd of the usual spectators which always gather when the public address system announces that an aircraft is in trouble. I also noticed the fire engines and the ambulance returning to their standby positions near the control tower.

As I raised the canopy and climbed from the cockpit, a sea of faces looked enquiringly up at me.

The Chief Instructor rather gruffly asked, "What was all that about then, Collard?"

My subsequent explanation obviously did not convince him, and I felt an air of unbelief issuing from the assembled group of senior officers.

My instructor, Flying Officer Larry Allen, was somewhat more accommodating. He put his arm on my shoulder and said, "Well done! At least you got it back on the ground and walked away from it, so it must have been a good landing. Let's have a coffee."

Having filled in the necessary report forms and been interviewed by various members of the hierarchy, I was left in no doubt that it had all been my fault and that I had mishandled the aircraft. The Chief Instructor was convinced that I had failed to raise my flaps when I initially climbed away from my practice forced landing and he even used my Final Handling Test, three days later, to make his point. As I climbed into the aircraft with the Wing Commander I was left in no doubt that I was not the favourite flavour of the month and that he considered he was about to fly with an idiot. His manner was dismissive, gruff and thoroughly off-putting. He made adverse comments about every attempt I made to fulfil his demands.

On returning to the circuit he took control, flew an approach and left the flaps down when he climbed away.

"There you are," he shouted "the aircraft's out of trim! You left your flaps down! Try it for yourself! You have control."

I took control and experienced the large amount of pressure required to prevent the aircraft's nose from rising, but I was able to hold it and even lower the nose against the pressure.

"Even if this was the case, sir, why did my elevator control jam?" I asked tentatively.

"Imagination!" he replied brusquely. "Nothing was found amiss with your elevator control."

This I could not deny, as the control column had full and free movement from the moment I got back on the ground and a subsequent strip inspection of the tail plane by the engineering staff found nothing wrong with the elevator.

The whole matter was subscribed to "Pilot error – an inexperienced student pilot mishandling his aircraft." The case was closed, and I was reprimanded by the Chief Flying Instructor. He ordered me to have two more flights with another instructor and then "Your Squadron Commander can give you another Final Handling Test. You've frightened me enough!"

On the following day, 24th April, I flew two revision sorties with another instructor, followed by another Final Handling Test carried out by my Squadron Commander. The revision flights restored my confidence, and the test flight confirmed my suitability to continue my flying career.

The junior course, meanwhile, was at the night flying stage of their training. Night flying required a thorough runway and lighting inspection to be carried out by the fire crews at the end of each day's operations to ensure that no runway lights were unserviceable and no foreign debris was on the runway; jet engines take a distinct dislike to ingesting bits of hardware!

A few evenings following my incident, during such a pre-night flying inspection, a fireman (bless his heart!) found a small bolt in the grass immediately alongside the left hand edge of runway 24. It had fresh, clean scratch marks on it. The bolt eventually reached the engineering staff that had previously stripped XE857 and they found that the scratch marks matched perfectly with the elevator control cables. Further scuff marks on the inside of the elevator itself were also found.

It was concluded that the bolt had loosened over a period of time and had worked its way along the Vampire's booms during my solo flight, eventually fouling the elevator control cable at its extremity. It had been dislodged when my left wheel hit the ground and had been ejected onto the grass through the elevator shroud. I was exonerated and there was even talk of a *Green Endorsement* being awarded for getting the aircraft safely down but this did not transpire. I sensed that certain senior officers were somewhat embarrassed!

The Graduation Day for our course took place on Wednesday 25th April 1956 in the No. 1 Squadron hangar. My mother and father, together with Elizabeth, attended. The reviewing officer who presented me with my wings was an army Major-General, the General Officer Commanding Northumbrian District. He wore the parachute brevet on his right upper arm. He presented me with the scroll holding my Queen's Commission.

Then, as he fixed the pilot badge to my chest, he said, "It was a proud day for me when I received my parachute wings, but these I'm pinning on you are the real ones. Congratulations! Well done!"

I considered it very generous of him to speak in those terms, but I would much prefer the way I got my wings to the way he got his!

Figure 13: We've made it! Wings Graduation at Middleton-St-George 25 April 1956. L-R. Wilson, author, Paul, Crosby, Grafham, Bainbridge, Joel, Gourlay, Shucksmith. [Photo: Northern Dispatch, Darlington]

Nine of us thus received our pilot brevet and became substantive Pilot Officers. Our Course Leader was awarded the Cup of Honour for gaining the highest aggregate of marks for flying, leadership and ground subjects. He also won the Vafeas Trophy for the student obtaining the highest marks in the final examination on ground subjects. Sadly, some months later, he was killed in a road accident at Waterbeach where he had been flying Hunters.

Our Deputy Course Leader was awarded the Flying Trophy presented to the student showing the greatest proficiency in general flying. He too was to die in a Hunter aircraft a few months later.

Following the Graduation Parade a service was held in the station chapel led by the Station Chaplain. The hymns were 'Who would true valour see' and 'Fight the good fight'. The reading was from Luke's Gospel chapter 6, verses 39 to 49. We graduates were asked to stand for the following dedication:

"To the end that those who shall enjoy the special trust and confidence of our Sovereign Lady Queen Elizabeth as commissioned officers of the Royal Air Force may, with our own mouth and consent, openly before God and this congregation, promise that by the grace of God they will endeavour faithfully to frame and fashion their lives on the principles of Christ's religion, so that by word and deed they may be wholesome examples to the men and women committed to their charge, especially the young, and be dutiful and fearless leaders in the service to which they are called, it has been thought good to ask as many as shall find it in their hearts to answer: Will you give your faithful diligence so to discharge the duties that shall be laid upon you as officers in the Royal Air Force of our Sovereign Lady Queen Elizabeth as to be a safeguard to her most Gracious Majesty the due order of this realm, and the great trust committed to your charge?"

We were asked to reply, "I will apply myself thereto, the Lord being my helper."

"Will you maintain and set forward whatsoever things are true, whatsoever things are honest, whatsoever things are just, whatsoever things are of good report, wherever you shall be appointed to serve?"

We were asked to reply, "I will do so by the help of God."

I particularly identified with the last challenge as it is, in essence, Philippians chapter 4, verse 8.

Luncheon followed in the officers' mess and my parents, Elizabeth, Larry Allen and myself sat at the first table on the left as one entered the dining hall. The menu was...

Grapefruit Maraschino
Cream of Chicken
Poached salmon with Mousseline sauce
Chicken Maryland
New potatoes
Brussel sprouts
Apple pie and cream
Coffee

...a delightful meal spoilt only by a steward accidentally spilling the cream of chicken down Larry's neck! I was full of admiration in the way he reacted with such dignity, grace and self-control whilst I, to my shame, was creased with laughter!

Thus I left Middleton St. George as Pilot Officer R. Collard RAF, the proud possessor not only of my pilot brevet but also the Queen's Commission, back-dated to 1st December 1954 marking the date on which I graduated from being an Officer Cadet. It also meant I qualified for pay as a substantive Pilot Officer with Flying Pay added! The thin blue ring on my sleeve seemed huge and my wings seemed to spread right across my chest!

In spite of my struggle with Maths together with my lack of natural flying ability, my boyhood lack of physical co-ordination and my lack of overall maturity and confidence, I had made it! I now awaited my operational posting.

The clouds of uncertainty, failure, fear and even death had lifted and I was on my way into the career to which I was sure I had been called by my Saviour, but I was to be constantly reminded that any success was of Him, not me. I also had a wedding to anticipate!

A Saint Goes Marching In

My next posting after gaining my wings was to No. 233 Operational Conversion Unit at Pembrey, on the Gower Peninsula, to undergo advanced training in air combat, battle tactics and air gunnery. All dual flying was in the Vampire T11 and solo work in the single-seater Vampire FB5.

The most memorable event during this three month course was my formal application to get married! In those days one had to obtain the written permission of one's Commanding Officer! I duly put my service writing skills to the test by writing a 'formal-official' letter to the Station Commander, asking that I might pursue marriage. A week later I was summoned before him. He held my letter in his hand.

Looking up from behind his desk he said, "I suppose if I refuse your request, you would get married anyway?" to which I simply replied, "Yes, sir!"

He rose from his seat, extended his right hand, smiled benevolently and said, "So would I! You have my permission and my good wishes." At that moment my life experienced a cloudless sky.

On 6th July 1956 the Chief Flying Instructor signed my log book and launched me as an operational fighter pilot. My assessments in pilot-navigation, air gunnery and as a fighter pilot overall were 'Average'. I was posted to No. 16 (Fighter) Squadron at Celle, in Germany, to fly the Venom FB1 - the front-line fighter bomber at that time.

This squadron had been formed on 10th May 1915 at St Omer, in France, and had been commanded by "Stuffy" Dowding who, in 1940, as an Air Chief Marshal, was the Air Officer Commanding-in-Chief Fighter Command during the Battle of Britain and the architect of that victory. Its badge was a couple of crossed keys: one gold and one black, representing day and night operations. The Latin motto was *Operta Aperta* meaning 'Hidden Things Revealed'. The mascot, which appeared on the tail fin of its aircraft, was 'The Saint' (a matchstick man with a halo around his head). A black band, edged in gold, encircled both the Venom's tail booms. The Squadron march was 'When the saints go marching in' and was arranged by Walford Davies for the presentation of the Queen's Colour to the Squadron by Princess Marina, a few weeks prior to my joining.

After seven days' leave I boarded the train from Purley that eventually delivered me and my large cabin trunk to Harwich where I embarked on the overnight troopship bound for the Hook of Holland. The ship was packed with service personnel all destined for the European continent, and I was assigned to a small cabin housing four other junior officers. The bunks were arranged along the sides of the cabin in two tiers. I was given the top bunk and found I was unable to sit up in bed due to the low height of the ceiling. I learned what a sardine must feel like in its can! We all shared one wash basin. The toilet was further along the deck.

It must have been a fairly smooth crossing as I slept reasonably well but was semi-conscious of the stifling heat, the throbbing of the engines and the general claustrophobia of the cabin. The ship's public address system hailed us early next morning, ordering us to make for the appropriate mess hall for breakfast.

Having docked, we had to identify our luggage on the quayside before boarding our appropriately colour-coded military train. Mine was red, bound for Hanover. There I would change to a civilian train which would take me to Celle.

The journey was long and tedious. As we chuffed our way through the Dutch and German countryside, evidence of the war, albeit twelve years past, was still to be seen, especially in the larger towns. Through Holland many people waved to us, but in Germany there was sullenness and even the occasional rude signs. The allies were still in occupation, and Germany was still licking her wounds. The young people particularly were antagonistic towards us. I wondered how I would be received on the civilian train, travelling as I was in the uniform of an RAF Pilot Officer!

Having left the red train at Hanover I found myself in the company of another Pilot Officer who had been with me at Pembrey. His posting was to No. 145 (Fighter) Squadron also stationed at Celle. I was glad of his company. Although so young he was a married man, quietly spoken and rather shy. He was hoping to get his wife, May, to join him as soon as he had settled down to squadron life, assuming a married quarter became available. I longed for the time when Elizabeth and I would be married and could be together. I missed her dreadfully!

150

At Celle we were met by an Air Force car which took us to the base where we presented our identity cards to a Royal Air Force policeman on gate duty. We were directed to the officers' mess which was a large building smelling of pinewood and polish. Apparently it had been the Luftwaffe Sergeants' mess, the officers having been billeted out in the town. We checked in at reception where a young Corporal steward took our particulars and asked us to sign in.

"Which squadron are you joining, sir?" he asked Pete.

"One four five," was the response.

"Oh! Congratulations!" said the steward. "And you, sir?" turning to me.

"Sixteen," I replied.

He said nothing but raised his eyebrows.

With this uncertain welcome I was shown to my room on the top floor of the building opposite. I mounted the wide wooden staircase, walked along the ample corridor with its highly polished pine floor and into a room overlooking the main entrance to the officers' mess. It was very spacious and comprised a bed, wardrobe, bedside locker, table and chair, easy chair and a wash basin. The toilet and bathroom were across the corridor and shared by three of us. I made myself at home and wondered what Luftwaffe Feldwebel, Oberfeldwebel or Stabsfeldwebel might have occupied it before me.

After a shower I dressed again in my best blue and returned to the mess where I asked a steward where I would find the Commanding Officer of No. 16 Squadron.

"He's in the bar, sir."

I went down the curving steps into the 'Keller bar' where I was faced by the pungent smell of tobacco smoke which hung heavily in the air and, through the haze, saw a noisy crowd of officers hooting and roaring in the manner one associates with military taverns. I threaded my way through beer-swilling, laughing pilots until I was able to see the actual bar against which a row of fellows was leaning. A hassled and red-faced bar steward was doing his best to satisfy the constant demands of his customers.

I accosted a prematurely bald young Flying Officer at the end of the bar and asked if he would point out the Commanding Officer.

"Who wants to know?" he slurred drunkenly.

"I'm Ron Collard," I replied, raising my voice to be heard above the din, "the new pilot!"

"Boss!" yelled the young Flying Officer. "We have a new boy among us!"

I was faced by a tall, lean Squadron Leader, with swept-back, dark hair, sporting a thin moustache. He held a beer mug in one hand and, with the other, extracted a long cigarette holder from his mouth. He looked down at me with penetrating eyes.

"What do you want to drink?" were his first words to me.

My reply was, "A fruit juice please, sir."

There was a sudden hush around the group at the bar, and I found myself the centre of attention.

"What did you say?" asked the Squadron Leader, incredulously.

"I said a fruit juice please, sir" I repeated.

The Squadron Leader placed his beer mug firmly onto the bar top and looked at me hard and long.

"Now listen carefully, Collard. You have joined a drinking squadron with a drinking tradition. You will drink like the rest of us. Now what will you have?"

Again all eyes were turned in my direction and no one spoke.

I had always avoided alcohol as I had seen what it can do even to the most intelligent and likeable people. I realise that this is a generalisation and that some people drink alcohol in moderation or "for their stomach's sake" without any detrimental effect on their personalities or behaviour, but in the Royal Air Force, where I had already seen the devastation it can cause, I drew my line very firmly at total abstinence.

I reciprocated my Commanding Officer's steady stare and replied, "A fruit juice for me, sir, but if you find that abhorrent then please let me get one myself and I shall be happy to buy you a beer."

By now the whole Keller Bar was silent. A pall of smoke drifted over the assembly, but few were actually smoking or drinking. They were fixed by the drama unfolding before them. Quite apart from standing up to the CO, I had committed a (then) cardinal sin in offering a drink to a senior officer!

Still looking intently into my eyes, the CO, without turning his head said, "Steward, pour this officer a fruit juice." He then added to me,

"Mark my words, lad. You will become a drinker like the rest of us before you're much older. It's a squadron principle."

"I doubt that, sir" I replied. "You see, I also have a principle to keep."

He gave me a steady but not unfriendly look and changed the subject.

"Do you play a musical instrument? We, as a squadron, are a dance band and all my pilots play something."

The atmosphere was less tense now as I replied, "No sir. I did take piano lessons as a boy but I gave them up." I felt the CO's attitude to be less hostile and so risked a flanking remark as I grinned, "I can play the gramophone, sir!" I sensed a flicker of a smile pass his lips and an easing of the frosty atmosphere.

After that the CO asked me more general questions about myself and showed particular interest when the conversation got around to sport. He seemed suitably impressed with my football, rugby, athletics, cross-country and boxing history. He immediately 'signed me up' for the squadron football team which subsequently won the inter-squadron trophy.

Gradually the Keller Bar got back to its normal level of noise and bustle. The din was such that I found it increasingly difficult to hear what the CO was saying, but he eventually dismissed me, ordering me to report to him officially after the main meteorological and air traffic briefing on the morrow. He suggested that I now circulate among the assembled company and meet some of the chaps. Before I had moved, a young, tall, blonde Flying Officer (in later years to become an Air Commodore) nudged my elbow and smiled down at me.

"Well done!" he said. "It's not easy standing up to the Boss."

That was my first meeting with the squadron adjutant who had, during training, had to bail out of his spinning Vampire FB5 and parachuted right into the middle of a girls' hockey match – he never lived that down!

Another chap, more my own size, also came over to me with a serious look on his face and introduced himself.

"We're all expected to conform on this squadron and do everything the same and together. You will have to dye your flying suit black and get yourself a yellow scarf and a black and yellow jockey cap, as we always dress alike. We attend all service functions together."

Someone who witnessed the scene in the Keller Bar was the young Roman Catholic Chaplain. He had only just been commissioned and Celle was his first posting. He was to feature again in my story in a few months' time.

On reporting officially to the CO the following morning, he informed me that he was about to lead the whole squadron to Sylt for an air gunnery detachment. As I had only just arrived and had never flown the Venom fighter bomber, I would stay behind and carry out my initiation with Station Flight. I was also given various jobs to do on the squadron, one being to look after Flying Officer Charlie Peace – the squadron mascot. He was a parrot having his own RAF identity card and a white instrument rating! In spite of my dislike for anything feathered, Charlie and I got on famously.

After cleaning his cage and topping up his victuals every morning, I would offer him my hand and he would hop onto it, squawking his delight. I would then launch him down the long corridor in our squadron headquarters, and he would enjoy a short and noisy flight, constantly losing height all the way. He would then waddle back to me, singing and shrieking, mount my hand and happily be returned to his cage until lunchtime¹ when the procedure was repeated. He only blotted his copy book once whilst in my charge; he swore at the Padre!

Having studied Pilot's Notes for the Venom FB1 and passed an oral examination carried out by the CO of Station Flight, I was shown around the aircraft and left to familiarise myself with the cockpit. It was basically the same as a Vampire FB5 but powered by the more powerful Ghost Mk 103 turbine engine developing 4,850 pounds of thrust.

Having been checked out in the dual Vampire T11 and introduced to the local flying area and air traffic patterns, I was authorised to fly the Venom for the first time. It was a sheer delight. The extra power was evident on opening the throttle, but the rate of climb took me by surprise. It went up like a lift! The initial climb to five thousand feet was made at three hundred and sixty knots giving a rate of climb of four thousand feet per minute, which in those days was shifting!

One of the exercises I was briefed to carry out was the *compressibility run*. It meant taking the aircraft up to forty five thousand feet and putting it into a steep dive. Pilot's Notes for this exercise read, "At above .86

Mach the wing drop is no longer controllable, elevator control is eventually lost and the aircraft steepens its dive, temporarily out of control. The attitude of the aircraft may vary and in some cases it may become completely inverted."

I proved all this to be the case on my first run but recovered as per the next paragraph in Pilot's Notes by closing the throttle and extending the airbrakes. Once the speed had reduced to about .84 Mach, control was regained. Aerobatics were a delight to perform. The loop was entered at 370 knots, the roll at 270 knots and the vertical roll at 400 knots.

When the squadron returned from Sylt, both my close and battle formation flying were checked out and, after a formal interview with the Wing Leader, Wing Commander Don Kingaby DSO, DFM**, I was deemed to be an operational fighter pilot. Wing Commander Kingaby was a Battle of Britain veteran who, as a Sergeant pilot, had shot down more Messerschmit 109s than any other pilot in the battle, during which he won his three DFMs. His only injury during the battle was on the ground. He lost the top of his little finger when he was strafed as he was running for cover on one occasion. He was a cheerful, lively commander with a good sense of humour - a typical fighter pilot. He was only my size but called me "Titch"! I was to meet him again on more equal terms some eight years later.

The front-line squadrons of the 2nd Tactical Air Force in Germany were gradually handing over to the new-look Luftwaffe under NATO. Like Wing Commander Don Kingaby, many of the German senior officers were war veterans. Occasionally at dining-in nights we would host such officers which seemed to some of us as rather bizarre. Don Kingaby, with his usual hilarity, frequently kept us in fits of laughter as he recalled having been in conflict with some of the very men who now graced our top table!

In spite of being sworn enemies just a few years ago, most of the veterans on both sides seemed to realise we were entering a new phase of history with the Communist Bloc being the threat to European stability, so experiences and expertise were pooled and a new international camaraderie developed. The only restriction on the new Luftwaffe was the wearing of medal ribbons – iron crosses, etc, were considered inappropriate!

Figure 14: My Venom FB1 at Celle. Part of the 2nd Allied Tactical Air Force safeguarding the eastern flank of NATO during the Cold War. Picture taken following the Luftwaffe General's visit.

One day we were notified that a Luftwaffe General was going to visit the squadron and we were to stand by our aircraft, in flying kit, as he inspected all three squadrons. We were informed that he was security cleared to NATO Top Secret so we were free to answer any of his questions.

Eventually the General arrived in his car and slowly drove up the line of aircraft. He stopped opposite me. His driver rushed round to open the door, and the General eased his tall frame from the little Volkswagen. He was the typical Luftwaffe officer with an arrogant bearing, inscrutable, slim and very smart in his field-grey uniform.

As he approached I came to attention and saluted. He returned my salute with his baton and asked various questions of me through his driver who acted as his interpreter. My answers seemed to satisfy him and with a brief "Danke" he began to walk back towards his car. He then stopped, turned, looked at me again, and spoke briefly to his driver who came back to me.

"Sir, my General wishes to know why you have a knife on your thigh."

I explained that some dinghies had been known to inflate in the cockpit whilst the aircraft was in flight and, as the pilot sat strapped to it, the only way for the dinghy to expand was from between the legs straight onto the control column. This immediately pushed the column forward and down went the aircraft. At low level this invariably proved fatal. The Air Ministry, not sparing any expense, had provided us with a piece of sharpened tin attached to a wooden block, which was in turn attached to a piece of string linking the wooden block to the flying suit. The knife, simply known as a *Dinghy Stabber*, was sheathed in a strong fabric patch on the thigh. In the unfortunate event of a dinghy inflating in flight, the pilot simply had to draw his knife and stab the dinghy!

The driver thanked me and set off to pass the information to his master, but he abruptly stopped in his tracks, turned to me and, with a wicked grin on his face said, "My General will be interested to hear your explanation, sir. He knows a lot about dinghies. He spent many hours in them in your Channel!"

Much of my subsequent flying with the squadron comprised low level sorties in pairs or four-ship battle formations, providing close support to the army, carrying out simulated rocket and machine gun attacks. We fired live rockets on the Fassberg range, where the target was an old Tiger tank, and carried out live air-to-air gunnery on a banner towed by a Mosquito on our frequent trips to Sylt.

On one of these excursions the correct use of radio procedures was brought home to us vividly. A Belgian squadron, flying Sabres, shared Sylt with us on this particular visit and they were known for their poor radio discipline. Instead of using call-signs they chatted away using forenames. A chap named Hank was taxiing out one day when his wingman, who was following him, noticed more than the usual amount of flame coming from his leader's engine.

"Hank, you're on fire!" he called.

Unbeknown to them, forty thousand feet above Sylt was a battle formation of four Sabres returning from the range. One of the pilots was named Hank! He became a very embarrassed and angry Belgian when, on eventually being plucked from the briny by a rescue helicopter, he learned that he had jumped out of a perfectly serviceable aircraft, which was now at the bottom of the North Sea for no reason at all!

As Welfare Officer for the squadron I was responsible for ensuring that the airmen were suitably cared for. Much of their welfare was the responsibility of their Flight Commanders, but I took up the slack. I was ordered by the Squadron Commander to arrange a football match between the officers and other ranks one Sunday afternoon. This put me in a dilemma!

As a Christian I had always treated Sunday as a special day - the first day of the week when we remember the Lord's resurrection. Usually I was attending or conducting services both in the morning and the evening, with Sunday School teaching in the afternoons. What should I do? – disobey the Squadron Commander or compromise my own principles? As always in such cases I resorted to prayer, asking that the Lord would guide me in making the right decision.

I found myself thinking positively rather than negatively. What would most of the fellows do if the match was not arranged? The answer to that was easy! Many would be off to the nearby nudist beach. How much better for them to be playing a healthy game of football! The words of Jesus, as recorded in Mark chapter 2 verses 23 to 28, seemed to answer my dilemma. Surely it is not so much a matter of what we do *not* do on the Lord's special day as what we *do* and our reason for doing it. The match was played, enjoyed by all, and I was still able to attend the station church for both morning and evening services.

I look back on my time with 16 Squadron with mixed feelings. It was certainly a learning experience for me. I was maturing, rather painfully, and finding my place in the world, but my main difficulty was tolerating behaviour with which I was not accustomed nor in agreement, without appearing to be a 'religious crank'. I made many mistakes and took some hard knocks from my squadron colleagues, but one incident assured me that I was on the right track.

I had become quite friendly with both the Church of England and the Non-Conformist Chaplains and had a number of talks with the young, recently appointed, Roman Catholic Chaplain who first witnessed my joining the Squadron in the Keller Bar.

One day he and I were discussing various issues when he said, "Ron, you can't expect the chaps on the squadron to take any notice of your faith unless you become accepted as one of them. You will notice that I often get drunk with the lads and join in some of their capers, but this is in order to be accepted. Then they will listen to what I have to say."

It sounded plausible but I knew the Bible's teaching on these matters and decided to weather the storm, remain faithful to my understanding of the Lord's will and leave the outcome to Him.

Towards the end of my tour I was well established as a combat fighter pilot, was fulfilling my secondary duty as Welfare Officer with relish and was Deputy Standard Bearer, responsible for maintaining the Squadron Colour. I was also the Deputy Adjutant and had become the stand-in drummer for the squadron dance band!

The Commanding Officer had accepted me for what I was and, save for a few snide remarks about religion on occasions, did not bother me. One day he invited me to accompany him and his wife to the cinema and to join them for dinner at his home. I could hardly believe it! Why me? Perhaps he was going to give me some fatherly advice about being more 'worldly'.

I enjoyed the film. It was a harmless western but featured a way-out preacher who frequently quoted the Bible (out of context, of course) and twirled a couple of six-shooters which he frequently used among his community! This, of course, brought a windfall of comments from the CO such as "There's religion for you!" But I parried by pointing out that I followed a person, not a religion, and that you could not believe everything you saw on a man-made film.

Following a very enjoyable meal with the CO and his charming wife, I was invited into their lounge. The CO hesitatingly introduced a confidential and personal matter into the conversation and, with some embarrassment, asked me what action I thought he and his wife should take. I was flabbergasted! 'Gob-smacked' in today's lingo! Here was I, a mere Pilot Officer, being asked for advice by my Commanding Officer and his wife!

After I had recovered from my initial surprise and, knowing that the CO's wife was a devout Roman Catholic, I asked if they had consulted the Roman Catholic Chaplain. The reply was most revealing, and served to suggest that my attempt to live to Biblical principles, even on a fighter squadron, had not been in vain.

"Him!" exploded the CO. "He's no different from the rest of us!"

During the early part of my tour with No. 16 Fighter Squadron, I was detailed to attend an Aviation Medicine course at Wildenrath, a Winter Survival course at Bad Köhlgrub and a Moral Leadership course at Cologne.

At Wildenrath I was again subjected to the decompression chamber, experiencing more anoxia and explosive decompression drills, together with the study of various physiological considerations associated with flying and survival. I also experienced firing myself up a 70 feet high ramp on an ejector seat. Being small and light-weight, I went up the furthest and was saved from shooting off the top by the braking mechanism!

At Bad Köhlgrub the course was housed in a small village hotel where the local Herrenvolk assembled every night to play cards, get drunk and generally create a commotion.

The Winter Survival course was run by a rather sadistic Squadron Leader - an Intelligence Officer who believed in preparing us not only for surviving in winter conditions but also surviving Communist interrogation. Happily, that part was only applied physically if we were caught on the escape and evasion exercise; otherwise it was classroom information and films. The guys who were caught were subjected to sleep deprivation, hunger, indignity and haranguing under powerful spotlights. They were also stripped naked and hosed for many minutes with very cold water. I was determined not to get caught!

The survival element of the course comprised classroom lectures and field experience. Armed with only a parachute, flying suit and the survival rations contained in one's dinghy pack, we had to pick a spot in a forest to erect a *parateepee* (a Red Indian type tent using a parachute) and set ourselves up as though we were to stay there indefinitely.

This meant trapping rabbits, recognising what vegetation in the forest could be eaten to supplement the survival rations, cooking over an open fire and sleeping on a brushwood bed.

After a couple of days and nights we were moved on to another area of the forest where we had to do the same things all over again but this time without erecting a parateepee. Our shelter on this occasion had to be constructed from wood and branches. Throughout the exercise, the instructors were continually correcting us and encouraging us in our efforts, giving us many pearls of wisdom on all aspects of staying alive in winter conditions with only the items we would have on us if we were to bail out over hostile territory.

By far the most difficult and testing aspect of the course was the Escape and Evasion element. The chief instructor for this was a survivor of the Great Escape from Stalag Luft III. We were dropped off at dusk from a lorry some miles from the camp site and tasked to get back without being caught by the instructors or the local police and German civilians who had all been notified of our presence. Even some British soldiers, on exercises nearby, were also hunting us down.

As soon as I was dropped off the lorry with only a water bottle, two chocolate bars and a small compass for company, I began jogging up the road in the direction the lorry was taking. I figured that I might meet up with the next guy to be dropped. This proved to be the case, so at least we both had company and could work on the principle that 'two heads were better than one'.

We agreed that we should make as much headway as possible during the night and get ourselves back into camp, undetected, by dawn if possible. If dawn beat us to it then we would hide up just short of the camp and make a thorough reconnaissance of the defences prior to making any attempt to penetrate them. We might even remain in hiding until the following night.

In spite of the darkness and encountering various obstacles such as rivers and bogs, we made good progress across country, avoiding roads and bridges. We occasionally had to melt into the ground as we came across a few civilians and once we had to avoid a squad of soldiers, but we remained undetected right up to the forest where the camp was situated.

Dawn was showing its first light on the eastern horizon, but it was still dark enough for us to have a go at getting through the defences. We guessed that the instructors would be the last line of defence and that they would be unlikely to have positioned themselves very far outside the camp, as this territory would be covered by the soldiers, civilians and police.

My colleague and I decided to split up in order to minimise our being seen or heard. I skirted the camp area, giving it a berth of some eight hundred metres, carefully listening and watching for any signs of movement. Occasionally I threw a stick or stone as far as I could either side of me to see if there was any reaction to the noise but all remained quiet.

Getting ever nearer to the camp I saw the trees thinning out and decided to make a dash over the last few hundred metres. Hardly had I got up speed than a yell came from my right and a figure lunged at me from the darkness. His hand brushed against me as I ducked and weaved my way onwards. The rules of the game were that a capture could only be claimed when an escapee was physically held. Ahead of me another figure loomed large but I dropped my right shoulder and side-stepped to the left (thank you rugby!) and finally made it into the safe area. My two assailants came panting after me to take my name and formally declare my success in evading capture.

After a thorough debriefing we were transported back to Bad Köhlgrub to embark upon the final element of the course: learning to ski. This was a necessity if escaping and evading in a European winter. I never did become very proficient, but at least I could make reasonable headway cross-country on the level and managed to stay upright for most of the time downhill so long as a change of direction was not called for! One of my most endearing memories of the course is that of a morning's hard cross-country skiing followed by a bowl of hot soup, crispy bread and rich butter eaten in a log cabin overlooking mountains and valleys clothed in sun-drenched snow backed by a clear blue sky. The final touch was the haunting sound of a zither being played by a *lederhosen*-clad local. Brilliant!

The Moral Leadership course at Cologne was conducted by the Chaplains' Branch. Some dozen officers of various ranks assembled for a long weekend and took part in various discussions centred around moral and ethical issues encountered in the Armed Forces. It also aimed to equip us with the appropriate know-how to deal with some of the problems encountered among the airmen and airwomen for whom we were responsible on our squadrons.

On leaving the course I made my way to the railway station. This necessitated my walking past Cologne cathedral which still bore extensive damage from Bomber Command's attentions during the war, and I felt very conspicuous in my RAF uniform. Walking through an underpass, I heard running footsteps behind me. I turned to see a youth approaching me, and I became somewhat apprehensive. Was this to be an assault? We frequently had to put up with rude signs and comments from some German civilians who resented our being in their country as the occupying force.

I faced him squarely and placed my suitcase on the ground between him and me. He held out his hand and smiled. I was still tensely cautious.

In broken English and still smiling he said, "Please sir, you R.A.F? Can I carry your suitcase?"

"Thank you, but I can manage," I replied.

"Please, you are going to train station, sir? I carry your case for you."

Still wary I asked why he was so keen to do so.

"You got rid of Hitler for us. I love the R.A.F and want to be a pilot myself."

This was enough to convince me of his genuineness, so I relented.

Our conversation, during the short walk to the station, was most enlightening. I shared with him my initial concerns and he laughed. He told me a little of his experiences as a child during the war; he could not have been much my junior. He was so very thankful for his freedom from Nazism and spoke as though I had been personally responsible for his liberation! I hastily corrected him and assured him I was only aged twenty one and did not fight in the war.

He then very generously said, "You and your uniform represent the liberation of Europe. You must know many people in Britain who fought in the war. Please tell them how much we thank them."

Ever since, whenever I have had the privilege of addressing war veterans, I have recounted this story and passed on the thanks of that German youth.

Catching the train for my return to Celle, I found myself in a compartment comprising of some rather dignified gentlemen and a rather less dignified-looking chap who was reading a German newspaper. Some comment was made about "these junior officers, travelling in uniform", and I informed them I was returning from a Moral Leadership course. This caused some hilarity, and various remarks were made which generally belittled such a course. I then learned that they had been on a course for Wing Commanders! – *Wing Commanders!!* – I was in a compartment full of senior officers! I excused myself and got up to leave, but they insisted that I stayed and they became friendlier.

In the course of their subsequent conversations, generic nouns were discussed. What were the collective terms for ducks, owls, ravens, goats, etc.

One wag among them said, "I wonder what the collective noun for Wing Commanders would be."

From behind his newspaper, the previously silent German quietly stated, in impeccable English, "A flush of W.C.s, perhaps?"

The *Cold War* was ever threatening world peace. Russia, with her communist satellite countries, faced the western allies across the border separating Germany into East and West. The 2nd Allied Tactical Air Force, of which the Celle Wing comprising 16, 145 and 94 Squadrons formed part, was tasked with maintaining the integrity of the western side of the border. This was accomplished by each squadron working with others on a roster basis, patrolling at high, medium and low altitude in fully armed battle formations.

We were under orders to intercept any unidentified aircraft on the western side of the border and to escort it down to the nearest allied airfield. Should it refuse or resist, we were to fire across its flight path. If this also failed to bring a favourable response, or if at any time we were fired upon, then we were ordered to shoot it down.

The border was certainly an *iron curtain* to us, and we had to be extremely vigilant that we did not stray over to the eastern side, especially as we had the disadvantage of the prevailing westerly wind which could easily drift an unwary aviator into the eastern sector where he could be faced with communist aircraft looking after their side of the fence!

Being sure of one's position was particularly critical over cloud when visual contact with the ground was only spasmodic. Thus we were frequently calling base for compass *steers* which would bring us back towards the airfield. As Celle was only thirty miles from the border, a steer giving a westerly heading was not good news, especially if the steer was repeated over a period of time! It meant that one was coming from the east and may therefore have violated the border unwittingly. Under such conditions your imagination played overtime as you visualised some hungry Mig 15 bearing down on you from behind! You were always looking over your shoulder and into your rear-view mirror!

As the atom bomb was the major threat, the allied air force was expected to get airborne within four minutes of an alert so that the majority of its aircraft would be safe in the sky and not destroyed on the ground when an airfield was hit. For this purpose, exercises were frequently carried out to ensure this capability.

In September, all three squadrons of the Celle Wing flew to Norvenich: a NATO airfield which was still under construction, although the runways and dispersal areas had been completed. We were to live, sleep and eat under canvas, flying our normal exercises and battle patrols in combat conditions.

One of these exercises was *Operation Stronghold* which was designed to test the efficiency of the UK's early warning system. Various raids, both high and low level, were to be made by squadrons stationed in western Germany, France, Belgium and Holland in order to test the efficiency and reaction time of the UK defences. It was tasked to identify such raids early enough to scramble its interceptors and get the valuable *V-Force* of Valiants, Victors and Vulcans airborne within the four-minute deadline.

On 22nd September 1956 I was authorised to fly with twelve other aircraft of 16 Squadron on *Raid 141*, which was a high level attack upon the UK mainland. We flew at forty two thousand feet in battle formations of four aircraft. My steed was the oldest on the squadron, and I had great difficulty in keeping up. Our orders were to return to Norvenich once we had crossed the UK coast or when intercepted.

Fortunately for the citizens of the UK, we were met by a squadron of Hunter aircraft about thirty miles out so 'for us the war was over' and we dutifully returned to base in spite of the overwhelming urge to have a dog-fight with them and get some photographic evidence on our camera guns of having scored a few kills. We were under strict orders not to do so, as mixing it with the Hunters might have left us with insufficient fuel to get back to Norvenich.

Just a week later, on 28th September, we were briefed for a practice atom bomb scramble. This entailed each flight being at cockpit readiness on a roster basis so that at least fifty percent of each of the three squadrons would be airborne well within the four minutes. We were briefed, however, that the exercise would end once we had entered the duty runway. We were then to taxi the length of the runway and return to dispersal. For this reason we were told not to change into flying kit but simply wear our helmets so that the control tower could call us if necessary; otherwise we were to maintain radio silence. In order to get the maximum number of aircraft airborne in the allotted time, 94 Squadron was to take off on the southern taxiway, 145 on the right hand side of the duty runway and 16 Squadron on the left.

When the time came for my stint at cockpit readiness, I got a lift in the squadron Land Rover out to the dispersal pan where I relieved the present incumbent of Venom FB1 WK399. I was dressed in my working blue, with blue webbing belt, revolver and ammunition pouch, heavy duty 'ammunition' boots, blue webbing anklets, and my flying helmet. I pulled it onto my head and plugged in the radio lead. I carried out my cockpit checks and waited for my hour's standby to pass. I did not strap myself to the ejector seat as I would not be taking off. All I had to do if the *scramble* call came, was to hit the start button, taxi down the runway and return to dispersal. Exercise over. However...

I was about a third of the way through my watch when a dispatch rider roared up to my aircraft and shouted that Operations had now ordered that all aircraft were to actually take off, should the scramble occur. In order to get properly attired in flying kit, I would be relieved within the next five minutes by another pilot suitably clad, whilst I returned to my tent to get myself dressed for the occasion.

I tried to put the obvious question to him, namely, "What am I expected to do if the scramble comes before I am relieved?" but he had already roared off in a cloud of fumes and dust to make his next call. Sure enough, just a couple of minutes later, the red and green flare ascended majestically into the blue sky and exploded with a resounding pop. The war game was on!

I was caught between two stools. On the one hand I could go without full flying kit, which meant no lifejacket, no personal first aid kit, no maps, no gloves, no airfield directory, no check-list, no Pilot's Notes etc, or I could hold on a little longer in the hope that my properly clothed colleague would arrive and have time to strap in and go in my place. Being a conscientious and task-orientated chap, I immediately hit the starter button, turned on my oxygen and, working like a one-armed paper-hanger, strapped myself in prior to removing my ejector seat safety pin. Pre-take-off checks were completed over the short distance to the end of the runway where I opened the throttle and took off. Controlling the rudders proved quite a challenge, as it was the first time I had flown shod in ammunition boots!

Rising above the trees that separated the runway from the southern taxiway, I found myself in formation with one 94 Squadron Venom on my left and one from 145 Squadron on my right. The other two decided to formate on me. Thus, a comparatively junior pilot was now leading his first three-ship formation!

By now radio silence had gone by the board. The air was full of radio transmissions as we all tried to make some sense as to what we were to do next, where we were to go and who was leading who. At last we were instructed by the ground controller that we were *not* to return to Norvenich but to divert to Wahn (a joint military and civilian airfield). So here was I, an unwilling formation leader, with no flying suit, no life-jacket, no gloves, no map, no airfield directory and now no sense of humour!

I saw another aircraft ahead, so I decided to lead my lot on to it. Others obviously had the same idea, so we all ended up following this chap. After more radio transmissions we discovered that our Wing Leader was in fact the youngest and most inexperienced pilot on the Celle wing, now riding point to eighteen aircraft!

Eventually we were able to establish who was in what aircraft, and our Squadron Leader fought his way to the front, took the lead and brought us safely towards Wahn where he gave the order to form echelon starboard in flights of three. This meant eighteen Venoms would roar into the Wahn circuit among both civilian and other military aircraft, monopolising the traffic pattern and air traffic control!

The civilian passengers awaiting their flights must have thought that the Russians had arrived, but the controller gave us landing priority so it was not long before we were all safely on the ground taxiing to the apron with marshallers going ape trying to deal with two or three aircraft each. Fuel bowsers rapidly became exhausted of supplies, and civilian aircraft captains were getting apoplexy as they missed their arrival and departure schedules.

We eventually made our way to the officers' mess, which was also the civilian 'airport hotel' and were given permission by the President of the Mess Committee (PMC) to enter in our flying kit. He took one look at me and nearly had a fit! I explained how I had been caught short by the scramble and did not even have a hat! My Squadron Commander put in a good word for me, but I felt extremely self-conscious as I sank my boots into the lush pile of the carpet and later walked hatless back to the flight line. I suppose I could have worn my flying helmet (we were still wearing the leather variety with goggles) but did not want to risk the smirks of airmen as they threw up their salutes, muttering to their mates, "Who does 'e think 'e is – Biggles?!"

After lunch we were ordered to return directly to Celle. This meant that most of our kit would still be at Norvenich, but we were assured that it would be packed for us and transported back by road. Our return flight to Celle was uneventful.

Twenty four hours later our kit arrived on a lorry and I was rejoined with my cabin trunk containing my flying kit and other personal effects, but as I sifted through the items I could not find my anti-glare spectacles which had been with the rest of my kit in my tent at Norvenich. Various investigations, which included questioning my colleague who had packed my cabin trunk, proved fruitless. I therefore had some explaining to do and much form-filling to complete at the Equipment Section before another pair of spectacles was reluctantly issued. Anti-glare spectacles were contained in a dark blue metal case lined with a soft blue cloth not unlike today's Velcro. I had imprinted my name in red biro on the lining in the lid.

The incident was forgotten until some weeks later when one of the airmen at Celle died. Still only twenty one years old I was detailed to be his Personal Effects Officer which was not an enviable task.

As soon as the body had been removed, I had to take custody of the key, enter the room (some airmen had their own private rooms in that barrack block) and start compiling a detailed inventory of all the lad's possessions. I then had to package them, sending certain items to his next-of-kin, others to various departments on the camp, and some to a central disposal unit in the UK. I also had to do the same for his possessions located at this squadron such as working overalls, tools, drinking mug, locker keys, etc. I had to check that he had nothing away for repair or at the laundry. My final job was to ensure the room was left thoroughly clean and empty, save for the regulation furniture, ready to receive its new incumbent. All actions and items had to be documented.

It was an eerie experience for me to fold the underclothes, shirt, and socks that had been cut away from the body by the medical staff and to handle the shoes which he had been wearing that same day. As I began systematically categorising and listing the various items, I became more intimately acquainted with this young man's life. I find it impossible, even all these years later, to share with you, my reader, the deeper personal secrets that I unearthed whilst carrying out my duties. Suffice it to say that the lad was obviously lonely, insecure and troubled. I had only known him by sight, but the incident touched me deeply and, as Squadron Welfare Office, I resolved to make it my business to know the airmen on my squadron as individuals, not just as 'the ground crew' - a practice that I adopted throughout the rest of my flying career.

After two days' work my task was complete. The inventory was finalised and each item annotated as to its destination. The deceased's private effects had been packaged and dispatched to his next-of-kin, his professional items returned to stores and other service items crated, awaiting shipping back to the UK. The room was empty but for the regulation furniture of bed with new mattress, wardrobe, bed-side cabinet, table and chair. All was in order.

I was about to leave the room when a thought crossed my mind. I had not checked the top of the wardrobe. Why bother? Who would put anything up there? It was obvious from ground level that no suitcases, bags or clothing were evident. However, according to training, "attention to detail" was paramount, so I pulled the chair over to the wardrobe and climbed up. Being short of stature I could not see behind the forward lip of the wardrobe top so I substituted the chair with the table. Now I could see everything. Tucked tightly behind the lip of the wardrobe top, in the far right hand corner, was an anti-glare spectacles case! On examining it, I found it to be unquestionably mine. Although the lining in the lid had been ripped out, parts of the red biro marks could still be seen, matching with my name.

Maybe the airman had recently found my spectacles and was keeping them in safe custody until he could return them to me. Perhaps that had been his intention but he had forgotten. Perhaps someone else had planted them. Maybe the previous occupant of the room had been involved. One will never know.

The final part of this tragic story was, of course, the funeral service and burial with full military honours. I was detailed to be the Family Liaison Officer who would look after them throughout the ceremony, explaining what was happening and seeing them off at the end of the proceedings. They said very little, wept very little, and seemed quite remote from each other. I felt very sad for them. In my heart I was praying that the Lord would, in some way, use me for their comfort and give me the right words to say and the right actions to perform, but I felt completely inadequate and a failure.

As they boarded the car taking them back to Hanover airport I shook their hands and saluted. Just then my Station Commander came forward to bid them goodbye. The father expressed his thanks for "all your escorting officer has done for us today." What had I done? It was a lesson that would be reflected through my later ministry when encountering pastoral situations involving tragedy: it is not so much what is said that matters but the fact that you are there, identifying with the mourners, making yourself available to them and being watchful for their practical needs. I suppose it is summed up in the simple words of the Saviour: "Rejoice with them that rejoice and weep with them that weep."

Now to happier memories!

On 14th March I flew my last sortie as a single man. On 1st April I was back in the air as a married man. Between those two sorties the most wonderful event of my life took place. I returned to the UK by air from Hanover to Heathrow, spent a night with my family in Purley, then took the train to Kirton-in-Lindsey. I shall never forget my feelings as the train puffed into that same station that had been my unknown destination back in June three years earlier.

As usual, the station was virtually deserted but for Elizabeth. The sight of her thrilled me beyond imagination, and I held her close. I remember saying to her, "Now we will never be without each other again" - words that were true in spirit but not in practice! We were to experience the clouds of much enforced and painful separation over the coming years.

Figure 15: 23rd March 1957 at Kirton-in-Lindsey Methodist Church.
[Photo: Hull Daily Mail & Times]

Our wedding was held on 23rd March 1957 in the Methodist Church in Kirton-in-Lindsey. Eddie Crew, our Minister and close friend, conducted the service, and the reception was held in the church hall. Among the generous gifts was an electric clock given by the Sunday School, Choir and Youth Group. It is still working in our lounge as I write fifty two years later! Perhaps it will "stop short, never to go again, when the old man dies!"

After just a few days honeymoon at the Prospect Hotel in Harrogate, I returned to Germany with my wife. We flew from Heathrow to Hanover in a Dakota aircraft, and I introduced her to our first home: a short-term, first-floor flat on the RAF station at Celle.

When I consider all that this meant to Elizabeth, I am still in awe of her love and loyalty. Uprooted from her country village, removed from her family and friends, whisked overseas for the first time in her life, and dumped into a totally different existence and social circle, she somehow remained the same Elizabeth. She had much adapting to do - not only to a husband (and me at that!) but to a foreign country, foreign language, squadron life, some days and nights on her own, and no transport other than a German bus.

Over a period of time we had the pleasure of sharing our home and our food, not only with members of the squadron but also with many airmen and airwomen who used to crowd into our lounge for a weekly Bible study and prayer meeting, often numbering thirty.

Elizabeth, quite understandably, wanted to look after our home herself and stamp her personality upon it. Not many days after taking over the flat, I was telephoned at the squadron by the Station Warrant Officer who asked me why my wife had refused the help of a German char-lady. Was my wife not satisfied with the individual concerned? Would she like another sent around?

I returned to the flat and found Elizabeth drinking coffee with a German lady who was as limited with her English as Elizabeth was with her German! Apparently the Air Force, in its generosity, employed a team of German cleaning ladies to 'do' all the married quarters once a week. Today was our day, but Elizabeth did not want, nor need, any help. She was perfectly capable of cleaning her own home and rather enjoyed it!

The German lady had interpreted the "Nein, danke" as being because the Germans and the British had been at war! Happily it was soon amicably resolved over another cup of coffee and we all parted with handshakes, nodding heads and smiles. The only one who remained confused was the Station Warrant Officer who could not understand why an officer's wife did not want waiting on!

My Commanding Officer wanted all his pilots to be drivers of motor vehicles. I was one of the very few who did not possess a driving licence, so I was duly assigned to our Squadron Motor Transport Officer, who was given the unenviable task of teaching me to drive on a left-handed Daimler Benz three ton truck using the 'wrong' side of the road!

He was a delightful chap with a good sense of humour, spaniel eyes and a very flat face adorned with a large handlebar moustache. He reckons that his face had been normal until he had asked me to try an emergency stop! Eventually I was signed up as competent to drive military vehicles on the base, and I particularly enjoyed buzzing around in the squadron's Land Rover. My early days of being a driver were to be given a life-long lesson that affected my future driving right up to the present time...

The station's mobile radar unit was situated in the centre of the airfield. It was staffed by ground personnel who worked in shifts around the clock. On this particular night the new watch had been collected as usual from the officers', sergeants' and airmen's messes by a Volkswagen mini-bus. There was a strict speed limit on the perimeter track around the airfield. It paralleled the main runway and was therefore straight for over a mile. Due to a party in the airmen's mess, some of the watch had been a few minutes late joining the mini-bus and the officer on board had been heard to instruct the driver to "step on it".

Unknown to the driver, a Venom aircraft was being towed from the compass-swinging base, way over the other side of the airfield, to the squadron hangar. In accordance with the Station Standing Orders, the Venom's navigation and downward identification lights were on, as were the towing tractor's headlights. It proceeded along the centre of the perimeter track with the aircraft's wing tips just overhanging the grass on either edge. It must be remembered that the perimeter lights bordering the edges of the perimeter track were amber on the outside and blue on the inside.

The tractor driver was concerned to see the lights of a vehicle coming towards him at a very high speed on his left hand side. He applied his brakes but could do nothing to prevent the horrendous crash as the mini-bus hit the aircraft's left tip tank which tore the roof off the vehicle. The impact separated the aircraft from the tractor's tow bar and turned the aircraft through ninety degrees. The mini-bus continued on its side for another fifty yards before coming to rest with all the occupants dead, the majority decapitated.

The subsequent Court of Inquiry concluded that the mini-bus driver would have seen a tractor on his left as he drove up the right hand side of the perimeter track (the correct side of the road in Germany) but had failed to see the aircraft, as its red navigation light would have been indistinct from the amber lighting of the perimeter's outside edge and its green navigation light indistinct from the blue lighting on the perimeter's inside edge. The pool of light cast by the aircraft's downward identification light would have been masked to a large degree by the tractor.

On the following morning, the bodies having been removed, our Station Commander ordered all personnel to view the accident site for at least five minutes. Every squadron, every department, from the Station Commander's own staff to the most junior German civilians in the *Works* Department, were escorted to the crash site in turn by RAF Police.

Many were unable to hide their emotions as they viewed the smashed mini-bus with its roof peeled back like an opened sardine can - the blood still fresh on the metal and seats and the remains of human brains, flesh and blood on the squashed tip tank of the aircraft.

The Station Commander was usually a very calm, composed and sedate gentleman, highly respected by everyone. He was, however, incensed by this unnecessary loss of life due to a speed limit violation and made his feelings clearly felt throughout the station.

In those days it was customary for young pilots to *prang* their car occasionally as part of the Fighter Pilot image, but after observing that scene, there was one young man who decided that a road accident could be as fatal as an aircraft crash. Thus my resolve was set to approach my driving with the same professional and responsible attitude as that required for my flying, a resolve which subsequently brought Elizabeth and me to undertake the Advanced Motorists' Course and gain entry into Membership of the Institute of Advanced Motorists - a step I would advocate for all drivers!

The Squadron was gradually being converted from the Venom FB1 to the Hawker Hunter. A few of our more senior pilots had already been on a conversion course at Jever and had returned to the squadron with great enthusiasm, longing for the day when we would be re-equipped with this sleek and powerful fighter capable of breaking the sound barrier.

One Hunter had been brought to Celle in order that we could familiarise ourselves with all the checks and become acquainted with the technical aspects of the aircraft before being authorised to actually fly it. In those days there was no Hunter Mk 7 with dual controls. A pilot new to the Hunter had to be thoroughly briefed by a Qualified Flying Instructor from a Hunter Squadron and then quizzed to ensure the briefings had been understood before being authorised to fly it.

One day I was up in the cockpit, familiarising myself with the checks and emergency drills, when the Adjutant called up to me, "You can forget it! The squadron is disbanding, and we're all going home!"

I met this announcement with mixed emotions. I was looking forward to flying the Hunter (the Pilot's Notes are still in my study as I write) but I was also glad to be going home, if only for Elizabeth's sake. At least she would not feel so isolated and could see more of her parents and brothers. What was in store for us - clouds or bright skies? One thing of which we were sure: we had each other for life and the Lord Jesus would be with us from here to eternity.

From Pillar to Posting

D ue to the 2nd Tactical Air Force in Germany progressively handing over to the new NATO Luftwaffe, a surplus of pilots resulted, all crying out for flying jobs. Many were posted to ground duties, and I was offered the job of editor for 'Air Clues', the Royal Air Force Flight Safety magazine, which I firmly turned down!

I held my ground against other attempts to sideline me from flying and was finally posted to Cosford on 14th July 1957 where, as a humble Flying Officer, I was put in charge of the airfield, two Ansons, three Chipmunks and four other pilots: two Flight Sergeants to fly the Ansons and two Pilot Officers to fly the Chipmunks. Our task was to give air experience to two hundred air cadets per week during the three months of summer camps. I thoroughly enjoyed myself, flying every day and supervising the whole show.

During my time as *Officer Commanding Flying* at Cosford, I was often requested to give air experience flights to other members of the Cosford staff when the cadet flying was less intensive. Not only was Cosford a Technical Training School, it was also a hospital, so there was no shortage of officers, airmen and airwomen queuing up for flights.

One nursing sister was a particular patron. She spent a lot of her free time at the airfield just waiting for a spare seat. I flew her nine times in the Chipmunk and she always asked for aerobatics. At first I simply did one manoeuvre, then reverted to straight and level flight before offering another, but she soon got fed-up with that and asked for an aerobatic sequence.

I began by stringing a few of the basic manoeuvres together with a rest period in between, but even that did not satisfy her! She asked for the full repertoire! I went into the complete sequence with some trepidation as I was sure she would throw up her lunch, but all I got over the intercom was a series of giggles and whoops of delight.

She eventually married a navigator who was later ordained in the Church of England. I was to meet up with the couple again some twenty five years later when I was visiting Wiltshire taking services and giving presentations on behalf of Mission Aviation Fellowship. Imagine my delight and surprise when, in 2004, I was given the new edition of the book 'Hope Has Wings' (the story of Mission Aviation Fellowship, written by Stuart King) and saw that one of its commendations was written by none other than my ex-Chipmunk passenger. Back in touch again, forty seven years after our last flight!

Whilst the flying brought me much satisfaction, the domestic scene was not so good. Elizabeth and I began our days at Cosford accommodated in a local inn and living out of a suitcase. Elizabeth spent her days looking for suitable 'digs' and eventually found some with a family in Shifnal. The accommodation comprised the front room as our sitting room, a bedroom upstairs and a shared bathroom and kitchen – not the best for a bride of only three and a half months!

Most of our leisure time together was spent going to the local cinema (when there was something worth seeing), walking, or listening to music on our Grundig TK5 tape recorder - a cheaply purchased souvenir of Germany.

On a couple of occasions we visited Molyneaux Park in Wolverhampton to see the Wanderers play. In those days Wolves were in the first division, and we had the pleasure of watching such famous players as Duncan Edwards and the rest of the 'Busby Babes', Billy Wright and even Stanley Matthews. Taking my new wife to a football match was not the problem it might be today. On one occasion I had cause to ask a fan three rows back to modify his language which, surprisingly, he did without a murmur!

My brief encounter with Wolves did not end when we left Cosford. Many years later, when visiting a church in Sussex on behalf of Mission Aviation Fellowship, I had lunch with the vicar: the Reverend Cullis, son of Stan Cullis, the Manager of Wolves and former England centre-half!

Sundays were spent at the local church, but we could not commit ourselves to much activity during the week as I often had to fly until dusk and we knew we would be moving on once the cadet camps were over - but where would I be posted? What accommodation would we find? In those days, an officer under the age of twenty five was not entitled to the full marriage allowance or to married quarters.

My next posting, over the period November 1957 to January 1958, was to Strubby, on the Lincolnshire coast, where I attended No. 131 All

Weather Refresher Course, flying the famous Gloster Meteor: the first British jet aircraft. All dual flying was done on the Mark 7, which had tandem seating, and all solo flying was in the Mark 8 single-seat fighter. On successful completion of the course I was scheduled to join No. 231 Operational Conversion Unit at Bassingbourn where I would learn to fly the Canberra, the aircraft I had always coveted!

The dual-controlled Meteor T7 had no ejector seats and no cockpit pressurisation. I found it an uncomfortable aircraft in many respects but the single-seat fighter version, the F8, was a beauty. An ejector seat, cockpit pressurisation and well harmonised controls made it a delight to fly. However, due to the engines being set well out along the wings from the fuselage, both versions of the Meteor could be tricky to fly on one engine. With an engine closed down, the thrust from the other resulted in a marked moment arm around the centre of gravity. A lot of pressure on the rudder was required to keep the aircraft straight. This was an added problem for me, having such short legs, so asymmetric flying proved very tiring! I was only just able to make the grade. Some of my previous colleagues, from Kirton Lindsey and Hullavington, were killed flying Meteors on one engine.

There were other idiosyncrasies with the aircraft. The left engine was fed by the front fuel tank and the right engine by the rear. By a control in the cockpit, the pilot could drop a baffle between the two tanks or lift it to allow fuel to flow freely between them. Thus, if low on fuel in a climb, one had to baffle the tank, otherwise all the fuel would pool in the rear and the left engine would fail! Similarly in a descent, the fuel would pool in the forward tank and the right engine would fail! If, on the other hand, an engine failed or had to be closed down in level flight, the baffle could be lifted to allow all remaining fuel to flow to the good engine.

One also had to remember to apply a boot of rudder when the landing gear was lowered, as one leg came down first, tending to yaw the aircraft. Applying all this when flying solely by reference to instruments, especially when on *limited panel* (master instrument covered) and with one engine closed down, was a real challenge. I had to have two attempts at the instrument rating test purely because of my struggle to cope with asymmetric flight on limited panel.

On take-off, the Meteor resembled a reluctant lorry! Both throttles were smoothly advanced against the brakes and one anticipated a kick in the back when they were released, but instead the aircraft slowly trundled along the runway, gradually gathering the necessary speed to lift off. Once in the air, however, it showed a clean pair of heels.

One design fault got a lot of pilots into trouble! The flap control in the cockpit was very similar to the ventral fuel tank release handle, and both were positioned adjacent to one another! Many a pilot completed his landing run, cleared the runway, and left his ventral tank behind as he taxied back with his flaps still down!

The flying, though a tough challenge, was enjoyable and I learned a lot. On the domestic front, Elizabeth and I had managed to find a holiday flat on the coastal road at Trusthorpe, just a few miles south of Mablethorpe. The only thing separating us from the North Sea was the sea wall. After our nomadic existence following our marriage, it was good to have a home of our own where all the rooms were ours exclusively. Neither of us could drive, so I was dependent upon a neighbour who was an instructor on the course to get me to the airfield. Elizabeth, as always, made the most of a rather lonely existence during the day and managed to occupy herself creatively and take frequent bus rides into Mablethorpe for a look around the shops.

Typically, I found myself detailed to be Orderly Officer over the Christmas! I decided that I would not be without my wife, so she came and spent the time with me at the airfield. But for the skeleton staff, the place was deserted, and my duties simply comprised security checks, patrols, raising and lowering the Ensign each day, and checking that the small staff were functioning appropriately and being well fed!

The two other officers on my course are worthy of note. Group Captain Norman Ryder was a veteran of the Battle of Britain and subsequently became a prisoner-of-war. He kept me spellbound with his anecdotes.

One story which stands out in my mind was the occasion when he was shot down and ditched in the sea. He had trouble releasing the hood, and he saw the outside world becoming an ever-deeper green as he and his aircraft sank. He fought hard and eventually succeeded in getting clear of the stricken aircraft but still found it took him an age, with lungs bursting, to frog his way to the surface.

He was a true officer and gentleman. I consider myself privileged to have served with him, if only for three months. Some thirty eight years later I was preaching at Acland Road Free Church in Dorchester when a gentleman approached me after the service and said, "Norman Ryder sends his kindest regards." Before I could engage him in further conversation he was gone, and other members of the congregation wanted to speak with me. It has remained a mystery how his name suddenly came into my life again, way out of context. How did Group Captain Ryder know I was preaching at that church? How could he have remembered me from all the hundreds of people he must have met and served alongside in the Royal Air Force?

The second officer with me on our course was Squadron Leader Peter Thorne who had been awarded the Air Force Cross and two bars for his work as a test pilot on the Supermarine Swift. He had a great sense of humour, was full of enthralling flying stories, but was a humble man with no airs or graces. He treated me as an equal rather than as a junior officer and did a lot for my morale when I was having a struggle mastering the Meteor. His encouragement and advice in the crew room was invaluable, and I have to thank him as much as my instructor for getting me through the course. I was to meet him in a different context some eight years later when, as a Group Captain, he attended the Senior Officers' Canberra Refresher Course at Bassingbourn where I was the Airmanship and Survival Instructor. He was about to take command of the famous Farnborough airfield where I had witnessed the demise of John Derry and Alan Richards in the DH110 thirteen years earlier.

On the night of 16th January 1958 I flew my last flight in a Meteor and so ended my conversion to twin-engine jets.

Elizabeth and I once again packed our bags and, walking in deep snow, vacated our flat at Trusthorpe and headed off to spend some leave with both sets of parents. It was time to think of our next posting to Bassingbourn and to make enquiries about accommodation.

On arrival at Royston railway station I telephoned a colleague who was already on the Canberra conversion course and asked if he knew of any accommodation. Unfortunately he could not be of much help but recommended the Black Bull Hotel as a start. Thus Elizabeth and I again began a new posting living out of our suitcases in another pub!

Every day I was away flying, Elizabeth walked the streets of Royston looking for somewhere to stay. Eventually we got a small room and bedroom above the coal offices, with a bathroom and kitchen shared with the landlady. Fortunately we had a good sense of humour! When we got down into bed that first night - and I do mean *down* (the bed was only one foot above the creaky floorboards) - we found that our heads were on the same level as our feet! The bed had a distinct V-shape with a marked sag in the middle. In fact, our backsides were on the floor!

Needless to say, the following day Elizabeth was again prospecting and, after about a week, found something better at 'The Nook' in Melbourne Road, Royston. Although we shared the bathroom and kitchen with the widowed incumbent, we had an ample bedroom and lounge to ourselves. We were even allowed to watch 'Match of the Day' on her television in the lounge on a Saturday night! This became our home for the next three months.

During that time we initially attended the Royston Methodist Church. The incumbent had been a previous Minister at Kirton Lindsey, known to Elizabeth. Through him we met other Christians in the Royston area, including Allon and Sonia Taffs at the little flint church on the hill in the small village of Therfield.

Allon had been a meteorological observer in the Royal Air Force in the Far East and was currently a design draughtsman with a company in Baldock. He was also the part-time pastor of the Therfield Chapel. Our friendship with Allon and Sonia was to last over many years, way beyond my service career.

Our stay at 'The Nook' in Royston was also marked by the most wonderful event we had experienced since our marriage. We learned that Elizabeth was to have a baby! What rejoicing! Not only within our families but in the wider family of the church!

The news also caused me some anxiety. Assuming I was able to master the Canberra, I would be posted to an operational squadron in the Far East, Near East, Cyprus, Malta, Germany or the UK. Would I be able to take my wife and child with me? The thought of an unaccompanied posting was unbearable. Even if my posting was accompanied, I was still too young to qualify for married quarters, which had long waiting lists. Where would we find accommodation?

As always, these matters were brought before our heavenly Father and we trusted Him to oversee our way forward. For the time being we had a comfortable and functional home close to Royston town centre and a church at Therfield to which we could devote our off-duty hours. Many longstanding friendships were forged there, and we are still in touch with some of those wonderful people.

My main focus now was to complete the Canberra conversion course and qualify as an operational pilot on the bomber or photographic reconnaissance force.

Crewing Up

I began my training on the Canberra in March 1958. In the tradition of Bomber Command, pilots and navigators were left to sort themselves out into crews, so my first task was to find a navigator brave enough to fly with me. As we were all milling around in the crew room I was quietly praying that the Lord would lead me to the right man.

I was soon aware of a short, dumpy, rosy-faced Flight Lieutenant coming my way. Smiling broadly he offered his hand and said in a broad West Country accent, "We little chaps must stick together!" His name: Derek Cavanah.

Our first flight together was on 20th March in the Canberra T4, the dual-controlled version. I took to the aircraft immediately! It was a beauty to fly, albeit more ponderous than the Vampire, Venom and Meteor fighters. Having a navigator in the back was a new experience, and I had to learn the new arts of crewmanship and captaincy. All our solo flying was done initially on the bomber version, the B2, then on the photographic reconnaissance version, the PR3.

Derek, with checklist in hand, would accompany me as I carried out the external checks, and would monitor my responses to his challenges to ensure the check was correct. This same pattern was followed with all checks inside the aircraft, be it on the ground or in the air. We had to be at the aircraft one hour prior to our take-off time in order to complete all the necessary checks! In the air, checks were similarly monitored and even emergency drills were executed with the checklist after immediate action had been taken.

Derek had his own work to do in addition to reading out all the checks. He was responsible for all navigation, which included dead reckoning, astro-navigation, operation of the main navigation aid known as 'Gee', and monitoring the fuel graph. He would also operate the seven survey cameras when we progressed on to the photographic phase of the course, while I operated the tactical cameras, the F95s.

His other job was to serve up the in-flight rations – usually diced sandwiches and orange juice drunk through a straw. It was quite a feat to take refreshments at altitude, as the oxygen mask had to be removed but only for a few seconds. Thus the pilot had to give his navigator a running commentary: "Removing mask! Inserting grub! Mask back on!" or "Removing mask! Drinking! Mask back on!" - the idea being that, should the last comment seem a long time coming, the navigator would first yell for a response and then, if none came, he would change his oxygen and radio leads to the *wander* connections, unstrap from his ejector seat, move forward along the cat-walk and slam the pilot's oxygen mask back on to his face before the aircraft went its own way! Happily this never happened to me! Should the same misfortune occur when the navigator was dining, then the pilot simply kept yelling at him as he put the aircraft into a descent to below a cabin altitude of ten thousand feet where oxygen was not required. The navigator would (hopefully) rapidly recover.

After five sorties, Derek and I were cleared to operate as a crew and were sent off on various general handling and procedural exercises, alternating with ever-longer navigational sorties, sometimes lasting as long as four and a half hours. Occasionally Derek would complain of headaches and a sensation of confusion, but after visiting the Medical Officer he was cleared to continue flying. However, on 16th April we were authorised for a navigational exercise from Bassingbourn with turning points at Barnstaple, Dungeness and Cromarty at heights around thirty five thousand feet. The sortie, which lasted three hours and twenty minutes, was our last flight together.

On the leg from Cromarty, Derek began to behave rather strangely. He did not seem to register what I was saying to him and his responses were increasingly confused and slow. I immediately suspected an oxygen problem and put the aircraft into a descent, asking him to check his supply and connections. This he did and assured me, rather sluggishly, that all was well. Having spent some minutes below ten thousand feet, Derek began to respond normally but had no recollection of having had a problem.

The incident was reported on our debriefing and the Medical Officer was again alerted. After many tests and a visit to specialists (during which time I flew with a replacement navigator) Derek was pronounced unfit for further flying above ten thousand feet. Apparently he had some problem with the make-up of his blood cells, which failed to provide his brain with sufficient oxygen under decreased pressure, giving him a sort of "internal hypoxia".

Derek and I had to part, and I was sorry to see him go. Where was God in all this? I had asked Him to ensure I got the right chap. He had only lasted ten sorties! Happily Derek went on to become a very competent navigator-cum-winchman on rescue helicopters and was awarded the Queen's Commendation for one of his operations. It could not have happened to a nicer chap, but what about me? The rest of my colleagues on the course were already crewed-up. I was alone. It would probably mean that I would be re-coursed and have to start the training all over again.

A few days later I became aware of a new fellow on the course. He was a tall, lean, dark-haired Flying Officer, sporting a navigator's brevet. He had a small and rather abrupt moustache and walked with a slight stoop as though he was subconsciously compensating for his height. I was sitting in the crew room when this fellow approached me with a welcoming smile.

"Ron Collard, I presume? Ian Bullock. At your service! I'm your new nav."

I stood up and was pleasantly surprised that his face did not fall and he did not immediately retract his offer when he saw how small I was.

"Delighted to meet you," I replied, "so long as you don't mind having only half a pilot! Yes, I'm Ron Collard - all five feet four inches of me."

Canberra navigators liked their pilots to have long legs in case of an engine failure when plenty of leg power and leverage would be required to keep the aircraft in the air!

Ian laughed and offered his hand.

"Good things come in small parcels," he replied generously. "I'm happy to crew with you if you are with me."

That sealed a very firm friendship which lasted until Ian's posting two years later. As I write, on 6th December 2009, I note with interest that it was just forty nine years ago that Ian and I made our last flight together - a sortie lasting two hours and ten minutes, photographing the floods in the Severn Valley, to make sure those farmers did not overcook their claims for compensation! Also, today, I have sent the usual Christmas card to his widow with whom my wife and I have kept contact over the intervening years.

I firmly believe that God answered my prayer in linking me with Ian. He was a most loyal friend, even on the occasions when I professionally let him down, and he contributed greatly to my confidence as he put his trust in me however poor my performance. I am proud to have known him as a friend and could not have wished for a more competent navigator.

Ian later retired from the Royal Air Force with the rank of Squadron Leader and became a Department Head with the Civil Aviation Authority. He became a Liveryman of the Guild of Air Pilots and Air Navigators, a Freeman of the City of London, and a Fellow of the Royal Institute of Navigation. He also gained his Private Pilot's Licence. Sadly, he later died of Alzheimer's disease - a true officer, gentleman and personal friend for whom I had the greatest admiration.

My first flight with Ian was on 6th May 1958 when my instructor checked us out as a newly constituted crew. We flew our first solo flight together that same day when we carried out a navigation exercise ending in a *Standard Let-Down* through cloud, landing back at Bassingbourn using the *Blind Approach Beam System* (BABS).

Flying with the same chap over a period of nearly two years not only resulted in a firm friendship but also in a mutual understanding that can rarely, if ever, be reproduced in other realms of professional life. Working under intense pressure and sometimes danger, in the confines of an aircraft cabin, brings out the real person. Mutual understanding, acceptance of each other's peculiarities, and unwavering trust in the other's professional abilities forms a bond that is comparable to brotherhood.

Although Ian never professed to being a practising Christian, he not only tolerated my faith but often stood up for me when I was targeted by the more atheistic and agnostic elements of the squadron. On detachments abroad he graciously observed a respectful silence in our room when I knelt by my bed for my Quiet Time with my Bible reading and prayer every morning and evening. We often discussed the deeper issues of life, and his questions, which I sought to answer from the Scriptures rather than simply giving my opinions, were always posed from a genuine desire to understand. He never used his questions to provoke a 'spiritual punch-up' as I had experienced from others. He was always willing to listen.

Ian had a quaint idiosyncrasy! Whenever he became a bit keyed-up, he would repeat the age-old nursery rhyme, somewhat modified!

"Twinkle, twinkle, little bat; how I wonder what you're at. Up above the world so high; like a tea-tray in the sky."

Sometimes "the tea tray" was substituted with "Canberra". I was to hear that ditty many times in the future!

The course at Bassingbourn was totally absorbing. There was much to learn and new challenges to face, but it was both enjoyable and satisfying. One of the new experiences was flying for up to four and a half hours without being able to leave one's seat! No autopilot! Looking back upon those days I wish I now had the size of bladder I must have had then!

Navigation exercises all around the UK gradually extended further afield with turning points at Nice, Calais, Bordeaux, and Cherbourg. Most also included some form of photographic exercise.

Having successfully completed my final handling test with the Chief Flying Instructor, I was duly authorised as a Canberra pilot in the Photographic Reconnaissance role. Ian Bullock and I were posted to No. 58 (PR) Squadron at RAF Wyton in Huntingdonshire. I had achieved my aim to fly the Canberra on Photographic Reconnaissance duties and, what is more, my posting was to the only Canberra PR unit in the UK. It meant that Elizabeth and I would be able to think about buying a house, but first we had to save enough money to place a deposit and secure a mortgage.

We decided not to put our name down for married quarters as the rent would have been dead money. Instead we bought a caravan and, having initially positioned it at Therfield, we moved it to a site at Oldhurst, a few miles from the airfield at Wyton. A caravan would be our home for the next three years!

Combat Ready

N o. 58 Squadron formed part of the Joint Air Reconnaissance Intelligence Committee (JARIC). Its badge was an owl and its motto "Alis Nocturnis", meaning "Always by Night". The squadron was formed at Cramlington in Northumberland on the 10th January 1916 and was one of the first to make a raid over Germany, on the night of the 3rd/4th September 1939, when it dropped leaflets!

As I entered the squadron crew room I was faced with a large wall map of the world and, in large letters above it, the statement "No. 58 Squadron's Local Flying Area". The squadron was, indeed, a widely travelled unit, much in demand not only from the Air Ministry but also from a variety of other government and civil authorities requiring photographic intelligence worldwide

Ian Bullock and I reported to the Squadron Commander who was a navigator - one of the first senior officers with a single-wing brevet to command a squadron. As we entered his office he was in the act of wiping the names of a crew off his operations board. They had been killed the previous week when they collided with an American aircraft from nearby Alconbury whilst night flying. We had been posted in as the replacements.

After the usual words of welcome, he informed us that the whole of 'A' Flight was about to leave on a detachment to Christmas Island to take part in *Operation Grapple* - the atom bomb trials - and that we would be temporarily attached to 'B' Flight for our initiation and familiarisation with squadron operations and procedures.

My first flight in the Canberra PR7, on the morning of 30th June 1958, was a most enjoyable and memorable experience. The flight lasted one hour forty minutes and was devoted to general handling, emergency drills, local air traffic procedures and 'circuits and bumps'. Being a combat aircraft it had no dual controls, so the squadron's Qualified Flying Instructor (QFI) sat alongside me on the fold-away *jump seat*. I admired his courage! He wore only a chest-type parachute, which had to be operated manually, and his way of escape was out of the door - not like Ian and I who occupied ejector seats with parachutes which operated automatically.

Happily, the flight went well, and the QFI talked me through the various exercises without ending up a nervous wreck.

After a thorough debriefing, he flew with us again that afternoon for fifty minutes to consolidate my take-offs and landings, including single-engine approaches, prior to sending us off on our own for forty five minutes. We were briefed to do some general handling, an instrument let-down procedure and a couple of circuits. Ian, of course, called out all the checks for me, as per standard procedure, and his voice remained firm and clear until the approach to land, when I noticed he adopted a quiet tuneless whistling, interspersed with the occasional muttering of "Twinkle, twinkle, little bat..." until we were safely on the ground.

Our experience was built up over the following weeks with long distance navigation and photo exercises in and around the UK.

The Canberra PR7 carried eight F24 survey cameras, operated by the navigator in his prone position in the nose and, for tactical work, two F95 oblique cameras operated by a thumb switch on the pilot's control yoke. The sighting of the former set was achieved by the navigator tracking the target line down a *banana sight*, so called because of its shape, and the latter by a less sophisticated method!

Before flight, an airman was asked to stand in line with the tip tank and the two radio aerials encased in the cockpit canopy. The pilot, using his chinagraph crayon, then drew a cross on the inside of the canopy at the point where the airman's feet appeared. A horizontal line was also drawn through the cross and extended forward by about six inches. On approaching the target, the pilot would track it along the horizontal line and operate the camera as the target coincided with the cross. Only a short burst was necessary, exposing some five frames. This was enough to get the target in the central frame and one third of the way up the print. Later the chinagraph lines and the cross were replaced by sticking thin orange *Dayglow* strips on the canopy. If one visits the Canberra PR3 displayed in the Royal Air Force Museum, even today one can see these strips in position. 'Heath Robinson' maybe, but very effective!

The Canberra had a *blister* cockpit canopy; that is, the coaming rose in front of the pilot and dipped on either side, which had the effect of forcing the pilot's eyes into the cockpit or giving him a false visual impression of the natural horizon. This led to cases of spatial disorientation that could be quite alarming. One has the sensation of rolling when in fact the aircraft is straight and level. The only answer is to ignore one's sensations and believe unfalteringly on one's instruments - a good example of true faith.

On 1st September 1958, crews were required to bolster No. 13 (PR) Squadron in Cyprus where a war against EOKA terrorists was in progress. Having acquired the necessary khaki drill and tropical flying kit, I bade farewell to a very pregnant Elizabeth and left our caravan home to join Ian aboard a passenger aircraft flying to Nicosia.

On arrival, the aircraft was boarded by an armed security officer who briefed us in a way that wonderfully concentrated the mind! He warned us about the atrocities being carried out by the terrorists and the need to be constantly on one's guard, day and night. He told us to keep our eyes open on the forthcoming coach journey south to Akrotiri and to report any vehicle that we saw following us.

We boarded the coach with other service personnel and noted with interest that we had four airmen and a sergeant with us, armed with sten guns. Their heads never stopped moving throughout the whole trip and their guns remained at the ready position. They directed us to be particularly vigilant when passing through ravines or wooded areas. The journey seemed endless but the concentration and awareness remained keen!

Once at Akrotiri we were given more briefings about personal and corporate security. Apparently terrorists had recently stolen a number of RAF uniforms from the dry cleaners and a few undesirables had been caught infiltrating aircraft dispersals at night and planting pencil bombs in the tail plane recesses of the aircraft. So far all had been discovered before detonation.

We were issued with ammunition and revolvers which we wore every waking hour except when actually flying. When we went to bed the revolver was within arm's reach, and we slept with a knife under the pillow and the door locked. Ian and I made it a practice to be awake before our batman, a local Cypriot, entered the room. We were told not to trust anyone outside our immediate squadron and staff personnel.

On one occasion a navigator from another squadron retired to his room and pulled the cord to put on the light above the shaving mirror. A grenade exploded and he was killed. On another occasion a mother in the married quarters became suspicious when a local plumber came to fix a problem with the water tank in the roof. She went into the attic as soon as he had departed and found a timed grenade set up right above the nursery where her baby was asleep.

One day, returning to Akrotiri from a photographic sortie against suspected terrorist hide-outs, I witnessed the disappearance of the mobile radar caravan in the centre of the airfield as it blew up. The brains behind the operation turned out to be a popular and friendly lady who worked in the officers' mess! Needless to say, she was nowhere to be found following the incident.

It is remarkable how, under such circumstances, one's sense of self-preservation becomes very acute! Anything that even smelt of EOKA was immediately suspect. Some of the more experienced members of the officers' mess utilised this to their advantage by marking one coffee pot with the dreaded initials. The newcomers naturally avoided it, thus ensuring that the 'old boys' never ran short of their coffee, even if they came in late!

Being a non-drinker I found my off-duty periods rather boring. Due to the security situation one could not go for a walk in the countryside nor explore the local towns and shops. I regularly attended the meetings of the Soldiers' and Airmen's Scripture Readers Association (SASRA) meetings and those of the Officers' Christian Union. I also enjoyed the officers' mess library and the games room where table-tennis and snooker were options. It was here that I had the privilege of meeting a remarkable chap who became a personal friend.

Neil Williams was a pilot with No. 13 Squadron (the resident Photographic Reconnaissance outfit at Akrotiri) - a quiet, thoughtful, softly-spoken Welshman, with a kind but inscrutable face. Neil also found the social life of the bar rather undesirable and was delighted to find a kindred spirit in me. We played endless table-tennis matches, went for walks around the domestic area, sat on the veranda sipping fruit juices, and discussed many and varied topics including, of course, flying and the Christian Gospel.

One of our favourite excursions was to join a beach party where, with armed guards in attendance, we would dive for sponges in the crystal clear water and glide leisurely over the underwater forests of green vegetation, meeting many exotic sea creatures. We wore flippers, face mask, nose clip and snorkel. Because of the security situation we were not allowed to go beyond two beach markers in order to keep within the protection of the armed guards, but we could go as far out as we wished, within reason. It is amazing just how far one can go, idly flapping one's flippers, with hands clasped leisurely behind one's back, viewing the submarine world.

Figure 16: The late Neil Williams.

Neil was an exceptional pilot and later graduated from the Empire Test Pilots' School. He also became the British aerobatic champion eleven times. Whilst serving on No. 13 Squadron, Neil had the misfortune to experience a complete landing gear failure at night during a flight over Libya. He had to make a wheels-up landing at El Adem, aided only by a *goose-neck* flare path (individual flaming cans of paraffin set every couple of hundred yards along the landing strip). Neil made a perfect landing with minimum damage to the underside of the Canberra.

In 1970 he was to experience a wing folding up as he practiced his aerobatic sequence in a Zlin aircraft at Hullavington. Immediately he saw the wing lifting, he inverted the aircraft, which slammed the wayward wing back into position. The Zlin had a negative-G fuel tank which facilitated his flying an upside-down approach to the runway. When he judged that he was about a wing-span's height above the ground, he rolled the aircraft the right way up. The left wing tip touched the ground and the last Neil saw of the world before he screwed himself into a defensive ball was the world going across his windscreen sideways. He survived! Sadly, seven years later he died with his wife and an engineer when the Heinkel he was ferrying from Spain crashed in the Guadarrama Mountains north of Madrid. Neil's memory lives on in the books he wrote and the films in which he flew, notably 'A Bridge Too Far'. He was the pilot flying the reconnaissance Spitfire.

All junior officers were detailed in turn to be in charge of the night guard at the squadron dispersals. A dozen airmen and a sergeant, suitably armed with sten guns, patrolled the compound from 18:00 hours to midnight and were replaced by another section that held office until 06:00 hours. The officer in charge was responsible for the security of the compound, the conduct and response of the guard to any emergencies, and maintaining radio contact with the operations centre.

It was during my watch, shortly after I had briefed the new section taking over, that I received a rather garbled call on the field telephone informing me that intruders had been spotted proceeding in the direction of my compound. I immediately briefed my sergeant and we both set out to locate and warn the patrolling pairs of guards that an infiltration was imminent. I ordered the patrols to insert their magazines into their sten guns but to keep the safety catches applied.

The Engagement Orders stated that an armed sentry faced with a suspect intruder was first to shout a warning (the usual "Halt, who goes there?") If no satisfactory answer was forthcoming he was to load his magazine onto his weapon and shout a further warning: "Halt or I fire." If this challenge also brought no favourable response, the sentry was to slip the safety catch and fire one shot well above head height. The last resort, should the response still be negative, was to shoot to kill.

All remained quiet for a long time until suddenly the stillness of the night was broken by one single shot on the other side of the compound. I checked that my revolver was fully loaded and that the safety catch was applied. I hurried in the direction of the shot, and my approach was challenged by one of my patrols. I replied with the code word, which was acknowledged, and asked for a report. Very shamefacedly one of the sentries admitted that he had tripped in the dark, his sten gun had fallen and fired accidentally. I reported the incident to Operations by field telephone.

The following morning I was called before the Wing Commander in charge of Operations and was 'hauled over the coals' for having ordered the guards to load their magazines instead of complying with the Engagement Orders. I was ordered to charge the offending sentry for not having applied his safety catch, and I was sentenced to a week's permanent duty as Station Orderly Officer. This included being on call every night and on duty every day outside the periods I was actually flying.

I was very angry about the sentry being charged, particularly as he assured me his safety catch had been on all the time, so I set out to defend him. I spoke with the Armaments Officer, and together we carried out some experiments on the firing range. We proved that a sten gun, if dropped, could fire a round even with the safety catch still applied. I presented the findings to the Wing Commander Operations, with the Armaments Officer as witness, and the charge against the sentry was subsequently dismissed.

I took full responsibility for having ordered the sentries to insert the magazines into their weapons but questioned the practicalities of the Engagement Orders as laid down. Rather cheekily I asked the Wing Commander if he would be willing to take part in an experiment to prove whether or not the Orders were practicable. I suggested he might act as Guard Commander one night and carry out the Orders to the letter whilst I would be the intruder, armed only with a knife. I challenged the Wing

Commander to get the third part of those Orders out of his mouth before he felt the point of my knife in his back!

In retrospect I displayed a surfeit of audacity and could well have found myself on another charge for insubordination, but after giving me a further dressing down and threatening me with another week of Orderly Officer duty, the puce-faced Wing Commander dismissed me.

However, I was interested to see that just a few days prior to my eventual return to England the Engagement Orders had been modified!

On 9th October I returned from Cyprus via Malta, and four weeks later Richard Andrew was born in Royston hospital. What a joy! I was a dad! In those days hospital matrons were omnipotent, and no father was allowed within a mile of the delivery room! Eventually I was able to see my firstborn son and managed to get seven days' leave. What a thrill it was to bring Elizabeth and tiny Richard home to our caravan, wondering what the future would hold for us all. Little did I realise then that in just over a year's time a little girl would be added to our family.

Back at Wyton, Ian and I continued with our various high level, low level, day and night navigation and photographic sorties which included photographing the floods at Salisbury and Christchurch from two thousand feet and photographing Newcastle and Cambridge from thirty thousand feet for the Ordnance Survey. We also took oblique pictures from two thousand feet of Tower Bridge, the building of new motorways, and the Deal and Walmer coastline for Town and Country Planning and Manchester Town Hall.

Throughout this period our navigational, photographic and general flying sorties were being constantly assessed. One of our last flights prior to becoming a Combat Crew was to find and photograph at low level "a bridge over some water" at a designated map reference in the Scottish Highlands. We were allowed only one pass at the target.

On studying the map there was no sign of a road or river at the given map reference. We double-checked the co-ordinates with the Intelligence Officer who had briefed us, and he simply reiterated his original briefing that it was rumoured there was a bridge over some water at that point – "Go and photograph it!"

Off we went and flew towards the reference point at one thousand feet above ground level in order to get an early view of any water or bridge, before dropping down to two hundred and fifty feet to take the photo with my oblique side-mounted F95 camera.

Ian had vacated his ejector seat and was standing alongside me in the catwalk, connected to the oxygen and radio wander leads. Our eyes keenly scanned the area ahead, coming at us at some four miles per minute. Suddenly he saw it!

"There's some water!" he yelled. "It's just a stream!"

A second later I saw the target. "There's the bridge! Look, it's just a plank!"

We trundled back to Wyton wondering if we might have misread the reference co-ordinates or simply missed seeing a whacking great bridge over a whacking great river, but Ian was sure of his map reading and neither of us had seen anything resembling a normal bridge.

On our debriefing, the Intelligence Officer, complete with the prints of our photos in his hand, congratulated us on having successfully completed our mission. Another invaluable lesson had been learned, namely to study all aspects of a briefing but not to allow your mind to be limited by convention, first impressions and pre-conceived ideas.

By now I had graduated from a White Instrument Rating to a Green, which was a further pre-requisite before we could be upgraded to a Combat crew. Sorties were flown further afield with night stops at various airfields in Germany and one at El Adem in Libya.

Operation Polar Bear concluded our work-up to Combat status. This was a navigational and photographic sortie to Stavanger in Norway with a Major from Military Intelligence occupying the *jump seat*. Ian and I did not realise at the time that this airfield would be our destination after photographing our war target should the Cold War get hotter! Major Thomas was to show us around Stavanger and introduce us to the appropriate Norwegian Air Force personnel, in particular the photographic interpreters who would be the first to see our films of the target. We would become very conversant with the airfield, its procedures and staff in due course.

After completing an escape and evasion exercise centred on Kinder Scout in the Peak District without getting caught, Ian and I were classified as Combat Crew on 31st August 1959, just over a year since joining the squadron, and we were given a war target. This meant a briefing from our

Squadron Commander followed by a further briefing from an Intelligence Officer who handed us a red folder marked "Top Secret" containing maps, photographs, codes, written briefs and flight plans which were to be kept up-to-date on a monthly basis. All combat crews had to carry out, in a sealed room, at least one hour of target study per month so that in the event of being ordered into action, only the winds would have to be entered on the flight plan and the appropriate headings, timings and fuel consumption calculated.

The first comment made by the Squadron Commander when he briefed us was, "Say nothing about your war targets or your individual operations to any living soul. To do so brings an automatic court martial. You are bound by the Official Secrets Act until thirty years after your last operational sortie."

This briefing put everything into perspective. Before being posted to 58 Squadron I had to complete a very comprehensive questionnaire concerning myself, my wife, my siblings, my mother and father and my grandparents. Subsequently I was interviewed by officers from the Special Investigation Branch, as were my three referees. As a result of all this I was eventually cleared to *NATO Top Secret* level and posted to the squadron. On my arrival, on 23rd June 1958, I signed an additional, appropriately modified version of the Official Secrets Act.

The enormity of my security status and the responsibility for maintaining silence regarding my operational flying came home to me very forcibly. For thirty years I kept silent and only in 1992 began to speak about some of those special sorties.

No such sorties were allocated to us immediately, but one of the first assignments Ian and I had as a Combat Crew was to take Canberra PR7 WH822 to Marham for the Battle of Britain day on 19th September 1959. We were to display the aircraft in its various configurations prior to carrying out a low level fly-past so that the spectators could enter a 'speed and height' competition.

Initially the aircraft was parked in the cordoned-off static display area, so that the public could view the Canberra. Eventually the time came for us to carry out our lengthy checks before taxiing out for the flying display. On this occasion I did the external checks on my own whilst Ian carried out a public relations exercise by conversing with the members of the crowd and answering their questions. One old lady asked him what I was doing walking around the aircraft, tapping panels, checking control surfaces, etc. Ian's answer was, "His sight's not too good and he's trying to find the way in."

Figure 17: Ian and I being briefed for a photographic sortie by army and RAF intelligence officers. [Photo: RAF Wyton / © UK MOD Crown Copyright 1960]

Further flights were made to Stavanger in Norway, including various NATO exercises, to prepare us for any Cold War eventuality. Some of the low level sorties among the Norwegian fjords were particularly enjoyable and challenging.

An even more delightful experience occurred on 21st November 1959 when our daughter, Helen Elizabeth, was born at Royston hospital just one year and thirteen days after her elder brother. Again, Elizabeth was subjected to the regime that was in vogue in those days. After the birth, little Helen was whisked away. Four hours later Elizabeth had to ask if she could see her baby!

Elizabeth and I were aiming to save enough money to put a deposit on a house in St. Ives, but for the present we had to make do with our Picador caravan measuring ten feet by twenty two feet situated in the garden of a friend's house in Woodhurst, near Huntingdon.

Although only a caravan, it was a comfortable home to us. A small coal stove heated our water. We had a tiny kitchen and bathroom, a lounge which doubled as our bedroom once we had lowered the folding bed from its wall space, and an end bedroom which housed the two children. We had a shed outside which housed the washing machine. Instead of a fridge we had an *Osocool* cabinet! It was a small box-like contraption which stood outside and was topped up with cold water poured into an indentation on its top. The water percolated through the porous exterior and the evaporation kept the temperature down sufficiently for milk to be kept fresh for a day or two.

On 24th December 1958 I managed to convince a driving examiner that I could negotiate Peterborough without turning his hair white! I purchased my first car: a light brown Ford Prefect having three forward gears, one reverse and a dynamo that ate carbon brushes hungrily! It proved to be a versatile vehicle which, when so needed, could transport eight of us from the squadron to the officers' mess and back again!

In January 1960 I flew out to Nairobi on a detachment detailed to carry out an aerial survey of Somalia. The transit flight was over France and down the western side of Italy and Sicily to El Adem: a desert airfield in Libya near Tobruk where we spent the night.

In the morning we continued our flight to Nairobi via the south-western corner of Egypt (known at the time as 'Nasser's Corner' after the then President of Egypt) and over the length of Sudan into Kenya.

We were based on the military airfield at Eastleigh, which was five thousand and six hundred feet above mean sea level. Because the runways were of *murram* (earth) rather than tarmac, we had to get airborne early in the morning when the air temperature was comparatively low. If we needed a full fuel load then we had to hop over to Embakasi (now Jomo Kenyatta Airport) to top up and utilise its much longer tarmac runways.

The detachment went without significant problems except for one occasion when I was not flying with Ian as my navigator. I was tasked to survey part of the extreme corner of the Somalia Peninsula between the

Indian Ocean and the Gulf of Aden. This meant a round trip of some two thousand two hundred miles which left us little time in the target area. When full of fuel (as we were on 18th February 1960) a Canberra carries 3,305 gallons or 26,440 lbs (at a specific gravity of .8). The all-up weight of the aircraft with full fuel load was 55,000 lbs, requiring at lift-off speed of 140 knots (161 mph) and that took a lot of runway!

The Canberra's endurance was quoted as six hours, assuming one flew as economically as possible. I achieved five hours and five minutes on that sortie, having cruise-climbed to fifty two thousand feet on the way home. In fact, in order to conserve fuel, I closed the throttles some forty miles from Nairobi, gliding until over Eastleigh and then entering the pattern in a spiral descent. I only applied the throttles again when I was on my final approach to land.

My performance caused my Detachment Commander's hair to stand on end. When he heard from the ground crew that only 1,500 lbs of fuel was left aboard my aircraft, he nearly climbed up the wall! It had been hardly enough to do a circuit of the airfield. If I had messed up my approach, necessitating going round again for another attempt, the chances are that both engines would have quit. I was duly and rightly reprimanded. However, unknown to him I had, just three weeks earlier, carried out another long distance photo task over the extreme end of Somalia, lasting five hours and forty minutes, landing with 1,900 pounds of fuel. In retrospect I should have cut both the tasks short and returned earlier when my fuel graph showed I was only just on the amber line, but cloud cover so often spoilt our chances to get the photos needed that I took advantage of the clear skies and only turned for home when my fuel graph was hovering on the red.

It so happened that Eastleigh was also the home of a squadron flying the large Beverley transport aircraft and one of its co-pilots was Peter Galyer from school days! Thanks to him I got a trip in a Beverley which made me even more thankful that I flew a Canberra!

Many of my off-duty hours were spent visiting Wilson airfield, just outside Nairobi, where the Missionary Aviation Fellowship was based. They operated their few Cessna 180 aircraft from a small corrugated iron hangar, supporting Christian missions and relief agencies throughout Kenya and Sudan. I spent many hours travelling around the Nairobi area on the pillion of a motorbike, enjoying the hospitality of the three incumbent families. Just being in their company and seeing their devotion to Christ and their love for the people of Africa, spoke to my heart. No vast technical support system for them! Pilots were also qualified maintenance engineers and the wives, in addition to their domestic duties, served as administrators and radio operators, keeping watch on the progress of every flight and organising the flying programmes to meet the needs of their customers. Modern and multi-facet missions worked as one to meet the physical and spiritual needs of people living in remote areas. Could I, as a serving Air Force Pilot, be of any use to this unique organisation? I was resolved to do as much as I could for it when I returned to the UK.

After a month away in Kenya it was a particular thrill to look out to the right of my cockpit as I made the final approach to the runway at Wyton and see my caravan home, snugly tucked away among the trees of Woodhurst, awaiting me. What a joy it was to hold my dear wife, little Richard and even smaller Helen in my arms once more. How I had missed them. I was amazed at how much Helen had grown during my absence.

In September 1960 the BBC television crews came to Wyton to shoot a documentary on photo reconnaissance entitled 'A Bird's Eye View'. The programme was to begin with a Canberra flying very low across the airfield, almost taking the head off the presenter, Geoffrey Wheeler. At the end of the programme our Military Intelligence Officer was to present Geoffrey with an enlargement of the picture taken by the pilot on the low pass. I was detailed to do the necessary flying, but it needed a few practice runs first!

I was authorised by the Station Commander to fly at fifty feet and get a picture of Geoffrey Wheeler standing by a Land Rover alongside the control tower. The first attempt was not clear enough to identify the presenter as Geoffrey Wheeler, so I was authorised to fly at fifteen feet to get his features clear!

My temporary navigator, allowing for the set angle of my F95 camera which was to do the job, calculated the required distance we needed to be from the target. It turned out to be fifteen yards!

"Fly as low as necessary to get the job done," said the Station Commander. "I want to see Geoffrey's handkerchief poking out of his top pocket." Then he added, "But I'll be watching you!"

Figure 18: One of the higher practice runs for the TV programme, with Geoffrey Wheeler by the Land Rover. Part of the aircraft's tip-tank can be seen in the top left corner of the picture. Note the Station Commander looking down from the balcony of the control tower. The final run was at 15 feet, and a little closer in, showing Geoffrey's pocket handkerchief and face more clearly.
[Photo: RAF Wyton 1960 / © UK MOD Crown Copyright 1960]

We laid a strip of white cloth fifteen yards from the position Geoffrey would be taking up so that my navigator could talk me along it from his prone position in the nose. The Canberra's wing span (including the tip-tanks) was 65.5 feet so it was essential that I pulled the aircraft up before applying any bank; otherwise a tip tank would be scraped along the grass! We came down to fifteen feet above the ground and roared towards the white line at 250 knots (290 mph). The photo was successful and showed not only Geoffrey's features but also his pocket handkerchief! The original print clearly showed the Station Commander leaning over the control tower rail supervising us from above!

In December 1960 Ian was posted and subsequently promoted to Squadron Leader. I found myself paired with a new navigator who had recently joined the squadron. John Buckland was another tall chap, a true officer and gentleman, and a first class navigator. We first flew together on 29th December on a photo task centred on Peterborough and Wolverhampton for the Ministry of Health and Local Government. This first sortie with John was marred by the right engine failing on the way home, but my short legs proved sufficient to get WJ819 home safely. John appeared suitably impressed!

Elizabeth and I, with our two children, moved into our first house at No. 10, The Pound, St Audrey's Lane, St Ives, Huntingdon, in April 1961. We bought it for £2,410. We were delighted with its three bedrooms, bathroom, dining lounge and spacious kitchen. It also had a garage and a sizeable garden - both front and back. No central heating, but never having had it we did not miss it!

John and I were scheduled for a night sortie on 10th April so I said 'cheerio' to the family and drove up to Wyton in good time to attend the meteorological and night flying briefings. Other crews also attended, but take-off times varied through the night. John and I were first to go, taking off whilst there was still some daylight evident in the western sky.

The weather briefing promised a good clear night. Winds were light and visibility was good. Just a routine four and a half hour sortie from Wyton, in Canberra PR7 serial number WJ825, to carry out a navigation and night photo exercise, to include approaches to some of the master diversion airfields in the UK – a piece of cake!

All went normally as we taxied to the threshold of the westerly runway 27. Pre-take-off checks were completed and, having obtained take-off clearance from the control tower, I moved the aircraft onto the centre line of the runway, straightening the nose wheel and applying the brakes. I slowly opened the two throttles, checking symmetry and ensuring the brakes were still holding the aircraft firmly at 7,000 rpm. All other necessary checks were completed before I released the brakes and opened up the engines to full power, each giving 7,400 pounds (3,367 kg) of static thrust.

I kept the aircraft straight initially with small asymmetric throttle movements and touches of brake until rudder control became effective at 70 knots (81 mph). As the flight was scheduled for four and a half hours, our fuel load was maximum. All eight internal fuel tanks were full together with the two wing tip tanks. The fuel weight totalled 26,440 pounds (12,018 kg) and the all-up weight of the aircraft was 55,000 pounds (25,000 kg). This required attaining a speed of 140 knots (161 mph) before the aircraft would lift off, using well over half of the available runway.

As the aircraft accelerated through 135 knots I began to ease back on the control yoke to lift the aircraft into the air. The rumble of wheels on tarmac ceased abruptly and we were airborne. At that precise second I sensed a loss of power in the left engine.

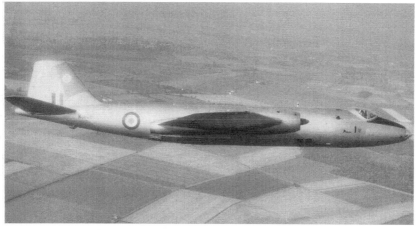

Figure 19: WJ 825. The Canberra PR7 that failed me on the night of 10th April 1961 and in which I flew up the Kuwait-Iraq border on 20th and 22nd July. [Photo: RAF Wyton / © UK MOD Crown Copyright 1960]

I immediately closed both throttles, replaced the aircraft firmly on the runway and applied the brakes as I called the tower: "Aborting take-off."

I could see the end of the runway approaching fast, and it looked as though I would not have enough runway left to stop the aircraft. I instinctively made to close the high pressure cocks on both engines to cut the fuel but fortunately stopped myself from doing so as this would have dumped two pints of fuel from each engine through the vent pipes which were situated directly above and in front of the wheels. If the brakes had caught fire due to the speed at which I had had to apply them, the addition of fuel would have doubtless caused an explosion at each wheel and augmented the fires already burning!

It was at this same instant that a squadron colleague, who was the duty pilot in the control tower, grabbed the microphone from the controller and yelled, "Do *not* close your engines down! Both your brakes are on fire!"

The *maxaret* brakes fitted to the Canberra were the forerunner of the automatic braking system (ABS) found in most cars today, giving automatic cadence braking. They were designed to be fully applied at a maximum speed of 95 knots (110 mph) but I had to call upon them at an estimated 130 knots (150 mph).

My speed was slowing, but the end of the runway was approaching fast. I resigned myself to the stark possibility of the aircraft going up in flames as it crashed through runway and approach lights and other obstructions in the over-run area. I yelled, "Brace! Brace!" to John, anticipating going off the end of the runway.

Happily, the speed dropped off sufficiently, and I was even able to use a small excess to turn the aircraft through ninety degrees off the runway and on to the taxiway. I clamped the handbrake on, as the aircraft was on a slight downhill slope, and yelled to John to abandon the aircraft. I had hardly got the last word out than John was flinging the door open and jumping to the ground with the portable fire extinguisher.

As I tore off my seat and parachute straps to follow him, John's ashen face and wide eyes re-appeared looking up at me from the doorway.

"You'd better hurry. We've a couple of bonfires out here, and I've broken the firing handle on the extinguisher!" (Such is human strength when under stress!) I virtually fell out of the aircraft and was faced by flames licking around both wheels.

The fire engines, which had chased us up the runway as soon as the alarm had been activated by the controller, arrived with lights flashing and sirens wailing. Powder was applied to the flames and the effect was dramatic! In a few seconds the flames were out, but the firemen continued to douse the wheels and the underside of the engine cowlings with powder whilst I climbed back into the cockpit to close the high pressure cocks and make the ejector seats safe. As I entered the cockpit I was aware of both engines idling normally. I checked both rev counters and saw, to my horror, that both engines were running smoothly with temperatures and pressures normal. Had I imagined a loss of power?

Having completed my close-down checks I vacated the aircraft to be faced by my Squadron Commander who had just arrived in his car.

"What's all this then, Ron?" he asked.

I explained the whole story, but he was obviously not convinced, especially when he said that both engines sounded to be idling normally when he arrived at the scene. I admitted that this was a fact, confirmed by the readings I had just observed on the instrument panel prior to closing the engines down.

My mind went back to Middleton-St-George when I had the elevator control jam in the Vampire. I was not the favourite pupil then, and I was obviously not the favourite squadron pilot now! The Squadron Commander said little but expressed his displeasure in a series of grunts with his parting shot being, "You realise you've just ruined the newest aircraft on the Squadron!" - WJ825 had recently been totally refurbished and only came back into Squadron service about a week before!

I felt utterly deflated. Here was I, a Flight Lieutenant in an elite intelligence squadron, working towards a 'Select Crew' rating, recently assessed as an 'Above Average' photographic pilot, standing by a smoking aircraft damaged by my apparent misinterpretation of events.

By now darkness was total as was my spirit. After the fire crews departed, their job well done, John and I walked back to dispersal to do the necessary paperwork. I hoped he could confirm the loss of engine power, but he reluctantly admitted that he had not been aware of anything out of the ordinary on the take-off run until he heard me close the throttles and felt the bump as I put the aircraft back onto the runway. He had no idea why I had aborted the take-off and only realised something was amiss when he heard my initial call to the control tower and the call from the Duty Pilot that our brakes were on fire!

Having filled in my Accident Report form I parted with John and drove back to my new home in a state of deep despair and confusion. I was convinced that the left engine had failed. What was the matter with me? I began to imagine all sorts of dreadful consequences resulting from the accident: a court martial, dismissed from the service, or at the best ignominiously posted away from the Squadron. "Ron Collard? – Oh yes, he was the idiot that thought he had an engine failure and ruined a perfectly good aircraft!"

I returned home and, having looked in on my two sleeping children, slipped quietly into bed, careful not to disturb Elizabeth. I resolved to say nothing about the accident to her. What would tomorrow bring? What would my colleagues think of me? How was I to face my Squadron Commander again?

As I lay silently in the peacefulness of the night, conscious of Elizabeth's warm presence alongside me and my two children blissfully asleep in their new bedroom, I made my concerns a matter of prayer. What a dreadful witness it would be for a Christian officer to be up before a court martial and to be found guilty of poor airmanship and endangering one of Her Majesty's aircraft, not to mention the life of a navigator!

As I prayed I slowly became aware of a deep sense of wellbeing and assurance. The 'Grim Reaper' had called on me tonight, as he had at Middleton-St-George, and I was still here. My clouds of concern and defeatism lifted. I felt euphoric. Nothing mattered. I was alive and had my lovely wife and family to live for even if I was cashiered from the Air Force!

The following day I reported to my Squadron Commander who had been joined by my Flight Commander and the Officer Commander Engineering Wing. I repeated my account of the previous night's event and answered their questions. They were stern but not unfriendly. The interview finished with my Squadron Commander telling me I would not be authorised to fly a Canberra again until the engine had been stripped down by Rolls Royce and the findings published.

Throughout my conversion training to twin-engine aircraft, I had been taught the importance of anticipating engine failures, especially on take-off and landing. Mental preparedness had been drummed into me from the very first flight on the Meteor, and this developed into my own self-disciplined drill which I repeated to myself before every take-off, even when flying a single-engine aircraft. It was called *The Captain's Brief*. The very act of thinking about the possibility of an engine failure and reminding oneself of the essential drill mentally alerts a pilot to any signs of abnormality in the take-off performance.

In a twin engine aircraft, especially one like the Meteor or Canberra with engines well offset from the centre line of the fuselage, an engine malfunction could be catastrophic, causing the good engine to impart a moment arm around the centre of gravity resulting in the aircraft yawing towards the dead engine. This yaw induces a rolling motion around the longitudinal axis. If no corrective action is taken, or the action is taken too late, the aircraft simply rolls and dives. If such an emergency happens close to the ground, the result is invariably fatal.

I was still convinced that a loss of power had occurred in the left engine and that I had taken the correct action, but I could not account for its subsequent normality when idling.

Whilst the engine was away being examined, WJ825 was cleaned up and its port engine replaced. Two new wheels were fitted, it was compass-swung, ground and air tested and put back on to the flight line. It looked as good as new – again! Apparently both sets of disc brakes had become so hot that each had split into two pieces due to contraction when cooled with the powder by the fire crews. Such is the power of sudden and extreme temperature changes on metal!

Eight days later the report came back from Rolls Royce. The Squadron Commander called me into his office, and I entered with much apprehension. He smiled and bade me be seated. He handed me the report from Rolls Royce.

Apparently, down in the bowels of the engine, a governor which controlled the swirl vanes that impart the correct angle of airflow into the engine had sheared at the precise instant I had lifted the aircraft into the air and thus closed the swirl vanes to their *idle* position. The loss of power was ratified, and the subsequent normal behaviour of the engine whilst idling was thus satisfactorily explained.

My Squadron Commander stood up and offered me his hand.

"Well done, Ron," he said. "Your handling of that emergency was exemplary. You are now back to full flying duties, and I shall be asking your Flight Commander to get you airborne again as soon as possible. By the way," he added, "I am recommending you to Group Headquarters for a *Good Show* citation."

The following day John and I were authorised to fly to Stavanger in Norway for a night stop. Maybe my Flight Commander had a warped sense of humour, as the aircraft he authorised me to fly was WJ825!

A month later my Good Show citation appeared in the Royal Air Force Flight Safety magazine, 'Air Clues'. There were a couple of inaccuracies in the original version so the corrected version appears thus:

SWIFT REACTION

On the night of the 10th April 1961 the pilot of Canberra PR7 WJ825 of No. 58 Squadron, Wyton, was making the initial take-off for a training flight at maximum all-up weight. Just as the aircraft left the ground the port engine failed. The pilot maintained control by swiftly closing the throttles, replacing the aircraft on the runway and applying steady braking.

At this time about 1,200 yards of runway remained. During the latter part of the run, both brakes caught fire but by now the speed was well down and the pilot was able to make a normal turn off at the end of the runway.

The aircraft was parked with brakes on as it was on a downhill gradient and then abandoned. The fire tenders arrived as the pilot got out and the flames coming from both wheels were extinguished. The damage caused was Category 2. [Category 5 would be a write-off.]

The technical investigation revealed that the port engine governor pump had seized and caused the drive to shear.

The pilot, Flight Lieutenant R Collard, had a very nasty situation on his hands when this emergency occurred and there are few worse than an engine failure at a critical point during a night take-off. He reacted quickly and correctly and is to be congratulated for averting what could easily have been a major accident.

On my annual appraisal as a photographic pilot, I was assessed as 'Above Average' and John was assessed as an 'Above Average' navigator. Our next upgrade would be to Select Crew status - the premiership of the air reconnaissance force - but meanwhile there was another conflict in which to engage...

On 16th July I happened to be working in the front garden when an RAF Land Rover pulled up and an Air Force policeman identified himself from Wyton Operations. (We had no telephone in those days!)

"There's a flap on, sir!" he remarked. "You're required immediately at Ops with your tropical kit."

I grabbed my *readiness bag*, checked its contents, and donned my uniform. A hurried kiss and embrace for each member of the family, and I was off. Where? How long away? Were we at war or what? Many questions crowded my mind, but it must have been even worse for Elizabeth, suddenly being left on her own with the children again and with so much uncertainty. For me the job would keep me occupied, but for her it was a different matter. Daily routine had to be maintained for the sake of the children but, within her own dear heart, there must have been much anxiety.

After the usual briefings, John Buckland and I calculated our flight plan and changed into our flying kit. I ensured that my *dog-tags* were around my neck - one designed to withstand burning and the other designed to withstand blast. Both had the same inscription: "R.COLLARD 3518711 OD." I also checked that I had my *skin chit* in the pocket of my flying suit. This was supposed to deter any would-be assassin from taking my life at a whim should we end up in hostile territory. The document promised a reward from Her Britannic Majesty should I be returned to her in one piece! The document when unfolded measured 39 cm by 32 cm and featured the Royal Coat of Arms and a Union Jack at the centre. The rest of the document contained useful phrases in Hebrew, Yiddish, German and Arabic, with the English translations and the foreign pronunciations spelt phonetically. The introductory paragraph stated, "I am a member of the British forces. Please assist me and help me to return to my friends. The British government will reward you." In most of the places where we carried out our covert operations, the opening sentence would have been enough to guarantee a very short life!

We were soon airborne and winging our way to El Adem (a flight of four hours fifteen minutes) for a night stop prior to flying on to Aden which we reached in a further five hours. The following day we set off for

Bahrain which took us three hours twenty five minutes. We thought El Adem and Aden were hot, but when the ground crew opened the aircraft door at Bahrain, the heat hit us like an oven. By the time we reached the flight office, both John and I were gasping. Water was supplied and we drank like camels. Never before, nor since, have I been so hot and thirsty. Happily our quarters were air conditioned, but the ground temperatures in the cockpit were extreme - kept to just tolerable proportions by cockpit shading and generators pumping in cool air.

We were then briefed on our task. We were part of *Operation Vantage* – the response to the threat imposed by Iraq on Kuwait. It was a miracle of military logistics that managed to position an all-British Task Force in Kuwait within a few days of the first signs of the Iraqi menace. I well remember the 'heart in mouth' sensations which accompanied me as I slowly opened the throttles at the end of Bahrain's runway to send the fuel-packed Canberra aircraft, loaded with long range oblique cameras, thundering into the sky for my first sortie into hostile territory.

It was a unique experience to find myself spending my 26th birthday flying along the border of Kuwait and Iraq. Our task was to photograph the threatening build up of Iraqi troops, armour and artillery.

My first sortie produced no results due to the desert haze, reducing visibility to a hundred yards in the target areas, but the subsequent sortie proved most successful and the air intelligence we gained, both photographic and visual, was soon being shared with the land commanders. Colonel Kassim, the Iraqi President, took one look at the forces facing him over the border and ordered a withdrawal. Not a shot was fired and not a life lost. As a result, Kuwait enjoyed thirty years of freedom until *Desert Storm* in 1991.

A month after our return from Operation Vantage, John Buckland and I, together with the rest of 'A' Flight, flew to Malta for *Operation Sunspot*. This was to practice night photography using the two F89 cameras mounted in the centre camera bay, combined with five photo-flashes stowed in the flare bay. Each flare had the luminosity of five million candle power and resembled a small torpedo. Our practice target was in the desert sands, near El Adem, in Libya. The round trip from Malta took about three hours and fifteen minutes.

Usually we took off in the daylight to arrive over the target area at thirty thousand feet by total nightfall. Once cleared by the Range Safety Officer at El Adem, John would vacate his ejector seat and use the oxygen and radio wander leads to take his prone position in the nose of the aircraft. He would navigate us towards the target which was an illuminated triangle. The trick was to fly at precisely the correct height, speed and heading, with the night camera rolling, and to release the five photo-flashes consecutively so that the light from their explosions lit up the target. The aim was to get the target slap in the middle of the centre explosion and thus in the centre of the five prints.

The run up to the target was virtually the same as for any bombing run. John would keep up a running commentary, directing me left or right to keep me on the centre line, allowing for drift. As we approached the flash release point his commentary of "steady... steady..." would become more rapid and intense until... "flares away!" At this point I would turn the cockpit lights to maximum, fly solely on instruments, lower my helmet visor and avoid looking outside the aircraft. John would also shield his eyes. Five lots of five million candle power on a dark night can play havoc with one's retinas!

After the fifth explosion, normal flying was resumed, the range cleared and the aircraft flown back to Malta. It was interesting to see, scattered around the target area, a number of tiny fires burning in the desert. This was not a result of our exercise but small groups of Arabs who would move in and collect the shrapnel which would end up in the local markets as cutlery and tools!

Occasionally a flare would fail to explode, and this caused a quandary as well as maybe giving some unfortunate Arab a terrible headache! Had the flare dropped but simply not detonated, or was it hung up in the flare-bay? A *doll's eye* at John's prone station would change from black to white, indicating that the flare had left the aircraft but even doll's eyes failed. If it remained black, there was only one answer: proceed to the jettison area off the coast of Tobruk and operate the flare jettison switch. Usually the appropriate doll's eye would confirm that a hung-up flare had dropped (even if there was no subsequent explosion) but sometimes there was no change of doll's eye and no explosion! – Was the rogue flare still on board?

In such an instance air traffic control at Malta was warned well in advance and necessary precautions put in place. It was possible that, on landing, the rogue flare could be jolted clear of its rack and be lying on the closed doors of the flare-bay! Thus one worked hard to ensure the smoothest possible night landing and minimum braking.

Once the aircraft was parked and the engines shut down, ground crew placed a deep mattress under the flare bay and slowly pumped the flare doors open manually. The hope was that if a flare was resting on the doors, it would be seen early and lowered ever so gently onto the mattress before the arming pin pulled!

On the same Operation Sunspot a year later, in May 1962, John and I had occasion, on two consecutive sorties, to attempt jettisoning a total of four flares. Of these only one left the aircraft; the other three hung up! Returning with three rogue flares did nothing for our morale but ensured the smoothest night landing I ever made!

Quite apart from facilitating our training for successful night photography, Malta also proved an excellent facility for sightseeing, swimming and topping up one's tan. Travelling by public transport, however, was an experience in itself. Every bus had a small altar to St. Christopher in the centre of the dashboard. The driver sat to one side of the wheel, steering with one hand. The other hand spent most of its time on the horn! The idea was that St. Christopher was really in control; the driver just helped him along! From the resulting driving standards, I was glad St. Christopher was not part of a Canberra crew!

Among the many colourful characters on the squadron was an eccentric Scotsman, inevitably called "Jock". He was reputed to have plunged the outer islands of Norway into total darkness by flying through the main power cable that spanned the gap, slicing off all the aerials and a layer of paint from the underside of the Canberra's belly!

Jock also turned his navigator's hair prematurely white on another occasion by performing a loop at night over the North Sea starting at low level! Jock's final claim to fame was to gain the high altitude record for playing the bagpipes! Neither his navigator nor the Squadron Commander were impressed!

On 17th September 1961 John and I were detailed to fly to Nairobi to set up facilities for a photographic detachment that would follow a week later. In the short time at our disposal, we had to organise, among other things, accommodation for the airmen, technical support, offices, transport and photographic processing facilities.

The Station Commander and his Wing Commanders knew of our task and were most helpful, but it proved to be a real test of our initiative, tact, and leadership. We had to get resident staff to sacrifice some of their precious time and equipment to meet our requirements.

We were able to get a whole hangar for the detachment, part of which we cordoned off with hessian to make a barrack room. Into this area we moved beds, bedding, wardrobes, bedside lockers, tables, chairs, bedside mats, screened partitions and everything necessary to make the airmen as comfortable and as private as possible. The area was positioned adjacent to the hangar ablutions and a rest room was also created with tables and easy chairs.

A detachment can be quite a burden upon the host station and staff, what with the extra catering, medical requirements, equipment demands and transport needs, but by the end of the week everything was in order, and I had the pleasure of meeting my Squadron Commander and the ground crew off the transport aircraft when it arrived at Nairobi airport, knowing John and I had done all we could. It was now up to the Squadron Commander to inspect everything and decide whether or not he could signal the squadron to fly from Wyton next day or whether more was needed to be done in preparation.

He was fully satisfied and generous in his acknowledgement of our work. He immediately signalled the rest of the detachment to proceed and we were released to return to the UK via civilian airlines. Job well done! Our next immediate task was to work up to our Select Crew category.

Select Crew

On 30th June 1962 John and I were awarded our Select Crew rating in the Photographic Reconnaissance force. In the intervening time we had flown many photo sorties at home and overseas. In addition to our high level night photography over the El Adem range, we also trained in low-level flare dropping on Saltfleet and Holbeach ranges off the Lincolnshire coast. The low level flashes were smaller than the high level variety and not as powerful. They fired obliquely from the flare-bay thus illuminating the area covered by both the F89s and my pilot-operated F95 camera.

We were now qualified to carry out any photographic sortie assigned to us, by day or night, high level or low level.

Our first clandestine sortie was preceded by a high-powered briefing. John and I were summoned before the Squadron Commander who informed us that we were being assigned to a special duty that was of NATO Top Secret status. He gave us the usual warning about keeping it to ourselves for the next thirty years.

He, together with the Station Commander, then drove us to Brampton where we were introduced to an Air Commodore and a couple of civilians: one from Military Intelligence and the other from the Foreign Office. We were given a lengthy and comprehensive briefing on the task, which was to position an aircraft at Khormaksar (Aden) and to report to the Station Commander who would be conversant with our assignment. He would give us all necessary back-up including a cover story should we have to eject and come down in hostile territory.

Once at Aden we were to photograph a road in a certain part of the Middle East which agents had informed us was near completion. It ran from the country's capital to the coast of the Red Sea and had been built by the Russians. The Foreign Office and Military Intelligence were keen to have pictures of the road to assess its strength, weak points, measurements etc, presumably to calculate whether or not it presented a threat to allied interests in the Middle East, especially in regard to the transport of military hardware from the coast into the interior where a war was already raging.

If this area fell to Communist forces, then Aden itself would be endangered.

We were to carry a third crew member who would be viewing the rear of the aircraft through a periscope, mounted in the navigator's escape hatch, to ensure we did not contrail at our operating height of forty two thousand feet. We were to stay as long as necessary in Aden until the job was done.

Once again we flew from Wyton across France, with beautiful views of the Alps and Mount Blanc, over northern Italy and down its leg to Sicily, across the Mediterranean Sea and to El Adem in Libya - a flight of four hours and twenty five minutes!

Before retiring that night I spent a while standing on the edge of the desert and marvelling at the silence, the blackness of the night and the brilliance of the stars. I tried to imagine what it must have been like for the Eighth Army in combat with the Afrika Corps, standing by for its assault upon El Alamein. I spent some time in prayer and, on returning to my room, read Psalm 8 verse 3, which was particularly significant: "When I consider your heavens, the work of your fingers, the moon and the stars which you have ordained, what is man that you are mindful of him, and the son of man that you visit him?"

The following morning we were up with the lark. Dawn was only just breaking as we made our way to the aircraft to carry out the comprehensive checks. The temperature was comfortably cool before the sun brought its cruel heat to the day.

From El Adem we routed to Khormaksar via the south-western corner of Egypt. The Egyptians were very sensitive about encroachment into their airspace, and some of my colleagues had, in the past, been accosted by Mig fighters of the Egyptian Air Force. John made sure we passed well clear of the area. Safely round Nasser's Corner we flew across northern Sudan, the northern tip of Ethiopia, across the Red Sea and into the Gulf of Aden.

Having arrived at Khormaksar, I was most humbled and pleasantly surprised to be met by Group Captain Alfred Knowles who I knew through the Officers' Christian Union and the Soldiers' and Airmen's Scripture Reader Association of which he was chairman.

He took us in his car to meet the Station Commander, then to the Operations Centre, prior to taking us to his home where his wife had prepared a delicious and most welcome meal.

Group Captain Knowles was special. He was not only a first class pilot and the holder of the Air Force Cross; he was also a highly skilled engineer and Fellow of the Royal Aeronautical Society. As an officer and true gentleman he had also been awarded the Order of the British Empire for his leadership and professionalism over many years.

More importantly he was a committed Christian whose testimony to the Lord was an example to all. He was highly regarded even by his most atheistic and agnostic peers and subordinates. With his aviation and technical skills he had not only built himself a beautiful electronic organ but had designed and built two small aircraft which he flew around the UK on his various visits.

The Station Commander was most helpful. He put his entire staff at our disposal and ensured our needs were promptly met. Servicing and replenishment of the aircraft, loading and unloading of cameras and film, priority with Air Traffic Control were all ours for the asking. He then gave us his final briefing which included our cover story, should we run into difficulties whilst in hostile airspace.

Assuming at least one of us survived an ejection or forced landing in hostile terrain, we were to be most apologetic to our captors and insist that we had experienced a navigational equipment failure which had caused us to encroach into the country's airspace. We were to keep to the usual drill of giving only number, rank and name, and were to present our government-prepared document, carried by all crew on special duties, which promised a significant reward if we were returned intact to Her Britannic Majesty!

In the event of our being faced with an emergency necessitating ejection or a forced landing, I was to transmit the one word "Checkmate" over the radio, if time allowed. This would alert a naval officer, comfortably sitting in a frigate positioned at the mouth of the Red Sea, listening in on our discrete frequency. He was briefed to immediately signal Khormaksar where the Station Commander would inform the Joint Air Intelligence Board in the UK and the Foreign Office. The latter would then begin the 'humble apologies' routine with the country involved, through the diplomatic channels, in the hope that an international incident might be avoided and we treated as accidental intruders rather than spies.

The Station Commander briefed us to file a flight plan from Khormaksar to Salalah which was a base in Oman with a British military presence - a flight of some six hundred and fifty miles. It was a route frequently taken by Royal Air Force aircraft, so should arouse no suspicion. It also meant that we would initially be flying away from our intended target.

After take-off we were to climb to a predetermined height which would ensure that any hostile radar would see us tracking east. Later we were to descend to two hundred feet over the sea, below radar cover, and turn on our reciprocal heading, tracking back towards Khormaksar before turning north up the Red Sea. Subsequently a rapid climb would be made to our operational height of forty two thousand feet and a turn made on to our target heading.

A constant check on contrails was to be made. Should any appear, I was to immediately throttle back and drop our height by two hundred feet before carefully re-applying power! By this method we would find a contrail-free height. Happily, we kept contrail-free from the start, so our operational height was maintained throughout the survey which would please the map-makers as their scale would not be compromised.

The road ran for more than one hundred miles, but as it twisted among the mountainous terrain we had to do two runs, laterally displaced, in order to get prints of the entire target area. This meant spending over an hour in hostile airspace. The Canberra was not fitted with an auto-pilot, so heading, height and speed had to be manually maintained with great precision. A small wing drop would throw the camera line from the vertical, resulting in asymmetric overlap and distortion on the prints. A change of pitch would give rise to asymmetric overlap in the longitudinal plane, and a change of speed would cause an inconsistent overlap longitudinally. All such errors would also affect the scale with which the photographic interpreters and cartographers would have to work.

Concentration, together with the constant awareness that a missile might be on its way towards us, called for strict self-discipline and self-control. Communications over the intercom were terse, brief and humourless. In spite of being in a pressurised and temperature-controlled cockpit, I sweated like a pig.

At long last John called out, "Cameras off!"

The relief in his voice was tangible, and the humour and rapport returned to our conversation as we carried out our post-photographic checks. Once clear of the coast we executed a maximum rate descent to low altitude, waggled our wings in acknowledgement over our watching frigate, and returned safely to Khormaksar.

John and I supervised the unloading of the cameras, and the films were placed in sealed containers for which we were personally responsible until reaching El Adem. Once I was in radio contact with El Adem I asked that the Station Security Officer meet the aircraft at dispersal. Sure enough he was there on his bicycle as we taxied in. He stuck his head into the cockpit and jokingly asked if we had been intercepted by Egyptian Migs.

"No," I said. "I simply want your signature for twenty cans of NATO Top Secret film which will be your personal responsibility overnight."

His grin evaporated. However, after a sleepless night he returned the films to me at the aircraft the following morning and breathed an audible sigh of relief when I signed for them.

A few days after our return to Wyton, John and I were summoned to Brampton where we were reintroduced to our films, this time in the form of photographic prints laid out on the floor of a large and secure debriefing room. The chaps from Military Intelligence and the Foreign Office were there, grinning broadly. They asked various questions of us, to supplement the reports from the Photographic Interpreters, and congratulated us on a job well done. We went home feeling satisfied that we had proved our worth as a Select Crew in a rather select force and done our bit in making the Cold War a touch cooler.

Such clandestine sorties were always fraught with danger and concentrated the mind wonderfully, but to see the results of one's efforts, and to know they were contributing significantly to maintaining a degree of world peace, was most rewarding.

It was during this same period of the Cold War that Gary Powers, a reconnaissance pilot with the Lockheed Company working for the CIA, was shot down by a missile over Russia whilst carrying out a photographic sortie in a U2 spy plane. It caused a heightening in the Cold War tension, as President Kruschev of the Soviet Union had all the trump cards in his hands. Gary was tried by the Soviet Supreme Court and was given an extensive prison sentence. Diplomatic bargaining eventually released him in exchange for a Soviet spy imprisoned by the Western Allies.

On 29th July 1962 Michael Philip made his arrival into this uncertain world. Unlike his brother and sister, he was born in our home and I had the joy of being present. Elizabeth had taken on quite a lot of gas during the delivery, and little Michael came out coloured blue! It was quite a spectacle seeing him gradually turning pink from his head to his feet as fresh Huntingdonshire air washed through his system!

Having taken a few days off around the time of Michael's birth I was soon back at work. Civilians might think that aircrew in the Royal Air Force are always flying, but this is not so. We are commissioned as *General Duties Officers (Flying)*, and the 'General Duties' take all forms! During my career I have conducted Unit Inquiries, served as a member of a Courts Martial, served on the board of Air and Road Accident Investigations, commanded Guards of Honour, acted as Personnel Effects Officer for a deceased airman, held a number of inventories, conducted *Marching In and Marching Out* procedures when married quarters change tenants - all in addition to the basic secondary duties that all officers have, over and above their primary duty of flying. Such secondary duties for me included being the *Air Cadet Liaison Officer* responsible for assisting local Air Training Corps and Combined Cadet Force squadrons, arranging of camps and flying experience for cadets allocated to the station during Easter and summer holidays, and holding the post of Station Flight Safety Officer. The latter appointment gave me direct access to the Station Commander, and I was responsible for all Flight Safety matters on the station including the arranging of Flight Safety meetings, the taking and promulgation of the Minutes, the following up of actions recommended and ensuring their implementation.

Most of us went into general duty or secondary duty mode when the weather was unsuitable for flying. Today was one of those days!

The cloud base was at roof level; the visibility was poor and the heavy drizzle continuous. The meteorological briefing that morning forecast a warm sector depression to be over the area for most of the day. The Photographic Reconnaissance Wing at Royal Air Force Wyton, comprising ourselves and No. 543 Squadron equipped with the four-engined Valiants for radar reconnaissance, was grounded. Even the birds seemed reluctant to get airborne - an ideal day for us to be about our general and secondary duties!

Some officers, having few if any such duties, kept themselves away from the attention of senior officers who might give them some onerous task, by drawing a *Classified* file from the Central Registry and walking busily around the station with it tucked under an arm! Usually the route they took, in prolonged stops, was to the officers' mess, their pals' crew room on the other squadron, married quarters, checking the weather at the met office, and visiting the section sporting the prettiest WRAF personnel!

Such activities were in swing on the morning of this grey day with lunch being a welcomed break. The clothes pegs in the officers' mess corridors were full of soggy raincoats and hats, and the various rooms were buzzing with loud and relaxed conversation. Games of snooker and table tennis were going full tilt in the games room. The ante-room was full of pipe and cigarette smoke as newspapers rustled continually. The dining hall echoed to laughter, chatter and the chinking of cutlery and crockery as hungry young men munched their lunch. The bar, of course, was humming with conversation and the clinking of glasses, although no alcohol was being consumed by aircrew on standby duties.

With everything in full swing the public address system suddenly announced, "All personnel to report to their place of duty immediately for a war exercise. The station is now on a war footing."

The noise level rose as scores of bodies downed their last drops of grog, discarded their snooker cues, table tennis bats, newspapers, beer mugs, coffee cups and half-eaten meals. The corridors suddenly filled with a noisy, running throng grabbing their outdoor clothing and hot-footing it to their place of duty. Within a few minutes the mess was virtually empty and silent but for the stewards tidying up after the mass exodus. The Church of England Padre slowly folded his newspaper and rose from his chair to return to the station church which, under war conditions, doubled as a second mortuary!

The clothes pegs were empty, except for one service dress hat. The Padre took it unthinkingly from its peg and stuck it on to his head - but it did not fit! He stopped, puzzled. He took it off and looked at it. Instead of the chaplain's badge on the front he saw the ordinary officer's badge. Wrong hat! He looked inside and there on the brown leather lining was the name "Flying Officer B. Moses" – a co-pilot on No. 543 Squadron.

"Never mind," thought the Padre. "I'll pop over to the squadron crew room and swap hats with Brian; he obviously took mine by mistake." Donning the ill-fitting hat, he strode out into the drizzle and made his way towards the squadron hangar. Who should he meet *en route* but the Station Commander coming the other way!

The Padre threw up the usual salute with a cheery, "Good afternoon, sir!" which the Group Captain acknowledged.

Suddenly the Station Commander stopped dead in his tracks and turned around. "Padre!" he yelled. "A word with you, please." The Padre duly retraced his steps and faced his Commander.

"Padre, you're improperly dressed! You're wearing the wrong hat. Where's yours?"

You can imagine the look on the Station Commander's face when the Padre innocently replied, "Moses has it sir, and I'm on my way to retrieve it!"

Grounded!

H aving served four years with 58 Squadron, it was time to be posted elsewhere. It was also time for me to be assigned to a ground job, as my career so far had been spent exclusively on flying duties. What had the Air Ministry in store for me? More to the point, what about the family? Would we need to sell our newly-acquired home and move to another part of the country - or even abroad? Happily we knew the One who knows every detail of our lives and whose plans for us are only for His glory and our good, so we asked Him, as on other occasions, to over-rule the posting.

I learned that a vacancy was coming up at Bassingbourn, where I had previously undergone the Canberra conversion course. The post was as a Ground Instructor in the Airmanship and Survival section. I mentioned this to my Squadron Commander who promised to pursue the matter, but I heard nothing for many weeks and my time on 58 Squadron was rapidly drawing to a close.

I was scheduled to night fly, so had been given the afternoon off in order to get some rest. I had fallen asleep on the bed and awoke to find I had a dull pain in my lumber region to the left of my spine. I thought it was probably indigestion and, bidding farewell to the family, drove to Wyton to meet up with John Buckland and attend the necessary briefings. By the time I arrived I was in agony, so I drove straight to Sick Quarters. The Medical Officer (MO) was playing cricket at the time, so an orderly went off to get him. On his return I was informed that the MO was actually batting and I would have to wait until someone got him 'out'! During the wait the pain became excruciating, then stopped. Eventually the MO arrived, and I had to tell him I was OK. I felt a real fraud and apologised for having troubled him. I continued with the night sortie which was uneventful.

Soon after this, my CO called me into his office and handed me my posting notice from the Air Ministry. I was to take the vacancy at Bassingbourn – I was jubilant! Not only could we stay in our home at St. Ives, with no disruption to the family, but my ground posting would be as near to flying as was possible. I would even be able to fly the Canberra occasionally to keep my hand in!

I reported to Bassingbourn in December 1962 and was introduced to Flight Lieutenant Leon Collingridge who was in charge of the Airmanship and Survival section. He was a cheerful, friendly and rotund gentleman who really knew his stuff. He had been a Wing Commander in Canada under the Empire Training Scheme, but had dropped two tiers of rank on returning to the UK in order to remain in the Royal Air Force.

As a Pilot Officer he had fought in the Battle of Britain with No. 66 Squadron at Coltishall and had been shot down on the 29th July 1940. He had crash-landed his Spitfire on a sandbank at Orfordness and, fearing it would catch fire, threw back the hood to escape. He was surprised how much difficulty he experienced in extricating himself from the cockpit. He ran about a hundred yards before realising he still had his parachute on! A chap in a boat picked him off the sandbank and rowed him ashore where he complained of a pain in his leg. He was eventually taken to Ipswich hospital where it was discovered his leg was broken!

Leon was well known throughout the Canberra force, as all the crews had come through his hands at Bassingbourn. He was a delight to work with, and I learned so much from him. After sitting in on all his lectures he gradually weaned me into the task and constructively criticised my own early attempts at lecturing on the various ejector seats then in use within the Canberra force, survival techniques for jungle, arctic, desert and sea, Canberra emergency drills, performance, and cockpit familiarisation.

During the days that followed I noticed I was passing blood, so I reported to the Medical Officer. From that point I was grounded and underwent many tests and consultations with specialists. I also experienced, on two more occasions, that same agonising pain that I had experienced prior to my night flight. I was diagnosed as having suffered renal colic. I was eventually referred to the Consultant Surgeon of the Royal Air Force, Air Vice Marshal, Sir Peter Dixon, who advised me that if I wished to continue flying I would have to undergo surgery and have the lower lobe of my left kidney removed as it was, in his parlance, "manufacturing calcium stones without a licence."

So it was that my flying ceased (at least for the time being) and my work as a Ground Instructor curtailed. Instead I became a patient at the

Royal Air Force hospital at Ely for three weeks. I had been there before for a couple of weeks during my time on 58 Squadron, to undergo an operation to remove fluid from the middle ear cavity, so I was familiar with hospital life and routines.

I cannot speak highly enough of the care and treatment I received on both occasions from the Royal Air Force Medical Branch. Not only did I have the personal attention of Sir Peter Dixon, who travelled up from London to perform my partial nephrectomy, I also had exemplary nursing from the Princess Mary's Royal Air Force Nursing Service.

Although a hospital, Ely was still a Royal Air Force station, so the discipline and service structure remained. So also did the cleanliness! No hospital bugs stood a chance of survival in that regime!

Three weeks after the operation the fifteen stitches were removed from the wound in my side and I was allowed home for two weeks' sick leave before reporting back to Ely for a consultant's appointment. I thought I might be cleared for flying again, but instead I was referred to the Central Medical Establishment (CME) in London to be medically re-boarded.

Whilst awaiting this appointment I returned to Bassingbourn for duty and was driving past Station Headquarters when a window was thrown open and the Station Commander, Group Captain T P Seymour, beckoned me.

With some trepidation I parked the car and hobbled to his office. He welcomed me most warmly and bade me sit down. He wanted to know all about my stay in hospital and whether or not I felt up to returning to work. He asked after Elizabeth, Richard, Helen and Michael by name. What a Commander! He knew everyone on his staff by name, their families and their situations. I later learned that over the breakfast table each day his wife would show him small photographs of various members of his staff and he would recite their names and details, which Mrs. Seymour would check from a nominal list. He was one of those leaders who instilled confidence and loyalty into his subordinates by his interest in them and support of them.

During my tour of duty at Bassingbourn, I took up the secondary duty of Air Cadet Liaison Officer (ACLO), responsible for organising and running Easter and Summer Camps for air cadets and helping the local cadet squadrons. When Group Captain Seymour was promoted to Air Commodore and posted to the Air Ministry, he wrote me a letter of thanks for all I had done in that role. That letter, which I still have in my possession, meant as much to me as a Queen's Commendation!

Eventually I had my appointment at the Central Medical Establishment in London. This entailed a number of tests, not only in relation to my kidneys, but covering all other departments of my body. It was, in fact, a total re-examination of my whole person similar to my initial medical examination back in 1954.

I was finally interviewed by a specialist holding the rank of Group Captain. He suggested that, as I had "had a good innings" as a pilot, it might be advisable, from a health point of view, to give up flying and revert to permanent ground duties. I was horrified! He informed me that the kidney problem could re-occur and that if I was in control of an aircraft when it happened, the results could be disastrous as the pain was so inhibiting.

I put up a vehement defence and assured him that I was not willing to come off flying duties unless I was ordered to do so and that I would do anything to get myself fully fit again. After some ponderous thought he told me he would have to downgrade me and that I would only be allowed to fly if accompanied by another pilot.

"However," he added, "if you have no further occurrences of renal colic during your current ground tour at Bassingbourn, we will re-consider an upgrade."

Other than periodic tests to follow up my nephrectomy, my health remained good, and I thoroughly enjoyed my tour as a ground instructor. I was even able to fly the Canberra T4 occasionally, accompanied by another pilot.

Hundreds of pilots and navigators, destined for the Canberra force around the world, passed through my hands. Among them were some warranting special mention: Peter Thorne, my fellow student on the Meteor course at Strubby, came through the course as a Group Captain, prior to taking command at Farnborough; Air Vice Marshal "Johnnie" Johnstone, top-scoring ace of the Battle of Britain, underwent the conversion course before taking up his post as Air Officer Commanding Malta; and Air Vice Marshal Spottswood became a student of mine prior to becoming Air Officer Commanding No. 3 Group of which Bassingbourn formed part. I was to meet him again on his inspection of the station at a later date. Another student of mine was a certain Wing Commander who had been my antagonist in Cyprus but, whether he recognised me or not, he proved to be most amicable!

Another interesting student on the course turned out to be the Commanding Officer of the School of Instructional Technique. He was one of the rare breed of Education Officers who was also a pilot. He came into my office on the day of his departure and very generously complimented me on my instructing. He asked me where I had learned my instructional techniques, and I was delighted to inform him that it had begun with the East Surrey Lay-Preachers' Fellowship and, more recently, through the mutual critiques carried out by the Christian Witness Team at RAF Wyton. He was, as one would expect, nonplussed but nevertheless awarded me an honorary A1 category!

The time came for Leon Collingridge to move on, and I had the honour of being his successor. This meant I had a large input into the Airmanship and Survival training of Canberra crews, liaising with such august units as The Royal Aircraft Establishment at Farnborough, the Handling Squadron at Boscombe Down, the Combat Survival School at Mountbatten and the Martin Baker Ejector Seat Company at Denham. I paid many visits to these establishments and underwent various courses. Among these was a Sea Survival Course at Mountbatten which was most informative and enjoyable, culminating in being taken beyond Plymouth Sound in an Air-Sea Rescue launch and, on the instructor's signal, leaping off the stern dressed in an immersion suit, flying overalls and parachute harness, complete with dinghy pack attached.

The launch was travelling at speed to simulate bailing out in a high wind. On hitting the water, the drill was to roll onto one's arched back with head forward, spread-eagle arms and legs, and surf-ride the water. When the instructor thought one had got the hang of it he yelled, "Release!" through his loud-hailer, at which point he started his stopwatch. The subject then released himself from the parachute harness, pulled in his dinghy pack, inflated the dinghy, threw out the sea drogue and clambered aboard. He then had to cover himself with the protective apron, at which point the instructor hit his stopwatch again and noted the time. The insulating cushions in the dinghy floor and in the protective body apron were then orally inflated to provide added protection from the elements.

In the North Sea, in winter, a survivor has less than a minute to get himself thus ensconced in his dinghy; otherwise he becomes incapacitated. Due to a keen sense of self-preservation, I managed to achieve the task in a time which broke the Mountbatten record!

A visit to the Martin Baker Ejector Seat Company also proved most interesting, particularly meeting with Benny Lynch who was the first man to test an ejector seat.

On his very first test from a modified Meteor he was fired out by a gun, having a terminal velocity of sixty feet per second. Once clear of the aircraft he had to release himself from the seat, push it away and deploy his parachute manually. He ended up in a field with compression of his spine and two crushed vertebrae!

Subsequent investigation found that the injuries were caused because his body had absorbed the power of the gun all at one instant. The next test seat was designed so that a smaller charge initiated its journey up the rails but caused the hot exhaust gasses to set off a secondary charge half way up. This imposed less initial impact on the body but accelerated the seat up the rails, giving the final required velocity of sixty feet per second.

The story goes that when Martin Baker visited Benny Lynch in hospital, he informed the amply-built Irishman that the solution had been found and would he be willing to try another ejection on his release from hospital. Benny's negative reply, though unprintable, could be summarised by the phrase "Not likely!" Martin Baker then offered him a substantial remuneration in addition to the original test fee, to which Benny replied, "Most likely!"

Subsequent testing proved the point, and all ejector seats today are designed to the same basic pattern of having a low-powered charge to initiate the firing, with secondary charges placed to accelerate the seat up the rails. The final velocity in vogue during my time was eighty feet per second, prior to the rocket seat being developed for such aircraft as the Harrier.

During my visit I was taken on a tour of the factory. At one point I noticed a young lad concentrating hard at a particular lathe. He was carefully aligning a bit with the centre of a star-wheel. When he had completed the task I asked what exactly he was doing. His reply epitomised the professionalism and ethos of the whole Martin Baker Company: "I'm saving a life, sir."

The Pilot's Handling Notes for the various marks of Canberra were constantly reviewed, especially if a significant modification had been implemented. With some seven different marks of ejector seat in use within the Canberra force worldwide, it was my job to liaise with the Handling Squadron at Boscombe Down, Martin Baker's and the technical writers of Pilot's Notes to ensure that the appropriate section of the publication was succinct, technically correct and 'user friendly' in the way it was presented (unlike a lot of today's computer manuals!)

In the course of introducing the Mark 2C ejector seat, I was visited by the designated technical writer who turned out to be Wing Commander Don Kingaby DSO DFM** - my wing leader from Celle days!

I thoroughly enjoyed my tour of duty at Bassingbourn. It was always a delight to enter my Airmanship and Survival Hall and see the highly polished floor, the four full-sized wooden mock-ups of the Canberra cockpits lined up along one wall, the ejector seats similarly arrayed and one suspended from the ceiling showing the full sequence of ejection with parachute and drogue streamed. Beneath it was a fully inflated dinghy with its associated equipment and around the hall various displays depicting survival techniques for arctic, desert, jungle and sea. At the rear of the building was the lecture room and cinema, complete with two 16mm projectors. At the front were my office and a small kitchen.

After Leon Collingridge left, Harry Joy joined me - a New Zealander from 58 Squadron with whom I had flown on a few occasions. He was also a Qualified Flying Instructor, and I was rather jealous of the fact! I decided that as soon as I had regained my medical category I would apply to attend the Instructor Course at the Central Flying School.

In the latter stages of my time at Bassingbourn, I was appointed Deputy Chief Ground Instructor, responsible for all the ground instruction received by both Bomber and Photographic Reconnaissance crews entering the Canberra force.

On one occasion a circular memo came from the Station Adjutant asking for volunteers to fill various posts including that of Officer in charge of the Guard of Honour. Being only five feet four inches in height, I felt confident that I would not be accepted, so I applied thinking I would get away with having no further secondary duties! I should have followed the usual service edict of never volunteering for anything! I was accepted and authorised to draw my gold-braided belt, white gloves and sword from stores - thus becoming Zorro in Air Force blue!

My first engagement in that capacity was the annual inspection of the station by the Air Officer Commanding No. 3 Group, Air Vice Marshal Denis Spotswood, my student of previous days. He, together with my Station Commander and most of the members of the Guard, stood over six feet tall!

One of the disadvantages of being a diminutive Guard Commander was that I ran out of arm before the sword had run out of sheath, so I had to improvise by drawing the sheath rearwards as I pulled the sword forwards!

As soon as the Air Officer had reached the saluting base I had to order the Guard of Honour to present arms. In unison with the last movement I had to lower my sword. Unfortunately, due to my short legs, the point of the sword dug into the ground ahead of me, so when I brought the sword up again, a small piece of tarmac was projected towards the Air Officer's left ear! If he noticed it, he did not react; nor did he say anything subsequently, so I must have missed him!

When he inspected the Airmanship and Survival Section he had a brief word with me, suggesting I should apply for a permanent commission. I considered this a huge compliment and, following his inspection, began making application. I was still not convinced that the Lord wanted me to stay in the Royal Air Force for the rest of my life, but I was open to His leading and had no indications at that point of any other particular calling.

I spent three very happy years at Bassingbourn, commuting each day from our home in St. Ives. As a family we continued to be involved with the church at Therfield. So far, so good – no recurrence of the renal colic and I was feeling as fit as ever! I played rugby regularly for Bassingbourn and was a frequent patron of the squash court. It was time to get airborne again!

Air Vice Marshal Sir Peter Dixon recommended my being medically upgraded for full flying duties, which the Central Medical Establishment in London subsequently ratified. My application to undergo the six-month flying instructors' course was accepted and I received my posting notice to report to the Central Flying School at Little Rissington, Gloucestershire, to join No. 232 Course in January 1966. Prior to this I had to attend a two-week flying refresher course at Manby, Lincolnshire, which introduced me to the ubiquitous Jet Provost: the basic training aircraft of the day.

As much as I was delighted to be in the air again with no medical restrictions, I found it hard being separated from the family. I rarely managed to leave Little Rissington before lunchtime on a Saturday, and I had to be back by midnight on the Sunday; such little time with Elizabeth and the children, but at least they were able to remain in a stable home environment for another six months and I was able to give my full attention to qualifying as a flying instructor.

One small cloud was to hang over me for the rest of my life as a result of my partial nephrectomy. I was told that my blood pressure would gradually increase over the years at a greater rate than brought about by normal ageing. When it reached an unacceptable limit, it would need to be treated with medication that might not be compatible with flying - a bridge ahead to be crossed, but for now my goal was to get the coveted initials 'QFI' added to my name: *Qualified Flying Instructor.*

"Follow Me Through"

My Flying Instructors' Course started in January 1966 and there was snow on the ground when I arrived at the officers' mess at Little Rissington. I was allocated a room which was to be shared with another student instructor. I hoped we would get on well together! I need not have been concerned. Into the room walked Peter de Bourcier, a Christian whom I had briefly known in previous days through the Officers' Christian Union. We both had our private times of prayer and the study of God's Word, but we also had many helpful discussions. In addition, I found Peter to be of great professional assistance as he was, unlike me, academically gifted and had a Bachelor of Science degree in Aeronautical Engineering.

There were seventeen of us student instructors on the Jet Provost element of the course, including two naval Lieutenants, a Lieutenant of the Lebanese Air Force and an A1 (exceptional) QFI who was undergoing a Refresher Course.

Our work began with an exam on all aviation subjects! The idea was to find out how little we knew, and to this end it was a great success! This was as much for our own benefit as that of the instructing staff. I ended up as 'Mister Average' but Peter came top of the pile!

The first few weeks were spent exclusively in Ground School, and I found the whole syllabus thoroughly stimulating. There was so much to learn. In spite of being a pilot with three operational tours behind me, flying took on a whole new vista! The intricacies of aerodynamics, meteorology, navigation, radio aids, compasses and magnetism, flight instruments, flight planning, aircraft systems for the Jet Provost etc. were all covered in even greater depth.

The additional dimension was, of course, not just knowledge but learning to impart such knowledge to others both in the air and on the ground. To this end the Instructional Technique sessions were particularly interesting to me and I found myself at the top of the form for this particular discipline. Speaking in front of others and imparting information seemed to come naturally to me, and I again looked back with much thankfulness to the grounding I had received with the East Surrey Lay Preachers' Fellowship.

A further exam was held prior to our starting the flying phase, after which we alternated ground school with flying, mornings and afternoons, until we passed our final ground exams about halfway through the course, concentrating thereafter entirely upon the flying.

If the Ground School phase had been challenging but enjoyable, the flying proved to be even more so.

My first two flights as a student instructor were simply to get back into the groove with the Jet Provost and familiarise myself with the local flying area. What a joy to fly over the beautiful Cotswold countryside, clad in snow! It brought back many happy memories of my days as a student pilot at Hullavington in the winter of 1954/55.

Three other elements, in addition to us, formed the Flying Instructors' Course: the Chipmunk element prepared instructors for duties at the Elementary Flying Training Schools which included the Army Air Corps Flying School at Middle Wallop; the Gnat element prepared instructors for the fast jet Advanced Flying Training School at Valley in Anglesey; and the Varsity element for the Advanced Flying Training School at Oakington, training pilots for multi-engine and multi-crew operations.

The Central Flying School is steeped in history dating back to the First World War. A Royal Flying Corps Lieutenant by the name of Smith-Barrie was the first to introduce a systematic approach to flying training. He had begun by showing his students the effects of the aircraft's controls before he had even started the engine. He then progressed his students through taxiing, take-off, climbing etc, so that all aspects of flying were covered. He also invented the instructional technique that was still in vogue in 1966. He would first demonstrate the complete manoeuvre, then break it up into easily digestible sections such as *entry*, *maintaining* and *recovery*, before progressively giving his student control to try each part of the manoeuvre for himself.

Virtually every Royal Air Force, Naval and Army pilot had been brought up on this system of instruction and the same profile was adopted on our course.

With tandem seating, as in most early aircraft, an instructor could not see what his student was doing unless he had a strategically placed mirror, which gave him only a very limited view - usually of his pupil's ashen face (as per my Tiger Moth) - so it was important that he knew when the student was controlling the aircraft and when he was just 'following through'. Thus were conceived the three stock phrases of the instructor: "I have control!", "Follow me through!" and "You have control!"

The first phrase meant that the instructor has complete control of the aircraft and the student's hands and feet were completely clear of all controls. "Follow me through!" ordered the student to lightly rest his feet on the rudder pedals, his right hand on the control column and his left hand on the throttle(s). Thus a student could learn a lot by simply feeling the movements of his instructor's hands and feet transmitted through his own set of controls. "You have control!" was the order for the student to take over the flying of the aircraft under the instructor's watchful eye. Most instructors also rested their hands and feet very lightly on the controls to monitor their student's movements.

The student's response to the command "I have control!" is "You have control, sir." The response to "Follow me through!" is "Following through, sir," and to the command "You have control!" is "I have control, sir."

To the layman this might seem unnecessarily pedantic, but it was vital for both the instructor and the student to know precisely who was in control of the aircraft at any one time. Ask Winston Churchill...

When this grand old man was being taught to fly in a tandem seat aircraft, there was an embarrassing moment! Only having Gosport tubes (as per my Tiger Moth) for communication, it was sometimes difficult to hear what was being said due to the noise of the engine and the buffeting of the slipstream in the open cockpit. Winston thought his instructor had control but the instructor had in fact asked Winston to carry out the landing. Each thought the other was making a bit of a 'pig's breakfast' of the approach, so contributed a prod here and there on the throttle, control stick and rudder. This resulted in a very heavy landing which broke off the wheels and smashed the propeller.

As they clambered from the wreckage and discovered the cause of the crash, the instructor summarised it by saying, "That was a typical case of falling between two stools," to which Winston immediately replied in his own inimitable style, "No! It was rather a case of stalling between two fools!"

Before being accepted for training as a QFI, a pilot had to hold the assessment of Above Average on his last three annual assessments in his operational role. In spite of this prerequisite, most pilots needed their own flying skills to be honed to an even higher standard, as a pupil will invariably copy his instructor's way of doing things. There is no place for an instructor who works on the principle "Don't do as I do; just do as I tell you!"

A pupil needs to see what he is striving to attain, so the instructor's demonstration must always be clear, correct, convincing, complete and conclusive. Edgar A. Guest's poem is as appropriate to flying instruction as it is to the Christian life:

> *I'd rather see a sermon than hear one any day.*
> *I'd rather one should walk with me than merely tell the way;*
> *The eye's a better pupil and more willing than the ear,*
> *Fine counsel is confusing but example's always clear.*
> *And the best of all the preachers are the men who live their creeds*
> *For to see good put in action is what everybody needs.*
> *I soon can learn to do it if you'll let me see it done;*
> *I can watch your hands in action but your tongue too fast may run.*
> *And the lecture you deliver may be very wise and true*
> *But I'd rather get my lessons by observing what you do*
> *For I might misunderstand the high advice that you may give,*
> *But there's no misunderstanding how you act and how you live.*

The poem could well be entitled 'Divine Instruction', as so much of the student / instructor relationship mirrors a Christian's relationship with his Saviour. He gives me control of my life but monitors me closely, ensuring that He takes control when I make a mess of things. I 'follow Him through' as He shows me, through my study of the Bible, how to operate my life. He is always with me in my training for heaven, even though there might be long periods of silence. Occasionally He might even shout at me for being a twit, but He will do it from a heart of love, not from vindictiveness, in order to improve my performance and keep me in one piece! A few staff instructors, even at the Central Flying School, seemed rather too full of themselves and tended to look down upon us lesser mortals who were trying to achieve what they had already attained. This did not help the relationship, but it served as a good lesson for the future when I eventually returned to Little Rissington as a staff instructor. I was always careful to treat my students as equals and to recognise their operational experience. It was up to me to channel that experience into their becoming instructors who could not only tell a student what to do but how to do it and, by their own demonstrations and general flying, be an impeccable example.

Whatever means of communication one employs, be it spoken, written or signalled, the four tenets of effective communication should be observed: Clarity, Relevance, Accuracy and Brevity. This was especially true when instructing in low flying where time is of the essence and every word has to be 'on target', but it equally applies in preaching sermons or simply contributing to a conversation. How boring rigmarole and irrelevance can be! No instructor should be a 'windbag'!

An instructor also has to choose his words carefully. Phrases well known to him may be meaningless to a student. Such a statement as "See that aircraft at two o'clock?" would probably be received by the student looking at his watch and saying, "But it's only half past one, sir!" To get the point across, the staff instructors would take every word their student instructors said literally, which gave rise to some interesting events...

On one occasion a student instructor, seeking to improve his student's lookout, exhorted, "OK, get your eyeballs out of the cockpit!" The response was for the staff instructor to wind back the hood and start to undo his seat harness! A similar response resulted when another student instructor ordered his student to put his feet on the rudder! *Rudder pedals* would have been the correct phase! The danger of badly chosen words used in instruction was further illustrated by the case of the airline Captain who, approaching to land, glanced across at the miserable features of his First Officer and exhorted him to "Cheer up!" The First Officer, with mind on his miseries, selected the gear up!

For me, the Instructor Course became more enjoyable as it progressed, and it certainly put a finer edge on my own flying as well as deepening my knowledge of all the associated subjects.

On 23rd May 1966, my Squadron Commander briefed me on the exercise he wanted me to give him as my final test. He would act and react as my student, and I was to give him a pre-flight briefing before taking him through the air-exercise just as I would if he were a real student. At the end of the flight I was to debrief him on his performance and answer his pupil-like questions.

All went well and I was both delighted and relieved to hear him pronounce me competent to instruct real students and to be posted as a staff instructor to a Basic Flying Training School, with a B2 category. This category marked me as a Qualified Flying Instructor on six months probation, permitting me to give air and ground instruction and authorise my own instructional sorties. I was not, however, permitted to send a student solo or to authorise any formation, navigational or night flying.

In those days there were many Basic Flying Training Schools to which a new QFI could be posted: Linton-on-Ouse, Church Fenton, Feltwell, Syerston, Cranwell, Acklington and Leeming, just to name a few. Where would I be bound? My destiny was in the lap of the Posting Officers at the Air Ministry - or so they thought! I believed there was One who would be directing their deliberations to fulfil His own will and purpose. I was not to be disappointed!

I was posted to Leeming in North Yorkshire. I had never heard of the place prior to going on the Instructor Course, but one or two of our staff instructors had been stationed there and they spoke well of it.

It was with a glad heart that I packed my bags and drove back to St. Ives via the Fosse Way and the A1 to inform Elizabeth that my immediate goal had been achieved and all the months of enforced separation had been worth it. I was now a QFI.

Leeming

After a couple of weeks' leave I loaded my Mini Traveller and made my way from St. Ives up the A1 to join the staff of No. 3 Flying Training School at Leeming in North Yorkshire. Once again I experienced the pangs of separation from Elizabeth and the family, but somehow I felt a deep peace that I was doing what I was meant to do and going to a place I was meant to go.

As I neared my destination I noticed I was running low on fuel so I stopped off at what was then a filling station at the Baldersby roundabout - now swallowed up by the new motorway. As I got out of the car I experienced an overwhelming sense of joy and satisfaction. I took a deep breath of bracing North Yorkshire air and viewed the distant Hambleton hills with relish. There was just something about the place that seemed to say, "Welcome home; this is where you belong."

Having gone through the usual arrival procedures, I reported to the Chief Flying Instructor who informed me that I was posted to No. 2 Squadron. I flew my acceptance flight with the Squadron Commander on 15th June. After further mutual flights with other new QFIs, just to brush off the rust of two weeks' leave, I flew with an A1 QFI from the Standards Squadron, who cleared me as "competent to instruct students at No. 3 Flying Training School!"

Thus, on 21st July 1966, I flew my very first instructional sortie with Acting Pilot Officer (APO) Preston on an instrument flying exercise in a Jet Provost Mk 3. Fortunately for me he was halfway through his course and performed well. It was very much like an instructor training session at the Central Flying School. I only had to pick him up on a few minor points and query a few matters of procedure with him.

It was a good ploy of the supervising staff to pair the new QFIs with the more experienced pupil pilots and this, for me, lasted another month before a brand new course arrived and I met the unfortunate young men who were allocated to me: Acting Pilot Officers Washington, McKenzie, Cockram, and Flying Officer Elwig, who was already commissioned as an officer in the Engineering Branch but had re-mustered for pilot training.

I now felt as Larry Allen must have felt when he was introduced to me as his first real pupil after all his instructor training. It was not just a matter of teaching a batch of young men to fly and get their wings; it was also a matter of changing overgrown sixth form schoolboys into Queen's Commissioned Officers and developing their characters, personalities and leadership skills - an awesome task!

I spent some time with my pupils getting to know them and outlining what I expected of them in terms of attitude, self-discipline and commitment. Privately I explained to Elwig, an officer only one rank lower than myself, the difference in our relationship to that of the other pupils, but he still insisted on calling me "Sir" at all times other than in the officers' mess. I appreciated the attitude he adopted and our pupil / instructor relationship could not have been better.

On 18th August 1966 I flew my first basic instructional sortie, Exercises 1 and 2, with the first of my pupils: APO Washington. This was to familiarise him with being airborne and showing him various landmarks, in addition to introducing him to the basic effects of the controls and how to use them to achieve and maintain straight, level and balanced flight.

So my career started as a *bone fide* QFI, and it was to continue for some further two thousand instructional hours both in the Royal Air Force, Commercial Aviation and Mission Aviation Fellowship.

Elizabeth and I sold our house in St. Ives and purchased No. 5, Admirals Court, in Thirsk. The children attended the local school and we were very happy there. Initially we attached ourselves to the Methodist church in Sowerby where the Rev. Malcolm Peters was the Minister. We appreciated his ministry enormously, and there began a life-long friendship with him and his wife Caroline. Later we had the privilege, with them, of being founding members of the Hambleton Evangelical Church which then met in a farm but subsequently bought the vacant Methodist Church at Carlton Miniott.

I flew with scores of pupil pilots during my time at Leeming. Sending them on their first solo, seeing them flying steadily alongside me in formation, and ultimately witnessing the presentation of their wings and Queen's Commission was most satisfying. Each had his own unique personality, strengths and weaknesses but a few stand out particularly in my memory...

One lad had been born of a Russian mother in a German concentration camp. He had big blue eyes which flashed at you from a rotund, smiling face. He made good progress through the course until we got to the spinning exercise. The idea of spinning is to ensure that the pilot can recognise it for what it is and take prompt recovery action. A spin is most likely to be encountered when pulling a tight turn at low speed or during aerobatics when large amounts of rudder are used in conjunction with 'up' elevator.

I showed a spin to my pupil at the end of another exercise, prior to returning to base, just to give him the assurance that it was 'a piece of cake'. I then gave him a thorough briefing before tackling the exercise the following day. At first things went quite well until I ultimately gave him control to execute the recovery. Nothing happened!

I said to him again, "Recover now!" but there was no movement and no sound other than some very rapid and pronounced breathing over the intercom.

I glanced at him and saw he was staring straight ahead with his big blue eyes standing out like chapel hat pegs. Nonchalantly I said, "OK, I have control," and tried to apply anti-spin rudder but it would not move! The rudder pedal appeared to be jammed. In fact it *was* - not because of any mechanical malfunction but because my pupil had frozen on it!

We were rapidly losing altitude and getting towards the point of no return when I would have to order an ejection. However, that might not be registered and obeyed by the pupil in his present state of seizure, so I tried another ploy. I hit him hard in the ribs with my left elbow and bawled at him! It worked! His legs and hands relaxed from the controls, and I affected a normal recovery from the spin.

A very subdued pupil and a rather shaky instructor talked about the incident over a cup of strong coffee. He admitted to having been terrified in the spin in spite of living through my original demonstration and two further spins which he had followed through.

I had to report this incident to the Flight Safety Officer who asked me to make out an Incident Report. As a result of this, a new instructional procedure was introduced to prevent such a situation happening again.

Pupils were instructed to adjust the rudder pedals in such a way that the knee was slightly bent when applying full rudder. In other words the knee could not be 'locked'. This gave the instructor a better chance of forcing the pupil's foot pressure off the rudder.

My pupils were not exclusively from the Royal Air Force. Some foreign pupils, mainly from the Middle East, also came to Leeming. Although I did not take any through a full course, I occasionally flew with some due to instructors being ill or on leave. One such lad was a Jordanian. I was detailed to take him on a *circuit and bumps* exercise, for which purpose we flew over to Teesside Airport as it was then known. It so happened that the runway in use was 24: the same one on which I had my jammed elevator incident on 20th April 1956.

It was a beautiful day with plenty of blue sky and 'fair-weather cumulus' clouds. It was moderately turbulent in the circuit pattern, so we were experiencing a bit of bumpiness. My pupil seemed to be coping well until he suddenly turned and looked at me with the whites of his eyes standing out in stark relief from his dark skin. His oxygen mask obscured most of his face, but I could see a distinct look of horror reflected in his features.

He thumped his chest with one hand and, with the other, pressed his mask even tighter onto his face. As both his hands were now off the controls and he had said nothing, I took over and asked, "What's the problem?" It soon became apparent! It can only be described as an acute case of projectile vomiting! His curried lunch spewed from the periphery of his mask like a bomb-burst and covered the inside of the cockpit, including me.

I slowed the aircraft to the limiting speed for opening the canopy and, winding it back, took off my own oxygen mask and breathed in a lungful of fresh North Yorkshire air. Meanwhile my pupil had released his mask which resulted in even more vomit being deposited liberally on to his lap and the control column. He laid his head back, his hands dropped to his side and, in spite of his natural colour, turned pale.

I spoke reassuringly to him on the way back to Leeming, and having secured the aircraft on the parking brake, told him not to touch anything but climb very carefully from the cockpit. Sounding like a vet at a calving, I asked the marshaller to go and get a large bucket of hot water, a towel and sponges. By now the pupil had recovered and realised the mess he had made.

"Sorry lad," I said, "but what comes up must be cleaned down. A bucket of water is on the way, and you have a job to do. See you when you've had a bath!"

I had occasion to fly with another foreign pupil who was undergoing the pre-solo phase. His regular instructor had been having trouble with him in regard to attitude. He was blasé and ill-disciplined. He was inconsistent in his performance, and thus his instructor had not been able to send him off solo. Among his many faults, this pupil seemed to have an aversion to actually *doing* his pre-landing checks. He would say them but not necessarily do them. On selecting the landing gear down, three red lights first appear, indicating that the three wheels have unlocked from the up position, followed by three green lights indicating they are locked down. The drill is to select the gear down, check the three reds turn to three greens and state, "Three green lights!" When turning onto the final approach the pilot is again required to look at his gear indicator, confirm that the three green lights are still showing, and call on the radio to the airfield controller, "Finals! Three greens!" Without that verbal confirmation from the pilot, the controller would not clear the aircraft to land, even if the wheels were visibly down. Pilots were also taught to again check the three green lights just prior to throttling back the engine before concentrating on the landing itself.

My foreign pupil would select the gear down, say, "Three green lights!" but not look at them. On finals he would call, "Finals! Three greens!" but not look at the indicator. However much I reminded him, corrected him and cajoled him, he seemed determined to do it his way.

I was about to end the flight and recommend him for suspension from further training when he played right into my hands! He selected the gear down by stabbing the button, but he did not stab it hard enough. The gear remained up! He dutifully stated, "Three greens!" and continued to fly the circuit. He turned onto his final approach and liturgically transmitted to the controller, "Finals! Three greens!"

I decided it was time to strike! I surreptitiously pulled out his radio lead so he could not hear any transmissions to or from the aircraft and made a call to the controller: "We do *not* have three green lights. The landing gear is still up, but I have to teach this guy a lesson. I will carry out a very low overshoot. Please do *not* fire any red flares!" (The runway controller, on seeing an aircraft approach without its landing gear fully extended would fire a red flare across the aircraft's path, prohibiting its continuation with the approach). I then reconnected the pupil's radio lead.

My comedian continued his approach and was beginning to throttle back the engine prior to landing when I leapt into action. I grabbed the controls and opened the throttle swiftly, yelling at him as aggressively and as frighteningly as I could, "LOOK AT YOUR LANDING GEAR INDICATOR!" He stared incredulously at the instrument for a moment, then said, "But I called, 'Finals! Three greens!'"

When the chap realised that he would have landed with his wheel up if I had not been with him, he seemed to wake up. In fact he began to physically shake and sob. I thickly laid on my censure of his actions and of his complacent attitude, not sparing him. I asked him what he thought I should do about the incident. Should I suspend him from further training (which would have been considered a disgrace by his fellow nationals) or should I recommend he be re-coursed and start his training all over again? (This would have meant a loss of face but not the same disgrace as suspension).

It was obvious that the lad had learned his lesson. He was contrite and broken. When he had composed himself, I spoke to him gently regarding his stupidity and lack of self-discipline. I pointed out that all the drills, procedures and even the verbal statements made during a sortie were necessary to ensure the safety of the pilot and his aircraft. One small mistake could cost him his life. I quoted the case of the Kiwi tin at Kirton-in-Lindsey. He had obviously not experienced that type of regime in his own Air Force prior to being recommended for flying training with the R.A.F.

A very subdued and distressed young man made his choice. He opted for being re-coursed, but I had one more card up my sleeve. "I'll make my decision in the morning," I said. "Meanwhile, we are going to fly again right now. I don't want to see you make even one mistake throughout the entire flight."

We repeated the circuit sortie, and it was like flying with a different pupil. He was alert, precise, accurate and thoroughly safe. He flew three consecutive circuits without my having to correct him for anything. I ordered him to land and return to dispersal. He was about to close the engine down when I stopped him and said, "Well done! Now go and do one circuit on your own - just like the ones you have just done with me - and *don't you dare let me down!*"

I watched him from the control tower, where I could also hear all his transmissions. He executed a very acceptable circuit and landing. As he opened the cockpit canopy on returning to dispersal, I climbed onto the wing and stood over him as he completed his parking checks. He looked up at me with tears in his eyes and a huge grin on his face.

"Thank you, sir!" he said.

Instructing can be very satisfying!

I recorded the whole incident in the Pupil's Report Book, so his instructor could catch up on events when he returned to duty. The pupil himself went on to have a full career in his national air force. Sometimes one has to be 'cruel to be kind'.

I served four years at Leeming and, in turn, was on the instructional staff of all three Flying Training Squadrons, ending my tour as a staff instructor on the Standards Squadron. This was a small unit, commanded by a Squadron Leader, and made up of four senior Flight Lieutenants holding A1 or A2 categories. Each held a Master Green instrument rating and was a qualified Instrument Rating Examiner (IRE).

Whereas the Flying Training Squadrons were responsible for taking student pilots through the course to Wings standard, it was the responsibility of the Standards Squadron to ensure the highest possible standards of instruction were maintained throughout the staff. Thus we routinely had a couple of QFIs from the Training Squadrons going through our hands - polishing up their flying, improving instructional technique, and deepening their knowledge of all associated subjects.

Periodically we also had a QFI in for two weeks, preparing for a visit to the Central Flying School where he would go through a gruelling period with the Examining Wing to upgrade from a B1 (average) QFI to an A2 (above average) or an A2 to an A1 (exceptional). In the latter case it was a three day event comprising two flights: one to prove that his own flying ability was exceptional, the other to prove his airborne instructional techniques were exceptional. He also had to give a lecture on a given subject and finally undergo a day of oral questioning on all associated subjects, in which he had to prove that he had exceptional knowledge and the ability to impart it in an exceptional way.

The other task we had on Standards Squadron was to fly with senior officers who were on non-flying appointments, in order to keep them current. This included subjecting them to instrument rating renewals comprising flying and oral examinations. It was occasionally necessary to downgrade a senior officer's instrument rating, or even fail him, if his performance was not up to standard – not an easy thing for a junior officer to do!

Visitors to Leeming were invariably directed to the Standards Squadron - some to be conducted around the station and others to discuss training techniques or safety issues. On one occasion we hosted the Secretary of State for Defence, Denis Healey, and I made him a cup of coffee - milk and one sugar, if I remember rightly!

The Station Flight Safety Officer (SFSO) was drawn from the Standards Squadron, and this role I happily accepted alongside that of Air Cadet Liaison Officer (ACLO). The SFSO had direct access to the Station Commander who was ultimately responsible for all flight safety matters on his station. It was my job to notify members of the Flight Safety Committee of a forthcoming meeting, prepare and promulgate the agenda, act as secretary and take the minutes of the meeting, distribute them and ensure all 'actions required' were followed up and completed by the appropriate members of staff prior to the next meeting. I was also authorised to carry out Flight Safety surveys and take the initiative on all Flight Safety matters, such as displaying suitable posters in crew rooms and notifying the Station Commander of any concerns I might have.

Occasionally I had to sit on Unit Enquiries and form part of the Board of Inquiry following an aircraft accident. Such was the case when, one afternoon, a student pilot was killed.

He had been briefed by his instructor for a solo navigation exercise in a Jet Provost Mk 3 with a full fuel load. The weather was good with a steady wind virtually down the runway which, orientated to the north east, was the shorter of the three intersecting runways and the one least used.

The pilot called for takeoff clearance but used his instructor's call sign instead of his own. When the air traffic controller corrected him for this error he replied, "Sorry, I'll try to remember in future." Those were his last words.

The runway controller, positioned in his red and white chequered caravan alongside the runway threshold, scanned the aircraft with his field glasses to ensure that the ejector seat safety pin had been removed and that there were no loose panels, no dripping fuel, oil, etc. He also logged the aircraft number and the takeoff time and checked that the flaps were at the takeoff setting.

The aircraft was seen to accelerate down the runway and lift off but adopt a higher than usual angle of climb. As the runway controller turned to survey the next aircraft positioning for takeoff, he heard a bang and, looking back up the runway, saw the first aircraft steeply banked to the left and descending. It disappeared behind some trees. The alarm was sounded and the emergency vehicles sped off across the airfield to the crash site.

The emergency crews found the aircraft wrecked in a field and only a few yards away a fully streamed but unopened parachute with the unconscious pilot attached. Unfortunately the pilot died in the ambulance on the way to Catterick Military Hospital.

The pilot had for some reason ejected whilst the aircraft was rolling to the left, so the ejector seat had fired almost horizontally, thus minimising the height for the parachute to stream and develop. The seat had hit the ground with the pilot still in it, and he died of multiple internal injuries.

The Board of Inquiry was immediately convened and a Wing Commander from another unit detailed to be the President. My immediate actions following an aircraft accident were to inform Group, Training Command and the Ministry of Defence by signal; inform the Station Commander and Chief Flying Instructor by phone; and brief the airmen detailed by the Station Warrant Officer to guard the wreckage. I also had to ensure that a room was made available for the Board of Inquiry and that all necessary furniture, writing materials, aircraft servicing log book, Pilot's Notes for the aircraft involved, Station Standing Orders, Command and Group Orders, Local Flying Orders, the authorisation sheet and the Pupil's Progress book were all available. The parachute and dinghy pack were also secured in case the Board needed to examine them.

On the following morning the Board of Inquiry assembled and the President briefed us and swore us in. I was detailed to act as Secretary, making a written record of the proceedings. I was particularly impressed with the professionalism of the gentleman from the Accident Investigation Branch (AIB), Mr. Stan Cuthbertson. Having briefly viewed the wreckage and after asking a few pertinent questions, he disappeared with a copy of Pilot's Notes and was not seen again until late in the afternoon. Meanwhile we set about our task as a Board, assembling witnesses, getting photos taken of the wreckage and the nearby ejector seat. The parachute and dinghy were also brought in for closer examination and the authorisation sheet and aircraft log book scrutinised.

Mr. Cuthbertson returned later that afternoon having absorbed Pilot's Notes for the Jet Provost Mk 3. There was nothing he did not know about it! His knowledge of all the systems, emergency drills, performance data, limitations and handling characteristics was profound.

Sworn statements were taken from all witnesses, including the Medical Officer conducting the post mortem, the Air Traffic Controller, the Runway Controller, the pilot of the second aircraft to enter the runway and many more who had witnessed the incident. Further statements were made by the deceased pilot's instructor, the marshaller who directed the aircraft away from the parking bay, the Senior NCO who signed the aircraft servicing log, a local farmer who witnessed the accident, etc. Gradually pictures began to emerge which pointed to possible causes of the tragedy, but each theory had to be pursued in minute detail until it either petered out or evidence proved the theory to be untenable.

One of these theories was that the aircraft had adopted an unusually high nose attitude on takeoff due to the pilot becoming distracted. It was the practice of some instructors to jam their map between the coaming and the windscreen prior to releasing the brakes, so that it was immediately at hand once the post takeoff checks had been completed. Many pupil pilots followed their instructor's example. There was a map pocket to the side of the pilot, low on the cockpit wall, but this necessitated the pilot having to reach down and fumble for his map, even looking down in order to locate it. Looking down into the cockpit soon after takeoff was not a good idea!

There was no sign of the map in the wreckage nor downwind of the crash site. Fields were searched extensively, even the boughs of trees, but no map materialised! Where was it? I was tasked to find it, if possible, and work out whether or not this was a contributory factor in the accident.

Stan Cuthbertson then 'threw a spanner in the works'! Previously we had heard from the Runway Controller, on a sworn statement, that the flaps were at the take-off position. Having examined the wreckage in more detail Stan was forced to the conclusion that the flaps had been fully retracted on impact! I was given the additional task of trying to establish why there was a difference in the witness statement and the mechanical evidence.

Various other theories emerged as the Board continued its deliberations - some easily dismissed and others plausible enough to be investigated. The big question was 'why did the pilot select a higher than normal takeoff attitude and why were the flaps at the takeoff setting at the start of the run and fully retracted on impact less than half a minute later'?

As Secretary to the Board it was my responsibility to lock up the room at the end of each day and keep the key so that evidence could not be tampered with nor documents removed. One evening I was casting my eye around the room prior to departure when I saw the kit bag containing all the pilot's clothes which had recently arrived from the post mortem. Was it possible that the map had been on the pilot when he was taken in the ambulance? Could it have been stuffed into the kit bag by one of the medical staff at the post mortem?

I emptied the contents on to the table and checked there was nothing left inside. As I went about my sombre business it reminded me of the time at Celle when I had been Personnel Effects Officer for the young airman who had died.

I put to one side the underwear cut from the body, his shirt, the chamois leather gloves, the flying suit (which I examined especially carefully), socks and the black leather boots. There was no sign of any map, but that left boot... something odd about it... There was a deep depression to the left of centre above where the third and fourth toes would be. It looked as though it had been hit by a hammer. What was the cause? I also noticed some slight scuff marks leading into the depression.

I telephoned Catterick Hospital and asked to speak to the Medical Officer who had carried out the post mortem. Had his examination revealed any map on the body? Could members of the ambulance team be asked to throw any light upon the map's whereabouts? I also asked if there had been any bruising around the third and fourth toe region of the pilot's left foot. In all cases the response was negative.

I puzzled over this boot way into the night. I thought through everything we knew about the take-off and the ejection. Suddenly it came to me! The pilot was six feet two inches in height. He had ejected whilst the aircraft was rolling to the left; thus he would have exited the aircraft with his left leg lower than his right and his trajectory would have brought his left foot very close to the flap lever situated on the left hand wall of the cockpit. His leg-restraining straps (designed to pull the legs in and together, to avoid flailing and possible breaking on ejection) were attached to the pilot just below his knees; thus the moment arm of a left foot would be greater on a six foot escapee than on one of my own build. Could his left boot have engaged the flap lever and selected the flaps up as he ejected?

I put this to the Board when we re-convened the following morning.

"There's only one way to find out," said the President. "We must simulate it."

I was given the job of arranging this. My first port of call was to the Wing Commander in charge of the Engineering Wing. I asked for a Jet Provost Mk 3 to be made available to the Board of Inquiry. The ejector seat was to have all its cartridges removed and a crane positioned so that the seat could be pulled slowly up the rails simulating an ejection. I also commandeered a six foot two inch pupil pilot and dressed him in the deceased pilot's flying suit and boots. The scene was set!

Slowly the crane lifted the seat from the floor of the aircraft, and I ordered the pilot to move his legs to the left as the leg restraint cords tightened. Sure enough, the depression in the toe of the left boot engaged snugly around the knob of the flap lever, set in the take-off position. The flaps fully retracted as the seat ascended the rails. Photos were taken, statements made and the conclusion documented that this was the cause of the discrepancy between the witness statements and the mechanical evidence found by Stan Cuthbertson. The flaps had been retracted by the pilot's left boot as the ejector seat rose up the rails with the aircraft rolling to its left. QED!

The Board was nearing its conclusions. Many different factors contributed to this fatal accident, but the root cause was found to be that the pilot had taken some extra yards positioning himself for take-off on a runway rarely used and shorter than those with which he would have been accustomed. A fully laden Mk 3 Jet Provost was slow to accelerate. Having lost some precious yards of runway due to his conscientious positioning and straightening of the nose wheel, the pilot would have seen, as he accelerated, the end of the runway approaching without having got as much speed as he would have anticipated. He therefore tried to lift the aircraft off the runway prematurely (thus the higher nose attitude seen by the witnesses) and stalled the aircraft trying to clear the trees beyond.

A more experienced pilot would have kept the aircraft on the runway until takeoff speed had been achieved and 'nursed' the aircraft into the air, keeping closer to the tops of the trees as he accelerated to climbing speed.

The Board made its recommendations and adjourned. I had the task of presenting everything for typing before proof-reading the typed manuscripts and duplicating all the documentation, including photos, to send to the Ministry of Defence, Training Command HQ, Group HQ, and many other departments and bodies.

Unlike my own flying training days, there were fewer fatal accidents during the years I was instructing. In fact this was the only one in which I was involved throughout my four years at Leeming. There were other accidents, incidents and unusual occurrences but no lives lost.

One such accident was a pupil pilot who returned to Leeming from a solo training sortie only to find his engine failed at one thousand feet when on the downwind leg prior to landing. He immediately realised he was in no position to try a *dead stick* (glide) landing, and any attempt to do so would point the aircraft towards the airfield which would endanger many lives.

He elected to turn the aircraft away from the airfield towards open ground and eject. This he did successfully, and the aircraft crashed into a field on the bank of the river Swale about half a mile from the airfield perimeter. The river formed a natural barrier to the emergency vehicles but fortunately there was no fire, and the young pilot, who landed in his parachute close to the aircraft, simply waited patiently until he was picked up. The Medical Officer subsequently found nothing wrong with him but, as a precaution, kept him in Sick Quarters overnight for observation. I visited him and got a statement from him for the Board of Inquiry. He was very calm, serene and clear-minded, giving a most detailed account of the problems he had faced and his reactions to them.

The Board of Inquiry found the Air/Fuel Ratio Control Unit (AFRCU) in the engine had failed. The pupil pilot was commended for his cool and correct response to the emergency.

My time as a QFI at Leeming was most enjoyable, especially on the Standards Squadron. Working professionally with such a cross-section of instructional experience and flying expertise was not only a challenge - it was also a means of learning. My professional knowledge and ability increased extensively during those years, and I look back upon them with much gratitude. I also had the privilege of serving with some delightful characters whose sense of humour, rapport and comradeship made every day something to eagerly anticipate. However, my time at Leeming was marred by another personal cloud which engulfed me...

Elizabeth and I, with our three children, had visited my parents in Purley during a short leave. Almost overnight I became very tired and nauseous. The following morning my flesh and the whites of my eyes turned yellow and I itched all over. Having sought medical advice it was concluded that I was suffering from Infective Hepatitis.

Thanks to a very co-operative and understanding father, mother and sister, we stayed at Purley until I felt strong enough to undergo the long drive back to our home in Thirsk. Elizabeth drove all the way, which included navigating through the centre of London as there was no M25 in those days. She purchased a headrest for me which clipped on the back of my seat and acted as a pillow for the journey. I was as weak as a kitten and would not have been much assistance to her should we have had any trouble with the car.

Once back home I immediately went to bed and was eventually visited by my Medical Officer from Leeming. He took one look at me and immediately arranged for my admittance to the Catterick Military Hospital.

I cannot speak too highly of the attention given me by the medical staff, especially by the consultant specialist (a Colonel) and the Queen

Alexandra Royal Army Nursing Corps. They were magnificent and relieved my suffering as much as they could, but suffer I did!

Infective Hepatitis is a vile disease. In addition to the constant itching from head to toe and the yellowing of the skin, one is subjected to virtually continuous cold sweating, nausea and depression. The symptoms just go on and on, night and day, with seemingly no improvement and no relief. I was usually given sleeping pills at night but these proved to be a mixed blessing. Although I got a few hours' sleep, I would wake up to find my body covered in weeping sores where I had scratched myself uncontrollably. Sheets and pillow cases had to be changed frequently each day and night due to the cold sweat which literally ran and dripped off my whole body.

As I agonised on my soggy bed, day after day, I could hear the muted *bip-bop* of the Wimbledon tennis going on in the television room down the corridor. Even today those sounds initially bring a brief feeling of unease and trauma.

There were times during my stay at Catterick when I was convinced I would never get better and I wanted to die. I frequently wept when on my own and cried out to God for His healing. The visits from Elizabeth, my brother Harold (who travelled up from Leeds to see me), and other kind friends, did a lot to keep me sane. On one occasion I heard new medical orderlies being briefed in a subdued voice by the ward sister.

"We have an RAF pilot in the ward suffering from Infective Hepatitis," she whispered. "This is a horrible disease and can bring about a deep depression. You are to constantly monitor Flight Lieutenant Collard and engage him in cheerful and optimistic conversation throughout your watch. Don't be surprised if you find him weeping sometimes."

These young orderlies did their job well. They sensed when I was open to conversation and when I wanted to be quiet and alone, but they looked in on me every few minutes. Once a week they all came to my bedside, one holding a particularly vicious looking hypodermic syringe. It was time for my weekly injection of vitamins, and it was a painful procedure! Whilst two of them held me down, the other inserted the syringe deep into my buttocks, then partially withdrew it and re-inserted it at a different angle, repeating the performance four times. Apparently this method was used to prevent an abscess forming. Some of the instruction I had received on various survival exercises came to my aid during this procedure. I adopted the mindset required for resisting enemy interrogation!

My illness prevented me from being able to read my Bible for some weeks although I was praying much and recalling passages and verses from Scripture that I had memorised over the years. I also sang in my heart various choruses and hymns. One morning I felt a little better and reached for my Bible resting on the bedside locker.

I turned to the passage that I had been studying prior to my illness and began reading Paul's second letter to Timothy, chapter four. I came to verse five and read, "But you be watchful in all things, endure afflictions, do the work of an evangelist, fulfil your ministry." OK, Paul was writing to his protégé Timothy, but God spoke to me in my own situation. I could well identify with the call to "endure afflictions" but, with some petulance, I asked God how He expected me to "do the work of an evangelist" and "fulfil my ministry" when I was sweating and scratching in a soggy hospital bed. In my heart I said, "OK Lord, if you want me to speak to somebody about you, you'll have to bring them to me. I can't go to them!"

The day itched on with nausea frequently welling up. I felt extremely fatigued and very low in spirit. As I lay in my cold sweat listening to the monotonous *bip-bop* of the tennis interspersed with the crowd applause, a young man in civilian clothes appeared in the doorway. He seemed hesitant.

"Are you Flight Lieutenant Collard, sir?" he asked.

"That's me," I replied rather disinterestedly. "What do you want?"

"Can I speak with you, sir... just for a minute or two?"

I bade him take the chair beside my bed and asked him to say what he wanted to say.

He appeared almost reticent to speak but then said, "I'm an orderly from the other side of the hospital and have this afternoon off. Word has got around that you have a Bible on your bedside locker. Why is that, sir? I really want to know."

I found it difficult to keep the tears from my eyes - not because of my low state of spirit, nor because of my affliction, but because my heart was so full of thanks that God had shown that He really had heard my unspoken prayer and even taken note of my petulant demand! He was still with me after all.

For about half an hour I was able to testify to this young soldier of God's grace in my life and "tell of all His wonderful works" as I had experienced them during the war, at school, in my home and even now in hospital where he had become part of that testimony. We prayed together, and he shook my cold and sweaty hand as we parted. I never saw him again.

After his departure I fell back onto the pillow and just praised God from the depths of my heart for the proof that He had not given me up; He had not deserted me and wanted my service even in my present state.

When my regular orderlies, the ward sister and specialist visited me later, they all commented on the improvement they saw in me.

"The lights are on again, Collard!" said the Colonel. "I can see it in your eyes. They're still as yellow as the No. 2 snooker ball, but you're on the mend!"

From that point recovery began. It was slow but it was evident.

In all, I was away from work for four months and in hospital for five weeks. Even when I was discharged and returned to duty, I itched - but to a lesser degree. After every sortie I found myself scratching those parts of my body which had been in contact with the ejector seat, and at home I had to take a bath frequently to relieve the irritation. It must have taken another month before I could claim to be back to normal, although the sense of fatigue took a few weeks longer to dissipate. What caused the illness? My Medical Officer attributed it to either using an infected communal towel or an infected needle when being updated with my routine 'jabs' (few disposable needles in those days!) Whatever the cause, I was glad it was over and could settle down to a normal life again, both in the air and on the ground.

Having completed two consecutive tours of duty at Leeming, time came for another posting. Where this time? Imagine my delight and surprise when I was informed that I was to return to the Central Flying School as a staff instructor. Back to the Cotswolds!

The Red Pelican

The armorial bearings of the Central Flying School comprise a Red Pelican (strong wings) surmounting a crown and tower (a reminder of its naval and military beginnings), a pilot's brevet, an anchor and a sword (representing all three armed services) and underneath, white and blue wavy lines symbolising the river Avon upon the banks of which the unit was formed on 12th May 1912 at Upavon.

Some pilots consider that the choice of a red pelican was made because of its big mouth and poor flying performance!

The motto is "*Imprimis Praecepta*" meaning "Our Teaching is Everlasting". Perhaps a slight over-statement; nevertheless, the teaching given at CFS is second-to-none in the aviation world, and I am proud to have been part of both receiving from it and giving to it. As a motto, perhaps "*Docendo Disces*" would have been more appropriate ("You will Learn by Teaching"), which was certainly true in my experience.

Once again I had to be parted from the family. Elizabeth and the children remained in our house at Thirsk, and I reverted to living in the officers' mess at Little Rissington, awaiting the completion of our house being built from scratch in Gorse Close, Bourton-on-the-Water.

Prior to my starting at CFS in April 1970, Elizabeth and I had made enquiries of the local builder who informed us that a house would take three to six months to complete and would cost £7,500. We decided to stretch ourselves financially and bite the bullet.

It was both a delight and a frustration seeing our home develop from a muddy patch of ground into a beautiful detached house built in Cotswold stone having four bedrooms, central heating, garage and a highly polished hall floor. Sometimes I would view it with impatience as I saw the work delayed because of inclement weather or a hold up in a specific phase of the construction, but the builder did a fine job, and in July we took possession of our lovely home and the children were initiated into their new schools at Northleach and Bourton-on-the-Water.

It was a proud moment when, having gone through the usual acceptance period with the CFS Standards Squadron, I was entitled to sew on to the right upper arm of my flying suit the large blue badge depicting the red pelican and the words "Central Flying School" in gold underneath. It was more of a placard than a badge!

Training experienced pilots to become instructors was hugely satisfying and challenging. In addition to pilots from the Royal Air Force we also trained aviators from the Army Air Corps, the Royal Navy and many foreign air forces.

Among my foreign student instructors I had the pleasure of training a Kenyan officer, Lieutenant Joshi. He was a real gentleman and a fine pilot with a very steady and serene disposition. He had a quietly wicked sense of humour and 'gave as good as he got' with my other students. It is remarkable how political correctness has dampened genuine, free and good-natured banter. I remember one of my RAF students, who had been a pilot on the Varsity transport aircraft, mercilessly 'taking the mickey' out of Joshi because he could not pronounce his 'V's. They came out as 'W's, so he would refer to the "Warsity". When my other white students lampooned him for his pronunciation, Joshi, chuckling, simply responded with "Oh shut up, you Pinkies!" No offence was taken by anyone.

Joshi, like other Kenyan students, would never be far from his hand carvings. Every spare moment would be used whittling away at a piece of wood with a penknife. The results were remarkable. African figurines, animals and small utensils would materialise, typical of those seen in any African market. Elizabeth and I still have a dish and stand which Joshi presented to us as a parting gift. The stand, though opening out into a three-legged support for the dish, was hand-carved from one piece of wood.

It was also my privilege to take a number of senior officers through instructor refresher courses. Each lasted only a few weeks and was designed for QFIs who were officers of Group Captain rank destined to take command of Flying Training Schools, and Wing Commanders destined to become Chief Flying Instructors (CFI).

Among my senior students was Group Captain "Kit" Carson AFC, a softly spoken Irishman who was being posted to take command of my old station at Leeming. As much as it can be possible between a Group Captain and a Flight Lieutenant, we became firm friends and had a mutual appreciation of each other's professionalism.

I saw in Kit Carson a man after my own heart - a true gentleman, an excellent pilot and the type of man you would not hesitate to approach should you wish to share a problem or seek advice. He was a natural leader. He seemed to appreciate my way of instructing and was never too proud or rank-conscious to accept criticism when it was due. He also knew his own limitations.

On one occasion we were flying dual in a three-ship formation and had been practising the instructional procedures with me acting as pupil and him 'correcting' me and 'instructing' me. In teaching a pupil to fly in formation, it is crucial that the instructor knows the exact point at which he should take control of the aircraft. The pupil will only learn by experience and patient tutoring. It is no good taking control too early - otherwise he will never learn from his mistakes - but it is equally important not to let the pupil continue with a dangerous situation. With aircraft separated by just a few feet, a split-second misjudgement could be catastrophic. We were involved in this very exercise with me going as far as I dare, with some pupil-like errors verging upon the dangerous, and monitoring the Group Captain's response to them.

He did extremely well, and the time came for us to complete a landing in *Vic* formation on the shorter runway at Little Rissington. He was 'demonstrating' and I was speaking words of encouragement to him and correcting him where necessary when, about a hundred feet from touchdown, he said, "Please take over, Ron; I'm losing concentration."

It is no easy thing to suddenly take control at such a late stage of an approach, but all went well and I completed a smooth landing still holding the Vic formation. The Group Captain did not spare his praise. He too realised he had put me on the spot by relinquishing control at such a late stage. I admired him for being honest enough to admit that he was losing it and was professional enough to hand back control. Some senior officers in his position would doubtless have pressed on through fear of 'losing face' and, at the best, frightened the life out of me!

When Kit Carson departed for Leeming he not only wrote me a very generous letter of thanks but also wrote a letter of commendation to the Station Commander. It was therefore with some surprise that I was called into the CO's presence one day and given a reprimand!

I was handed a copy of the 'RAF Link-Up' newsletter. It kept Christians in the air force linked together and notified everyone of postings and other news items. I had written a short article about the conversion of five fellow officers who had asked if they could come to the Bible Study group which met in my home at Bourton-on-the-Water. Some of the local Christians, who regularly attended, welcomed them warmly.

I had shown a series of 'Fact and Faith' films which were sermons from science. These were interspersed with more conventional studies of the Bible but based on the questions raised by the group. Over a period of time each of these five men had committed their lives to Christ and the changes in lifestyle immediately became noticeable. I reported this in 'Link-Up' as an encouragement to other Christians in the RAF.

Somehow this publication had been handed to my Station Commander who told me, in no uncertain terms, that I was not to "engage in changing other people's lives" and that "this sort of thing would not be tolerated on my station."

I pointed out that the men concerned had simply asked questions and had of their own volition come to my home to join the Bible Study group already in existence. He took the line that I was obviously a 'religious maniac' and opened a file on me. He seemed to take a dislike to me as I was on the receiving end of a number of onerous tasks dished out through my Squadron Commander.

Ultimately the Station Commander ordered me to undergo a consultation with the Medical Officer (MO) and, dependent upon his report on my state of mind, would then decide whether or not to suspend me from flying.

In all, I had some two hours of interviews with the Station Commander and nearly an hour with the MO, who I knew had his own difficulties in life. My interview with him initially followed the usual pattern of personal questions but then progressed to more specific issues, such as how I reconciled my faith with serving in the armed forces. My answer seemed to soften his attitude and we began to discuss matters in a more relaxed manner. Ultimately I found myself giving my testimony in which I used the phrase "inner peace".

At that point the MO folded his file, put it to one side, and leaning across his desk said, "Inner peace? Interview over. Tell me more. I've never known any."

God had completely taken control of the interview. The MO and I simply chatted as though we were friends. I was able to enlarge upon my testimony and point to the words of Jesus, especially John 14:27: "Peace I leave with you, My peace I give to you: not as the world gives do I give to you. Let not your heart be troubled neither let it be afraid."

The interview ended with the MO standing to shake my hand and saying, "I'll forward my report to the Station Commander as he ordered, but you need have no fear of it from my point of view. Thanks for coming to see me."

A couple of days later I was again called to the Station Commander's office. Having given the customary salute, I expected the usual censure but none came.

"Sit down Ron," he said quietly. (This was the first time he had addressed me by my Christian name.) "It seems I was badly informed about you. You are free to go and continue your flying duties. Perhaps we could speak together about these matters sometime."

I thanked him and assured him that I would always be ready to respond to his invitation to talk. From then on the Station Commander always addressed me by my Christian name whenever we met but he never asked for a further chat.

Two other significant events occurred during my time at the Central Flying School. The first was the birth of our fourth child, Christopher Duncan. Elizabeth, as usual, had carried her baby without fuss and was looking forward to getting her figure back! On Friday 29th January 1971 I went to work as usual, flew a solo aerobatic exercise in the morning then a flight to Leeming and back in the afternoon. I came home to find Elizabeth on the verge of delivery. The midwife was called, and it was not long before Chris arrived and the three children were ushered in to view their baby brother, eight years junior to Michael. Elizabeth and I find it remarkable that men are now given weeks of paternal leave after the birth of a child in order to 'bond' with the new arrival! On 1st February I was back flying and Elizabeth, as usual, was efficiently and lovingly managing her new baby, three other children, the house, the garden... and of course me when I was there!

The other very significant event occurred on 8th June 1970. I was in the process of strapping myself in for my first flight of the day when an airman came to the aircraft and informed me that I was wanted on the telephone.

"Can't it wait until later?" I asked.

"No sir," replied the airman. "The Squadron Commander wants you now."

On entering the operations room, my Squadron Commander, without a word, handed me the phone. It was Elizabeth.

"Hallo, darling. Your dad went to be with the Lord at 8 o'clock this morning".

My very first thought was, "While I was listening to the daily briefing, Dad entered the Lord's presence!" I experienced a strange sort of pride. My dad - in Christ's presence!

In his lifetime, especially in the army, Dad had been 'quite a lad' and 'one of the boys'. In fact, in spite of his small stature, he had been a natural and well-accepted leader - very popular with his comrades-in-arms. He and his pal, Harold Fewtrell, had served in France and Belgium together and married the Laker sisters; Lilian was my mother and Ethel became Harold's wife.

Although my father was a man of respect and religious observance, he could hardly be described as a Christian for most of his years; however, something happened that changed him...

In my parental home, Dad's study was at the end of our upstairs corridor. One was not allowed to enter without first knocking on the door. Even if the door was open, one had to knock and wait permission to enter. On this occasion the door was slightly ajar. I quietly knocked but there was no reply. I knew Dad was there and became anxious that he might have been taken ill, so I eased the door further open. Dad was kneeling at his chair with an open Bible in front of him. I quietly withdrew, full of joy. It was soon apparent that a notable change had taken place in his life.

As soon as I passed the news of Dad's death to my Squadron Commander he offered his condolences on "losing my dad" to which I replied, "Thanks Boss, but we know where Dad is." I then added a phrase which I have used countless times since, especially when conducting the funeral of a committed Christian: "You haven't lost something if you know where it is. It may be temporarily inaccessible but it is not lost."

I was immediately granted leave for a week. My sortie was cancelled! I changed out of my flying kit and briefly visited my room in the mess to gather up a few items before driving off to Purley.

Arriving at Brancaster Lane I was met by Mum and Betty who seemed relieved to have me there to take the initiative from them. I checked that my brothers had been informed, that the doctor had called, a death certificate had been issued, and that the undertaker had visited. I was told that he had been for a first visit but was returning very soon. The significance of this statement was not at first obvious to me until the undertaker arrived and asked where the body was situated. I thought it would have been removed on the first visit. Hesitatingly I led the undertaker up the stairs and approached my parents' bedroom. Instinctively I knocked on the door before opening it. On the far side of the room, dressed in carpet slippers and dressing gown, was my father's body sitting in his chair by the window - head slightly to the left, eyelids partly closed and both forearms resting on the sides of the chair. He looked peacefully asleep.

My first reaction on seeing him was, "That's not my dad. He's not here anymore." Paul's words came to mind from his second letter to the Corinthian Christians, chapter five and verse one: "For we know that if our earthly house, this tent, is destroyed, we have a building from God, a house not made with hands, eternal in the heavens."

Clearing the garage and Dad's study was a challenge, particularly the latter! Although only a very small room, it was packed with memorabilia from both World Wars. Items included a German steel helmet, his ARP warden's helmet, a three inch calibre cartridge full of poppies (one for every year since 1918), a beautifully engineered brass nose-cone from an anti-aircraft shell which had landed in our fish pond one night during an air-raid, and various pieces of shrapnel. The walls were virtually papered with photographs. In his wardrobe hung his cavalry uniform, complete with cap and brown riding boots. Most of these military items were given to the regiment, which was currently equipped with tanks instead of horses. Much of the rest fed a bonfire in the garden, lasting three days!

So ended a life of seventy nine years! Considering he was at death's door with rheumatic fever as a child, Dad had a full and healthy life, serving his country in two World Wars and fathering four children, all of whom would come to know Christ as their Saviour before him. However, there was no doubt that Christ knew Dad and had a purpose for giving and sustaining his life, not only through serious illness in his boyhood but also in that foxhole in no man's land!

My days at CFS were drawing to a close, as was my career in the Royal Air Force. Although I held a permanent commission, it was as *Specialist Aircrew* which meant I would never attain a rank higher than Wing Commander. I had passed my exams for promotion to Squadron Leader back in 1962 but, due to the limited promotion ladder, there was no guarantee that I would even be appointed to that rank. Elizabeth and I were constrained to look for a more settled future. My service contract gave me the option of leaving the Air Force on my 38th birthday, so I notified the powers-that-be of my intention to do so. Being a regular officer I had the privilege of indicating my geographical choice of posting for my final tour of duty. Where else could I choose than North Yorkshire!

Group Captain Carson, whilst undergoing his refresher course at CFS, had told me I would always be welcome on his staff at Leeming. I telephoned him, asking if this invitation was still open and, on his confirmation, immediately put into writing my desire to go back to Leeming for my last year of service.

Whilst I awaited the outcome, there was still plenty of work to do at CFS. Not only did I have the regular task of taking pilots through the instructor course, I also had the delightful job of occasionally giving air experience to young British Airways co-pilots and army officers from the Staff College. One army Major who was in command of a squadron of tanks, knowing I had been on a ground attack fighter squadron in Germany, specifically asked to be shown a simulated rocket attack so he could appreciate it from the pilot's viewpoint. He came across as a rather eccentric and cocky chap who was rather put out to find he had to fly with such a small pilot! He was a six-footer! He chatted endlessly, mainly about himself - a malady known in the Royal Air Force as *verbal diarrhoea*.

It so happened that the Royal Air Force Regiment from Catterick was encamped on the derelict airfield at Wombleton on the North Yorkshire moors. They had their anti-aircraft guns with them and had given Leeming an open invitation to attack them at any time to test their reaction and drills. For me this was just what the doctor ordered, especially as I knew the treatment that would doubtless cure the Major's malady!

Having briefed him on the use of the ejection seat, the location of the sick bag and other necessary information, I strapped him in and off we went. I flew at the lowest permissible height (250 feet above ground level) at maximum permissible speed to Wombleton. Locating one of the gun emplacements I flew up-sun, hugging the trees on the airfield boundary, and began my 'patter' explaining the actions I was taking and the reason for them.

"In an attack like this the key element is surprise. The gunners will be looking into the sun as we attack, and our steep climb, followed by a steep descent, will give them great difficulty in getting their guns to bear. Here we go then!"

As the target passed by the left wing tip I pulled up into a near vertical climb to three thousand feet and wheeled the aircraft around its left wing tip to bring the target into the centre of my windscreen. At nine hundred feet in the descent I simulated the release of the rockets and at seven hundred feet pulled up momentarily before dropping back to treetop height and away. The last pull-up over the target registered 5g on the accelerometer. The Jet Provost was limited to 6g. At 5g a person's weight is multiplied by five... which includes his lunch!

As I settled back to normal flight I turned to the Major and asked, "What did you think of that then?"

No answer was forthcoming, but he hastily removed his oxygen mask, grabbed his sick bag and filled it comprehensively! He slowly turned a white face towards me and with vomit trickling down his chin said, "Sic in transit," which I thought was most appropriate for the occasion and showed him to be a man of character and humour!

He quickly recovered from his throw-up and appeared completely cured of his original malady! A very subdued Major slowly eased himself out of the aircraft!

After landing he insisted on having a 'before' and 'after' photo taken. 'Before' portrayed him standing with me at the aircraft with his arm round my shoulders looking down at me with a patronising smile. 'After' portrayed him on his knees, face in a sick bag, with me standing over him, hand on his shoulder, looking down on him with a smirk on my face. Apparently he wanted the photo for inclusion in the Staff College magazine!

Another most interesting duty was to work with a specialist Medical Officer, himself a pilot, specialising in the rehabilitation of pilots who had suffered what is now called post-traumatic stress disorder. Some came to us as a result of a combat situation (then we were still supplying pilots to other air forces locked in conflict, such as Saudi Arabia) or chaps that had experienced a particular air emergency, usually including an ejection, which had left a psychological wound.

After carrying out his initial interviews and treatment, the MO would gradually wean such pilots back into the air with progressive exercises. This is where I came into the picture. A lot of patience and gentleness was necessary, yet also a firmness which exuded security to those feeling confused and under-confident.

One particular case was of a pilot who had ejected from an aircraft because it got into a spin from which he was unable to recover. His ejection was so low that his parachute had only just developed prior to his hitting the ground. Thereafter he had had a phobia about spinning and could not get himself to fly at all for fear of the same thing happening again.

My particular remit from the MO was to gradually get this pilot back into an aircraft and ultimately get him spinning again!

At first I would simply ask him questions which got him talking freely about the flying he had enjoyed prior to his accident. Gradually I would get him discussing aircraft design and technicalities which required our viewing an aircraft close up, clambering around it and eventually entering the cockpit. Slowly the pilot became more comfortable in the cockpit environment until we were able to get him to start the engine and close it down again. On one occasion an aircraft required a compass swing, so I asked if he would like to help me. This resulted in his not only starting the engine but actually taxiing to the compass base way over the other side of the airfield and bringing it back to the hangar.

By using these progressive steps, and in close consultation with the MO before and after every phase, we were able to get the pilot away from his terror zone, through the fear zone and into the healthily apprehensive zone. At this point all his previous training, knowledge and experience tended to take him over the last hurdle and get him back into a comfort zone, tinged with sensible caution rather than illogical phobia.

Eventually came the day when, after further discussion with the MO and many dual sorties, the pilot was authorised to fly solo again. This was just an enjoyment trip. The brief was simply: "It's a beautiful day! Go and enjoy yourself. Only do what you want to do and keep the flight within 45 minutes."

Following further solo flights which extended the pilot's confidence came the day when I flew with him to try a spin. I assured him that he would not need to take any part but simply sit through one turn of a spin. All went well until the point of stall when he reacted adversely. I immediately applied pro-spin control but recovered at the incipient stage before the aircraft had time to complete a full turn. The poor chap was sweating and clawing the air.

"Can't cope with this! Let's land!" he gasped.

"Sure," I said comfortingly. "Get your map out and see if you can locate our exact position. I know roughly where we are."

In fact I knew exactly where we were, but this little bit of responsibility, which was well within his comfort zone, was designed to bring him back to reality and make him apply his mind to something he knew he could do. Once he identified our position I gave him control and we returned to base without further difficulty. On the debriefing I reminded him that he had come through the first phase of a spin. To him that was some accomplishment, but we had encountered a hurdle that was just too high for him. What next?

The MO, with a delightful twist of psychology, suggested to the pilot that he need not go any further, as spinning was not something one set out to do in normal flying practice, and that he could be recommended to return to flying duties as a co-pilot on an aircraft type which was not designed for manoeuvres that could lead to spinning - perhaps a posting to Coastal or Transport Command.

"Go away and think about it," advised the MO.

Both the MO and I knew that this chap was a devoted fighter pilot. He even looked upon the coastal and transport pilots as bus drivers and was of the personality that, having been on fighters all his career, could never countenance being a co-pilot. It was not long before he was back with his answer. The MO's subtle challenge had brought the fighter instinct to the surface.

"Let's have another go!" he said stoically.

The next flight proved to be successful. He took a one-turn spin. Subsequent sorties saw him progress to the point where, still somewhat reluctantly, he was able to complete the whole procedure himself. I finally asked him to enter and maintain a spin, only recovering when I told him to do so. As we spun through the first two or three turns I could tell by his increased breathing and whole demeanour that he was itching to recover, but he maintained his discipline and held on. I let him sweat for six turns but he executed the recovery perfectly.

I immediately took control and bawled congratulations into his ear! I slapped him on the thigh and made him feel he had conquered Everest - which, in his mind, he had! As I flew the aircraft back to base I let him talk the tension away but gave him control for the landing. This was to check that he could make the abrupt transition from relaxation to a high level of concentration and performance. He executed a perfect landing and maintained his discipline and concentration as we taxied back to dispersal.

As usual the MO was in on the debriefing.

"What would you like to do now?" he asked.

"Oh, I think I deserve a bit of a break. Probably have a game of squash," replied the pilot.

"You've certainly earned yourself a break, lad," said the MO, "but before that game of squash I want you to go off again solo and carry out five spins, each having four turns."

The pilot's face fell and I wondered if the MO had demanded too much. There was a moment's hiatus before the pilot grimly got up, swigged the rest of his coffee and walked resolutely towards the aircraft.

Having authorised the sortie, the MO called me aside and said, "This is where I have kittens! I don't see why I should have them all by myself; come and worry with me!" We had yet another coffee and kept well out of the young pilot's sight. He had to do this alone from start to finish. If he succeeded he was back to normal. If he failed, his career would probably be over as a pilot - certainly as a fighter pilot.

Sending any student solo is always a time of tension for an instructor. This proved just as bad, if not worse. We wound our way up the steps of the control tower and watched our subject through field glasses. We were able to hear his every transmission over the radio. His voice sounded firm enough. He made no verbal errors. His take-off and climb away were well executed. His airborne calls remained confident. All was going well.

Having cleared the airfield frequency, we were unable to hear any more of him so we made our way back to Standards Squadron for yet another coffee, asking the controller to inform us when our man was back on the airfield frequency. Meanwhile we waited, with some apprehension, hoping we would not hear a crash alarm or an announcement from the controller that an aircraft was overdue.

An hour later the controller informed us that our subject was back in the circuit and had elected to do a couple of touch and go landings to end the flight. Had he completed those spins, or had he chickened out?

We went to meet him from the aircraft and at first we were concerned. He walked towards us with his head bowed and his shoulders slumped, helmet dangling listlessly from his hand – a picture of failure! As we got nearer, however, he suddenly looked up, straightened up and with a broad smile yelled, "Eureka! I did it - six five-turn spins!"

I cannot adequately explain the deep satisfaction I felt on occasions like this. To see a man brought back from the depths of despair and failure to his rightful place as a confident, professional pilot was exhilarating. Sending a pupil on his first solo, seeing him awarded his wings, and getting a professional pilot his qualification as a flying instructor were all hugely satisfying, but nothing could replace the job satisfaction this rehabilitation work gave.

In all, I was involved with six cases, five of which were successful. Two of those 'patients' also became committed Christians during their stay at CFS.

On 6th June 1972, after two weeks' preparation with the CFS Standards Unit, I reported to Examining Wing to undergo my attempt to upgrade my instructor category to the ultimate A1.

The first examination tested my abilities as a Ground Instructor and Lecturer. My examiner tasked me to give a lecture on the workings of the ejector seat in front of an assembly of other CFS staff and students. Having lectured regularly on the subject at Bassingbourn, I was more than happy with his choice of assignment!

Later that morning my abilities as a Flying Instructor were examined. I was given a training sortie to complete with the examiner acting as the pupil. I had to give him a classroom tutorial on the sortie to be flown, followed in the afternoon by a pre-flight briefing before flying the sortie itself. This was in turn followed by a post-flight debriefing which included some searching questions from the 'pupil'.

The next phase of the examination took place in the form of a general handling sortie which included aerobatics, stalling and spinning, low flying, a practice diversion to another airfield, emergencies and various types of approaches. The examiner put me in at the deep end by closing the throttle on me just after we had entered cloud on the initial takeoff. The subsequent turn back towards the airfield and *dead stick* (engine off) landing went well as did the rest of the flight.

It ended by my examiner saying, "OK Ron, let's call it a day. Get back to Rissy [Little Rissington] as fast as you can, low level."

I opened the throttle fully, carried out all the necessary checks and roared across the Cotswolds at maximum permissible speed and minimum permissible height. It was a great sensation and brought the flight to a very enjoyable end.

The final day comprised an oral test of my knowledge of aviation subjects. This included spending some time going around and over an aircraft as part of the technical examination, in addition to questions on aerodynamics, instruments, meteorology, navigation aids, aviation medicine, compasses and magnetism, aircraft design, rules of the air, aircraft performance, etc. By the end of the day I felt I had been through a wringer!

The time came for my debriefing on all the three days' examinations. My lecturing and ground instruction were assessed as exceptional, as was my airborne instruction, but the assessment of my knowledge of aviation subjects and of my overall piloting abilities fell short. My examiner was generous enough to say, "If there was a category between A1 (exceptional) and A2 (above the average) I would happily award it." His parting shot was to commiserate with me for having failed but congratulating me on achieving a high level within the A2 category.

I considered his decision very fair. I knew I had fallen short of the 'exceptional' standard and would have lost some confidence in the examining system if I had been awarded it. During the debriefing we discussed the specific items that brought about the failure.

At the end of my general handling flight, when I was asked to return to Rissington at maximum possible speed, I had failed to notice that the slip indicator was not central. In a jet aircraft rudders are rarely used except for taxiing and aerobatics, but a Jet Provost at full speed can fly slightly out of balance, needing a small amount of rudder to compensate. It had escaped my notice! In addition, during my aerobatic sequence, I 'fell out' of a couple of stall turns. Not good enough for an exceptional pilot!

The aviation knowledge was a mixed bag for me. Most of the questions were straightforward enough, but aircraft design proved to be my weak point. Questions were centred upon the design of Concorde, which was actually undergoing its air tests from Filton at the time. Brian Trubshaw, Concorde's test pilot, had been to CFS to give a most interesting and informative lecture about the new aircraft, but some of the questions I fielded on its aerodynamics, especially in regard to the change from supersonic to subsonic flow of air through the engines, had me floundering.

I am glad I gave it a go. It was a good experience to have one's abilities and knowledge tested both in depth and width, even though the outcome was a disappointment. However, there was no disappointment about my new posting which had just been announced; it was back to Leeming!

During my last few weeks at CFS, a Squadron Leader, two other Flight Lieutenants and I were given the task of reviewing the instructional techniques used at CFS and to recommend changes. It meant standing back and taking a new look at the whole matter of pilot selection and training.

We realised that the days of the *wizard prang* - moustachioed, brave but reckless young extroverts that characterised war-time fighter pilots that pranged their cars regularly - had gone. We were entering an age of increasingly complex technological sophistication which required systematic management and close teamwork - both by aircrew in the cockpit and controllers on the ground. The whole personality profile of the pilot was changing. He had to be far more aware of his place in a team rather than his individuality, and he would be required to be much more responsible and accountable than ever before, with an analytical mind.

His training and the training of his instructors would need to reflect these changes and prepare him for them. We began by looking at the projected 'pilot of the future', listing the qualifications, experience and personality required. We then looked into the existing philosophy and ethos of our current instruction system, seeing where it was contrary to these new requirements.

Our research, experimentation and consultation with other bodies and individuals within the education and training disciplines were most interesting and satisfying exercises. They resulted in the *tutorial system* being adopted, more akin to the university approach to learning.

The original system at CFS was for a staff instructor to demonstrate an exercise to his student. The student would then fly a mutual sortie with another student and practice his 'patter' before flying a third sortie with his staff instructor, giving the exercise back. Thus one exercise took up three sorties. It was very much a matter of "Do it like this" and "I want to see you do likewise".

In contrast, the tutorial system began on the ground by asking the student instructor to analyse how he went about his flying. For example, how did he, as an experienced pilot, go about flying straight and level in balanced flight? The usual response to this was, "I just do it!" Getting a pilot to analyse just *how* he did it was the basis of the tutorial method. What was the pilot thinking about to ensure straight and level flight? Where was he looking, and what was he looking for?

It would take a whole book to give the full story of our research, but the outcome was that much more talking was done on the ground, less in the air, and the student instructor was encouraged to use his own experience, ability and knowledge in teaching a pupil pilot to fly. The earlier "Do it like this" system was replaced with a more personal and analytical approach with the onus being upon the instructor motivating the pupil to learn and the pupil being treated more as an intelligent individual than the rather buffoon 'Joe Bloggs' of yesteryear.

One more very interesting event occurred before I left CFS for my final posting back to Leeming.

I was Duty Pilot in the control tower one morning when the telephone rang. I identified myself as usual by stating my rank and name.

There was a notable pause then a voice said, "Would that be *Ron* Collard?" When I replied in the affirmative and asked who was speaking, the voice said, "Never you mind! Just meet the JP [Jet Provost] coming to you from Cranwell in about an hour's time!"

The phone went dead. Thinking it might be a senior officer visiting the station, I made various enquiries, including contacting the Station Commander, but nobody knew of any pending brass-hat's visit.

Eventually a Jet Provost from Cranwell roared into the circuit, announcing its arrival by doing a low and very fast run parallel to the runway before executing the tightest of turns onto *finals* and landing. Through the field glasses I could see the aircraft was being flown solo. I asked if the controller had a record of the pilot's name from the movement order, but he had none - just a callsign. The movement simply stated that a pilot from Cranwell was coming on a liaison visit to Standards Squadron at CFS.

I slapped my cap onto my head, ran down the steps of the control tower and made my way across the dispersal pan. As I approached the aircraft, the pilot levered himself out, jumped off the wing and walked towards me removing his helmet. It was Dick Bell, the guy from Hullavington days!

He was obviously delighted with my surprise and, as he offered me his hand, simply said, "John chapter nine - the blind man!"

What a joy it was to meet Dick as a Christian brother, not having seen him since our short time together eighteen years before. What an encouragement it was to see how the Word of God, preached very inadequately one evening at Hullavington, had taken root and eventually done its work in a life that was thereafter used extensively in the Lord's service.

Dick not only gained the Flying Training Command aerobatic trophy but became a test pilot on the Lightning aircraft and eventually retired from the Royal Air Force as a Squadron Leader to set up a Christian Conference centre in Seaton which is still operating today.

Figure 20: Dick Bell with Jet Provost.
[Photo: courtesy Dick Bell]

My time with the Red Pelican had come to an end but I was still entitled to wear the *placard* on my flying suit as I took up my final posting as a Standards Officer at Leeming in May 1972.

Once again it meant moving house and the children moving schools, but in many ways it was like going home. We had no difficulty selling our lovely Cotswold stone house in Bourton-on-the-Water, and we settled into an equally lovely house in Springfield Close, Ripon. Richard, Helen and Michael were all successful in their transfer to the Ripon Grammar School.

I was able to take terminal leave over the month of May 1973 which was devoted to completing the Commercial Pilot's Licence (CPL) Course at the Sir John Cass College in London. Although primarily a maritime institution, it also had an aviation faculty which prepared candidates for the Civil Aviation Authority's (CAA) CPL examination. I also had to present proof to the CAA that I had undergone a successful *type rating* on a specific aircraft. This was achieved by flying a sortie in a Chipmunk with a CAA approved examiner who was also a QFI on the Elementary Flying School at Church Fenton.

Whilst undergoing the CPL course in London I stayed with my mum and sister in South Croydon, returning to Ripon every weekend. I am indebted to them for their gracious hospitality, and particularly to Betty, who gave up her room so that I could have a bedsit study whilst she slept on the lounge floor.

The course itself was straightforward but for 'Radio Aids' which was new to me. We had to study such navigational aids as Loran, Decca and Consul. Lectures were given by a gentleman who knew his subject inside out but had little idea how to communicate his vast knowledge to the uninitiated. He addressed the blackboard in a monotonous voice, steadily filling it with white chalked diagrams and formulae, whilst we classmates looked at each other and shrugged our shoulders.

After some forty-five minutes he turned to the class (for the first time) and said nonchalantly, "Any questions?"

One brave student replied, "Yes. What have you been talking about? I haven't understood one word you have said!"

That guy spoke for all of us. It was an outstanding example of the need for those who teach and instruct to learn *how* to teach and instruct. Pure knowledge of one's subject is not enough. I suggest the same goes for preachers!

The CPL examination was held some weeks later at a centre in London which necessitated my having to find overnight accommodation nearby. I managed to get a reasonably priced B&B but had very little sleep as the noise of the London traffic kept me awake most of the night. I went into the exam feeling very tired and sluggish but managed to achieve the necessary standard in all the subjects. Subsequently the CAA issued me with my Commercial Pilot's Licence which, unlike my Private Pilot's Licence issued after my Flying Scholarship, entitled me to fly for "hire and reward"; in other words, I could fly fare-paying passengers.

It was with mixed feelings that I flew my last sortie as a Royal Air Force pilot on 21st June 1973 in Jet Provost Mark 3. It was a standardisation flight with a Flight Lieutenant Hencken. Although it was an instructional sortie I took control for my final approach and landing. I found it quite an emotional moment.

My last few days in the Royal Air Force were spent visiting the various sections at Leeming, returning publications and kit, and handing over my Flight Safety Officer duties to my replacement. I was also a guest of the officers' mess at a 'Dining Out' night when various humorous and generous comments were made on my contribution to No. 3 Flying Training School over a total of five years' service. I had served as a QFI on all three training squadrons and twice on the Standards Squadron, in addition to being the Station Flight Safety Officer and Air Cadet Liaison Officer.

Figure 21: The final photo before leaving the Royal Air Force. 21st June 1973.

My very last visit prior to departure from Leeming was to the Station Commander, Group Captain "Kit" Carson AFC. As I entered his PA's office, Margaret looked up with her usual cheery smile and bade me good morning.

She then added, "I'm just in the process of typing up your citation, sir." I genuinely did not know what she was talking about and looked at

274

her vacantly. Her elucidation struck me speechless: "You've been recommended for the award of the Air Force Cross for services to flying training."

Obviously someone else in Training Command was considered more worthy of the award as the recommendation was not ratified but, in itself, the recommendation was a huge honour, particularly as it originated from Group Captain Carson.

As was the custom when a regular officer left the Royal Air Force, I was interviewed by an officer of the Air Secretariat. The Wing Commander who spoke with me was most helpful and congenial but obviously had the brief to try to talk me into re-considering my decision to leave. He outlined my likely pathway should I change my mind. First, I would be posted as Squadron QFI on a frontline squadron flying Buccaneers. Then I would be promoted to Squadron Leader and given command of a training squadron either on a Basic Flying School or at the Central Flying School. It all sounded very attractive, but I had that inward constraint and conviction that my time with the colours should end.

So my Royal Air Force career terminated officially on 20th July 1973. What next? At least I had a Commercial Pilot's Licence, so it seemed logical that I should embark upon a career in civil aviation but to do so also required me gaining the instrument rating recognised by the Civil Aviation Authority (CAA). Although I had a Master Green instrument rating in the Air Force and was an Instrument Rating Examiner (IRE), this was not recognised by the CAA.

Overnight I found myself in a brand new world, and it was most uncomfortable. I was unemployed, with a huge financial hurdle to overcome in order to get the CAA instrument rating. Every flight and every course undertaken now had to be paid out of my own pocket. It also meant more enforced separation from the family. What had I let myself and my family in for? Yet I had that sense of assurance that I was doing what must be done.

The Oxford Blues

It was a humbling experience to be a Queen's Commissioned Officer one day and the member of a dole queue a few days later. Overall I was unemployed for seven months during which time I paid out a lot of money to equip myself for some sort of employment in civil aviation. The first task was to gain the CAA Instrument Rating which necessitated undergoing a course of instruction at the Oxford Air Training School at Kidlington Airport.

At least I had a gratuity of £1,500 from the RAF and I commuted half of my pension in order to have available cash, but it was not a happy experience having to pay invoices in excess of £110 for each one hour flight on top of the course fees. Every examination I underwent carried an additional fee.

I was able to stay at the vicarage at Witney during my time at Kidlington. I had frequently taken Bible studies there when I was stationed at CFS, and the vicar was a personal friend of my brother Fred. I am ever indebted to Howard and Ruby Cole for their kind, understanding and generous hospitality through July 1973.

The course was conducted on the Piper Twin Comanche (P39) which was a light twin engine propeller aircraft. It was a new experience for me to fly such a machine and to operate in airways. It was also a new and initially unnerving experience to find myself sitting in an airborne armchair rather than being trussed up in a maze of straps sitting on a parachute and the ever dependable ejector seat!

Flying solely on instruments was not in itself a problem to me as I had done so much in the RAF, but joining and flying airways with all the associated air traffic procedures, and flying into airports such as Birmingham, Cranfield, East Midlands and Bournemouth was a new and challenging experience, especially with an engine closed down.

On 26th July I underwent the test. I met my examiner, a CAA Captain, resplendent in his uniform with four gold braid rings round his cuffs and two rows of medal ribbons beneath his golden wings. He was a Scotsman who spoke very crisply and gave the impression that he would rather be doing something else somewhere else and was suffering from an acute bout of ennui.

Having completed my external and internal checks he informed me, disinterestedly, that I had carried them out satisfactorily and that I was now to proceed by starting the engines – I was planning to do that anyway! He then began to do the Daily Telegraph crossword! I frankly felt belittled. He was certainly not behaving as we had been taught to behave as examiners in the RAF.

He continued with his crossword until I had completed my pre-take-off checks. I then repeated the *Captain's brief* which I had been taught to do.

"Should an engine fail during the takeoff run I will close the throttles and use moderate braking! Should an engine fail after lift-off with runway still available I will replace the aircraft on the runway and use braking, as required! If an engine fails after take-off with no runway left available I will correct the yaw and hand control to you, sir!" (This was because the take-off was carried out visually until two hundred feet, at which point a screen was lowered to obscure the pilot's view, simulating entry into cloud.)

I had only just managed to get the word "sir" out of my mouth at the end of my Captain's brief when he turned on me furiously and, in his broad Scots accent yelled, "Ye'll di nae sich thing!"

I was flabbergasted! I had never before been spoken to like that by an instructor or examiner. I apologised and explained that I was only following the training I had received. I must admit that this exchange threw me. I found it very difficult to keep my focus, especially as he then reverted, muttering, to his crossword and continued doing it until he closed an engine on me later in the flight. I knew I had failed, particularly on the asymmetric phase which was disastrous, and this was confirmed by a surprisingly mellower examiner at the debriefing. I felt dreadful, not only for failing but for having wasted nearly £300 on that flight alone.

I came away from the debriefing feeling very low. I think the examiner realised how much I felt the failure, and he was almost sympathetic as we parted company. It took a while for me to compose myself or (more correctly) to be composed through a time of prayer over a coffee in a quiet corner of the cafeteria.

I drove back to the Witney vicarage and shared my lot with Howard and Ruby who immediately embraced me and prayed with me. In their prayers they reminded me that we serve a sovereign Lord who could even use failures to keep us in the centre of His will and purpose. The crucifixion at Calvary was, to all appearances, the classic example of apparent failure… but the One who 'failed' was actually fulfilling God's will. Three days later the 'failure' was swallowed up in victory! I also remembered another failed exam at Kirton-in-Lindsey which resulted in a victory!

My instructor at Kidlington suggested I had two more flights, concentrating on the asymmetric element of the test, before attempting it again. On 1st August I met my next examiner, Captain Sercombe, who was to test another student on the outbound route Kidlington to Bournemouth prior to conducting my test on the return flight. This meant I had to 'stew' for over two hours, sitting in the back of the P39 and in the crew room at Bournemouth, awaiting my execution!

At last Captain Sercombe called me in and gave me my briefing. His whole demeanour was professional, polite and encouraging. The occasional "good" and "nicely done" put me at ease and motivated me as he accompanied me around the aircraft on my external checks and supervised my starting procedures and taxiing. He even said, "Thank you!" after my Captain's briefing!

At the marshalling point for runway 26 we were held for some ten minutes (representing nearly £20) due to priority traffic landing and taking off. It was a very hot day with hardly a cloud in the sky so we opened the windows in an effort to keep cool, closing them when we were eventually cleared to enter the runway.

After take-off, with the screen closed on me by the examiner at two hundred feet, I was required to climb to three thousand feet, home back on to the Bournemouth beacon and carry out a four-minute holding pattern before commencing a let-down to join the Instrument Landing System (ILS) as per the Bournemouth approach chart. At decision height I was to execute the *Missed Approach Procedure* and climb away to join the airways that would take us back to Oxford via the Southampton beacon. It was on this latter leg that Captain Sercombe closed an engine, introducing the asymmetric element of the test.

Overall I was reasonably content with my performance but apprehensive about the result. The tolerances to pass the test were uncompromising. I did not know how I would face another failure.

Eventually Captain Sercombe called me into the Examiner's Office, stood up and offered me his hand.

"Congratulations, Mr. Collard. You have satisfied the CAA's requirements for the issue of an Instrument Rating."

I mumbled my thanks and felt an enormous load lift off my shoulders.

"Please sit down," he added. "I have some comments that might be of help to you."

Captain Sercombe then gave me a thorough debriefing, pointing out the strengths and weaknesses of my performance. I learned a lot from him - not least how to be a first class examiner! He also had the decency to deduct ten minutes off the chargeable time for the flight to allow for our being held at Bournemouth's take-off point! He saved me twenty quid!

My first port of call was a public telephone box where I called Elizabeth, announcing the good news, then back to the vicarage to rejoice with Howard and Ruby before hot-footing it home! Mission accomplished - at a price!

I decided to stay on at the Oxford Air Training School to get my CAA-approved Instructor Rating. This was very straightforward and followed the same profile as the preparations carried out in a Standards Squadron in the RAF. Flying was done in the Piper Cherokee (PA28) and after seven sorties I qualified as a Civilian Flying Instructor on 10th August 1973.

This qualification could only be used to instruct students undergoing training for their Private Pilot's Licence. If I wanted to instruct commercial pilots (those flying for hire and reward) I would need to get the Commercial Instructor's Rating! More money! I returned to Oxford in February 1974 to undergo this course which was carried out on the PA39 (Twin Comanche). After six sorties I passed the test and thus became a Commercial Flying Instructor - at a price!

Whilst I was about it I decided to get as many rubber stamps on my licence as possible, so I also applied for the Aerobatic Rating. This was easily achieved in just forty-five minutes in a Fuji 200/160 - the one and only occasion I flew that type of aircraft.

Now what about a job? Who would employ a thirty-eight-year-old re-tread from the RAF holding a shiny new Commercial Pilot's Licence, Instrument Rating, Commercial Instructor Rating and Aerobatic Rating?

I made application to a number of air operators including an experimental establishment at Llanbedr, Flying Clubs at Leeds and Teesside, an executive air taxi service at Leeds, and Air Bridge Carriers operating Argosy transport aircraft from East Midlands. All in their turn accepted me but none seemed right. I had no sense of peace about any of them.

To fly with a scheduled airline I would need the Air Transport Pilot's Licence (ATP) which was the top of the licensing league, but this would mean paying out even more money on another full course of academics and undergoing more examinations where the pass mark in each subject was eighty per cent.

Hey ho! 'In for a penny; in for a pound!' Although it meant another eight week course at Sir John Cass College in London, with further separation from the family, Elizabeth and I bit the bullet and agreed I should give it a go. This necessitated commuting between London and Ripon by rail at weekends.

Getting the ATP would be the ultimate licence, said by some to be the Ph.D. of the piloting world, but the CAA do not give such qualifications away without a fight! Unfortunately for me I found virtually every subject was mathematically loaded. We even had to use log tables for Meteorology!

The subjects themselves were the same as for the CPL but much more thorough and complex. The only new challenge was an examination called *Performance A*. This was the highest level of aircraft performance, requiring the interpretation of graphs and other data featuring weight and balance, take-off, climb, cruise, descent and landing calculations based upon a typical airliner. If one passed this exam there would be no requirement to undergo any further performance exams for any other aircraft type. Happily, I passed it first shot - at a price!

Once again my mum and sister Betty graciously accommodated me during the working week. Mum, bless her, even donated some of her savings to help me with the cost of the ATP course but, in spite of all the blessings which I readily acknowledge, this was probably the worst time of my life thus far. The stress of yet more separation, the uncertainty of the future, the responsibility of trying to be a husband and a dad only at weekends, the intensity of the studies and the crowded bustling environment of London, which I hated, all began to take its toll. The black clouds were surrounding me. Every day was a mountain to climb, except for Friday afternoon when I ran for my train at Kings Cross to take me home for thirty six precious hours before the soul-wrenching 'goodbyes' late on Sunday afternoon. Life seemed to be a repeat of my initial flying training days when being with Elizabeth was a beautiful but all too brief oasis in a week of struggle, stress and uncertainty.

The day came when the results of my ATP exams were made known. I had achieved a partial pass having failed in Navigation Plotting. I would have to re-sit the exam - at a price! The fact that I had achieved at least eighty per cent in all the other subjects seemed insignificant. I had not qualified for my ATP licence.

Once more I pulled myself up by my bootstraps and went back to London for some concentrated tutorial work at Cass College on the subject of Navigation Plotting. This subject was done on both the Mercator and Lamberts charts and involved much work with the Dalton Computer, the Douglas Protractor, dividers, parallel rulers and, for me, an eraser!!

As I walked towards the examination room on the day of my re-sit, who should I see coming towards me but John Buckland, the second navigator with whom I had served during my time with No. 58 Squadron at Wyton.

"What are *you* doing here? John called as he held out his hand.

"I'm re-sitting this wretched Navigation Plotting exam that I failed," I replied. "And what are *you* doing here?"

John threw his head back and laughed. "I work for the CAA," he announced. "I've written this exam paper! I'm invigilating it and marking it!"

It was a strange experience to see my navigator standing at the front of the hall briefing us for the two hour exam. I worked like a Trojan when he started the clock, checking and double-checking my calculations before drawing any lines on the charts. I was a bit put out to find one or two candidates handing in their work after about thirty minutes. I thought they must be 'whizz-kids', but it transpired they had just given up!

At the end of the two hours, feeling like a wet rag, I handed John my answer paper and charts and bade him farewell. We remained totally professional by not making any comments about the exam. Sadly I have never seen John since that day.

Although I managed to complete the paper I was not confident that my performance had been good enough. Happily, I did not have to use my eraser extensively but the maths involved had again been quite a challenge. If I failed this time I would have to take all the ATP exams again - at a price!

A couple of weeks later the results came through. Much to my surprise I had passed with eighty per cent! I would like to think that this was all my own doing but I have always had a sneaking suspicion that John might have given me a mark or two for getting my name correct and for not killing him when he daily risked his life with me on the Squadron! However, I knew John to be a true professional and a man of integrity, so perhaps it was all my own work after all!

At least I could now offer an employer an Air Transport Pilot's Licence, 4,500 hours of flying experience (including 2,000 hours as an instructor), an Instrument Rating, a Commercial Instructor Rating, and an Aerobatic Rating.

Unlike a few years earlier, when airline operators were crying out for ex-service pilots, I found myself as one small pebble on a very large beach. Vacancies were few. I had a nasty feeling that I had spent an awful lot of money, time and trouble, not to mention the stress and family separation, to no avail. Seven months after leaving the Royal Air Force, I was still unemployed, and money was flowing out of the bank with very little flowing in. I experienced an overdose of 'the blues'. It was a dark time for me – dark blues. Is that not appropriate when spending so much time at Oxford?

It was at this juncture that I received a telephone call from Tom Frank, the UK Director of the Mission Aviation Fellowship.

"I hear you've left the RAF and wonder if you would be interested in joining us. Perhaps we could have a chat about it sometime."

God moves in a mysterious way...

Wings with a Difference

I first heard of Mission Aviation Fellowship (MAF) when I visited the small Congregational Church at Buntingford in Hertfordshire back in 1958. A filmstrip was being shown entitled 'Mid-Century Martyrs', the story of five missionaries killed by the Auca Indians in Ecuador two years earlier. It had hit the headlines at the time.

One of the five was Nate Saint, the MAF pilot who flew the others into Auca territory, landing on a small sand bar on the Curaray River. The full story is told in 'Jungle Pilot', 'Through Gates of Splendour', 'Shadow of the Almighty' and 'The Savage My Kinsman'.

As a pilot and a Christian, I found this simple filmstrip stunningly interesting and deeply challenging. As I watched each frame come up on to the screen I found myself becoming increasingly aware that more than a filmstrip was speaking to me. The same Lord who had called these five men into His service, ultimately to give their lives for His Gospel, was calling me. One particular frame, not in itself hugely significant, was the point at which I knew, beyond any doubt, that I was to give my experience and qualifications back to the One who had enabled me to get them. The frame in question showed Nate's little yellow Piper Cruiser flying over a canopy of blue/green jungle.

From that evening onward I sought to learn more about this mission organisation and asked to be placed on its mailing list. Subsequently I responded to an open invitation to attend a conference at which the proof version of a motion film was to be shown for the first time. The film was eventually produced under the title 'Conflict in the Sky', the story of MAF's pioneering work with an aircraft in Sudan.

At that conference I met other serving and retired officers of the armed forces, test pilots and other civilian aviators, in addition to the small MAF staff. All were enthusiastic to see MAF develop further as a tool in God's hand to spread the Gospel and bring relief to the suffering in the more inaccessible regions of the world.

When on detachment to Nairobi with No. 58 Squadron in January and February 1960, I visited the small MAF base at Wilson Airport as mentioned on pages 200 and 201. Thus I gradually became more involved with the work of MAF and experienced that deep conviction and constraint that this was a work to which I should eventually give my future service; meanwhile I got a job with the Oxford Air Training School which in those days had a base at Carlisle Airport. I joined the staff as a Commercial Flying Instructor in March 1974.

Yet again this meant enforced separation from the family. At first we tried to sell our house in Springfield Close, Ripon, but without success. In the meantime I commuted at weekends along the A1, A66 and M6 in my little green mini traveller. Initially I managed to get 'digs' with a family in the village near the airport, but I missed my family and home dreadfully.

I was constantly trying to find accommodation for us in Carlisle, in the hope that our house in Ripon would eventually sell. Rented accommodation later became available in Lynne Close, Carlisle, so Elizabeth and I decided to move there with Helen, Michael and Christopher. We were reluctant to move Richard as he was approaching his GCE 'O' levels, so he became a boarder at the Ripon Grammar School. It was a very difficult decision to make, and I found it particularly painful saying goodbye to Richard and splitting up the family.

Hoping for something more permanent, Elizabeth and I put a deposit down on a spare piece of ground in Aglionby, a few miles out of Carlisle. We even engaged an architect to design a house similar to the one in Ripon but, as no purchaser was forthcoming, no building work could start. Eventually our time ran out and we had to relinquish the plot and forfeit our deposit.

Virtually all my fellow instructors at Carlisle were ex-service pilots from the Royal Air Force or Royal Navy. Some had flown during the Second World War. Two had been interned as POWs. One chap had been a Lancaster pilot who had been shot down on the day he should have been on leave! He was unfortunate enough to be caught in the crew room by his Flight Commander just as he was about to go home. Another pilot had reported sick and Bob was detailed to take his place, so instead of getting a week's leave he spent the next few years in a German Stalag Luft. He was not a happy bunny!!

The Chief Flying Instructor at Carlisle turned out to be a Christian which was a pleasant surprise. Sadly he was later killed with his student when his aircraft was caught on takeoff in the wake of an Argosy aircraft which had departed minutes before. His wife, Audrey, working as his PA in the office, heard the crash alarm. She instinctively knew it was David who, less than half an hour before, had left his office, placing his hand upon Audrey's shoulder saying, "See you at lunch."

It was a remarkable testimony to God's upholding grace that even as the emergency services were attending the scene, Audrey was making cups of tea and coffee and consoling the staff instructors, many of whom were in tears. Her faith in Christ shone through her grief.

The Oxford Air Training School at Carlisle took airline-sponsored cadets and trained them to Commercial Pilot's Licence standard. Young men from Algeria, Indonesia, Japan, Iraq and Greece were among the nationalities we trained. Some had never flown an aircraft before and others had received only ten hours of assessment flying prior to coming on the course. Occasionally, when the British Airways College at Hamble was overflowing, we would have a few British Airways cadets join us.

It was not all instructing! I had to get two more ratings: the Commercial Instructor's Rating for twin engine aircraft and type ratings on the PA28, P39 and Beagle Pup - at a price!

My very first instructional flight as a Commercial Flying Instructor was on 13th March 1974 with a Greek student from Olympic Airways named Meimaris. I was also given two other Greek students - Stefas and Tzagarakis - the latter, an ex-policeman. I flew exclusively with these three until another course came to Carlisle from Air Algerie when I added to my flock Laissaoui and a lad simply called "SNP" which stood for *Sans Nom Personna* ("Without a Name").

The Greek lads exhibited an interesting characteristic! They always wanted to move on to the next exercise on the syllabus even if their performance of the current exercise was substandard.

"But we did that yesterday, sir," was the frequent cry of complaint, to which I responded, "You did indeed, but it wasn't good enough, so we do it again until it is!"

How true are Paul's words in the book of Acts, chapter seventeen and verse twenty one: "For all the Athenians and the foreigners who were there spent their time in nothing else but either telling or hearing some new thing."

My flying career very nearly came to an abrupt end one afternoon. I had briefed and authorised Stefas to carry out a solo navigation exercise which was timed to leave Carlisle about two hours after I had taken off with Tsagarakis to fly to Prestwick.

On our return leg I had asked Tsagarakis for our position.

"There sir," he said, stabbing a finger at the map on his knees.

I briefly glanced down then looked up again. I was horrified to see, not twenty feet below us, passing obliquely from left to right, a PA28 with Stefas looking down at his map! I could clearly identify his features. It was all over in a split-second, but I remained speechless and wide-eyed for seconds afterwards! I had experienced a few near misses before in my flying career but nothing as close as that! What headlines it would have made: "Instructor and two of his students die in mid-air collision!"

On debriefing Stefas, I confirmed that he had not seen me. I informed him of our near fatal collision and he turned pale.

"A lesson for both of us, Stefas! Good lookout is the number one priority *before* you glance into the cockpit!"

In June 1974 a course of Indonesian cadets from Air Garuda joined us, and I took on Purwoko, Sujoto, and Suhurijono, the latter excelling himself by being the first on his course to go solo. It has been a tradition on such occasions to cut a length off the student pilot's tie, but the Indonesian lads showed us a new variation: they kicked Suhurijono all round the aircraft dispersal!

One morning I was approached by an instructor who was almost literally tearing his hair out!

"I can't do a thing with him!" he yelled to all and sundry. "He's impossible! He never does the same thing twice! He's so inconsistent! Would anyone like to give him a go? I've had my belly-full of him!"

It sounded an interesting challenge and I was a pupil short that day, so I accepted. The pupil in question was morose, uncommunicative and given to spitting (happily not in the aircraft)! During my briefing he seemed to be in another world and only answered my questions reluctantly. I briefed him to fly this sortie as though he was solo and to forget I was in the cockpit. I asked him to carry out a general handling flight including steep turns, stalling and circuits. I would just enjoy the ride and see how he performed. Whenever I flew with another instructor's pupil I liked to see how he operated without giving much, if any, instruction on the first flight.

After signing the authorisation sheet and the aircraft servicing log, we went to the aircraft. He walked around it, removed the static vent plugs and pitot head cover but made no further examination of the aircraft. We strapped in, and he started the engine without any checks being done. He called the tower for taxi clearance, made his way to the take-off point and, without further checks, requested take-off clearance and went!

As we accelerated down the runway I closed the throttle and asked the pupil to return to dispersal. I notified air traffic control that we were cancelling the sortie. The pupil said nothing but looked quizzical.

Having shut down the engine, I asked him why he had failed to do any checks.

His answer was, "But you told me to forget you were in the cockpit. I did what I normally do when solo."

It is hard to believe such stupidity and ill-discipline.

When the Chief Flying Instructor interviewed him, having read his instructor's reports together with mine, he asked, "Don't you want to succeed on this course and get your Commercial Pilot's Licence?"

The answer was "No! I want to be a butcher but I was made to apply to be an airline pilot."

Needless to say, this fellow was sent home and a very stern communication made with his sponsor airline!

The cultural difference among the pupil population was interestingly diverse. At one extreme you had the Arabs who generally had a very low opinion of women and spurned authority. They were happy to 'go along' with the system, albeit reluctantly, providing it achieved their own agenda in the end; self-discipline, responsibility, respect and conscientiousness were frequently lacking. At the other end of the spectrum were the Japanese. They would not ask questions of an instructor as they considered it would be an insult, implying that the instructor had not fully done his job. The Japanese took every word literally and were driven by honour and loyalty, not common sense. A typical example follows...

Two Japanese and two British Airways pupils had been briefed by the same instructor to carry out identical mutual flights in two PA39s to Edinburgh, using airways via the Talla beacon. The flights were scheduled for a Saturday. The weekend Duty Instructor checked that the weather forecast was compatible with the exercise and authorised the two Japanese to take off one hour after the British Airways pair.

On the Monday morning the instructor checked the weekend's authorisation sheets. The Japanese' entry simply read, "Duty carried out." The entry for the British Airways lads read, "Duty not carried out. Returned to base. Severe turbulence and icing over the Talla beacon. De-icing equipment not coping."

The instructor called the British Airways couple into his office and asked pertinent questions. It was confirmed that the weather conditions over and around the Talla beacon had been unexpectedly severe. The instructor congratulated them for exercising sound judgement and good airmanship by curtailing the flight and returning to base.

He then called in the Japanese couple, asking them the same questions.

"Did you encounter any severe turbulence over the Talla beacon on Saturday?"

"Yes, sir."

"Did you experience any icing?"

"Yes, sir."

"What category would you consider the icing to have been?"

"Severe, sir."

"Was your de-icing equipment dealing adequately with the icing?"

"No, sir."

"Why did you press on instead of returning to base?"

"Because you told us to fly to Edinburgh, sir."

There is no answer to that! The instructor had failed to brief them to return to base in the event of adverse weather! Briefing Japanese students was a hazard in itself. They took every word literally and considered it a dishonour to their instructor not to carry out his instructions to the letter. One can understand how the nation could obey orders in war conditions without a second thought, no matter what those orders might be! Immediate and precise obedience was a sign of honour to both the superior giving the order and to the subordinate receiving it. To question an order or adapt it would be dishonourable. To disobey it would be unthinkable.

What a breath of fresh air were the British Airways students - keen, conscientious, well-motivated, teachable and intelligent! I only had the pleasure of flying with three of them during the latter stages of their course, but I enjoyed every minute of it. Payne, Wallis and Lovitt are probably all retired Senior Captains now, but then they were my boys and I was proud of them.

Figure 22: The PA39 at Carlisle Airport with my three British Airways students: Payne, Wallis and Lovitt.

Other students came my way with such exotic names as Boudalia, Hammadouche, Economopoulis and Alexandropoulos. Even though some were a challenge to any instructor, each taught me a lot about cross-cultural understanding. Instructional techniques suitable for western pupils did not necessarily score with eastern and middle-eastern lads. One had to find new ways of getting the instruction over in a way which meant something to the individual pupil.

Why was our house not selling at Ripon?! Elizabeth and I put great importance on being together as a family, but here we were with Richard boarding at Ripon and the rest of us in rented accommodation in Carlisle.

In spite of much prayer there seemed to be an impasse and we had lost money on our efforts to settle in Aglionby. We decided to re-unite the family again, returning to our home in Springfield Close. Richard ceased to be a boarder and I reverted to commuting every weekend. Thanks to the kindness of the vicar of Scotby, his wife Margaret and their two little daughters, Catherine and Elizabeth, I had, for my last seven months at Carlisle, a super Christian home to return to for the working week.

Unknown to me things were moving within MAF, and after a meeting with the General Director and UK Director, it was agreed that I should join MAF in two capacities: first, to build up a national network of well-informed volunteer representatives to make MAF better known and thus widen the support base; second, to assist in the selection and preparation of pilot candidates.

It was agreed that I should remain in Ripon, as it was central to the British Isles and had good north-south communication. It was also agreed that I should go to Ethiopia immediately in order to see a frontline operation at work. Elizabeth and I thought that joining MAF would cut out a lot of the separation, but it was not to be; however, we now saw why our house in Ripon had not sold!

On 2nd of May 1975 I flew my last sortie with the Oxford Air Training School and on 28th June flew my first sortie with MAF, a flight in a Cessna 185 from Addis Ababa to Kirimu. The pilot was Verne Sikkema and our passenger Jud Threlkeld, an 'MK' (missionary kid) returning to his parents for the school holidays. The advantage of the aircraft was immediately obvious. Without it, Jud would have spent a good proportion of his school holiday trekking over wild and mountainous terrain in order to join his parents, then repeating the performance on the return journey back to school. Using the aircraft meant the family could be reunited in a couple of hours. It also gave the parents that peace of mind that they were only an MAF flight away from their son during term time.

The change from Royal Air Force life to civil aviation had been traumatic. The change from commercial instructing to MAF was even more traumatic. Financially, the former change brought a significant increase in salary but, understandably, the latter brought a significant decrease to below the level of my terminal Air Force pay. Belts had to be tightened, and although MAF paid a salary, it was up to me to endeavour to create at least some personal financial support.

Life was a brand new ball-game! For the next fourteen years I extensively travelled the British Isles (including the Channel Islands), presenting the work of mission in general and MAF in particular, to schools, colleges, universities, military establishments, and churches of most denominations. Over those fourteen years I averaged one week at home per month.

Elizabeth and I thought that leaving the Royal Air Force would give us a more stable home life, but the commuting to Carlisle had prevented that. Joining MAF separated us within the first two weeks with the visit to Ethiopia. Now, although home based, separation loomed large again.

Wherever I went I had a photo of Elizabeth in my wallet. It was her passport photo when we went to Germany after our wedding. It clearly showed her wonderful smile which has always meant so much to me. I carried it with me constantly from the moment we were married. Our frequent goodbyes on a Monday morning were very hard for me. I hated being parted from her and the children but saw it as a necessary sacrifice in the service of the One who sacrificed so much more for me. I still have the poem before me which accompanied that lovely photo:

Morning: the world, the flesh, the weary blood,
Revving again to the weekday pace;
The hurried dressing and the snatch at food,
The bungled kiss upon your Monday face.
The weekend peels and vanishes away
Borne upward out of sight by the tornados of necessity.
There is too much to do before tonight; even tonight
Though now it seems as far away as Saturday
Is just a breathing space before the week fully engages gear
And grinds and crushes loveliness and grace,
Gained on time's island for a little while
But gained and held in your remembered smile.

(Author unknown)

My usual profile over those fourteen years was to target a particular area of the British Isles for anything up to a three week visit and 'saturate' it with pre-arranged engagements, also undertaking other *ad hoc* opportunities that might present themselves. Each weekend away would be taken up with pre-planned visits to a church, normally giving a visual presentation on the Saturday evening, speaking at both services on the Sunday, with maybe additional events in the afternoon and after the evening service. I would also visit schools, colleges, universities, military establishments, clubs, coffee mornings, etc. as opportunity afforded. After two or three weeks away I would return home for a full seven days in order to see something of the family, catch up on administration and prepare for the next 'safari'.

At first I had to use my own car, a Renault 5, reclaiming mileage, but eventually I was authorised to purchase a car for MAF work and, with the kind attention of Colin Baines, a Christian car dealer in Harrogate, I purchased a Datsun Estate. Similarly my initial presentation equipment was borrowed from friends in my church in Ripon until, some years later, I was authorised to purchase a 35 mm slide projector, a 16 mm motion projector and a screen. Money was very scarce in MAF!

I had to create my own display in such a way that it would fit into the rear of my car and yet be easily erected. This accompanied me on virtually all my visits and featured at the various mission conventions and exhibitions I attended. Overall this display measured some ten feet long, two and a half feet wide and six feet high. The centre point of the display was a motion film showing through an aperture measuring eighteen inches by fourteen inches, with greaseproof paper acting as a screen. The film was back-projected via a mirror with the cine-projector and speaker situated at the rear.

Those fourteen years of travelling the British Isles resulted in the establishment of many local church and area volunteer representatives and prayer support groups for MAF. They also meant meeting some very wonderful people who not only welcomed me warmly to their groups and churches but gave me generous hospitality which was frequently repeated on subsequent visits.

Many and varied were the homes into which I was welcomed, but most became 'home from home' and many of my hosts have become life-long friends. My only regret is that I did not keep a record of all my visits to churches and the homes that were opened to me. In any case they would be too numerous to list in this book, but I must make special mention of a few who were outstanding.

I first met John and Sheila Paul when visiting their church at High Wycombe for a Missions' Weekend. I have lost count of the number of return visits I made to both their church and home. In spite of John having to commute to London every day, starting early and finishing late, both John and Sheila always had time in their precious evenings not only to feed me sumptuously and to give me their time but also to accompany me to meetings they had arranged in the local area. They also organised visits to schools, coffee mornings, etc for me during the day. John and Sheila were totally committed to MAF as they still are today.

John and Maureen Chacksfield were another couple who frequently entertained me on my various visits to the Fylde area of Lancashire. Not only did they organise comprehensive programmes for my visits to churches and schools, they also arranged for me to speak at the Workers' Christian Fellowship at the British Aerospace Establishment at Warton and to the Preston branch of the Royal Aeronautical Society. Unfortunately, in those days when I had to use my voice so extensively, I regularly suffered with very sore throats and headaches. On one occasion I had to spend most of my stay at the Chacksfield's in bed, with Maureen supplying me liberally with drinks, paracetamol, oranges and throat lozenges. I only surfaced to take the various meetings before collapsing into bed again with my throat on fire!

Another family that was outstanding in its service to MAF was Chris, Linda, Gavin and Lauren Matthews. Not only did they open their home near Heathrow to me, they also hosted one of our largest and most dedicated prayer groups. In addition they acted as a transit hotel for MAF personnel travelling in and out of the UK. Frequently Chris would meet a family off the aircraft at Heathrow and entertain them at home until I could collect them. Overnight accommodation would also be given to MAF travellers prior to their outward flight, with Chris taking them to the airport often at antisocial hours.

In those days MAF had an arrangement with a number of airlines enabling personnel to travel on standby. This significantly reduced the fares but was no guarantee that one would get a seat on the aircraft as MAF was at the bottom of the standby pile. Sometimes families had to be split up and travel in separate groups - not an ideal arrangement! Luggage frequently got on board and the owners did not, or vice versa!

Chris and Linda were absolute gems! Frequently they would drop passengers off at Heathrow only to be telephoned an hour or two later to be told the travellers had been 'bumped' and the next flight would not be until tomorrow night. Chris and Linda would retrieve the wayfarers from Heathrow and put them up for another night, feeding them royally. What a service this family gave to MAF over the years!

On one of my many visits north of the border I stayed with a Church of Scotland Minister and his wife who owned a beautiful sandy-coloured Labrador.

Having first introduced his wife, the Minister then turned to the dog, saying, "And this is Bob. Say 'how-do-you-do' to Mr. Collard."

Bob dutifully sat back on his haunches and offered me his right paw. At lunch I was conscious of a pair of baleful eyes watching my every mouthful. Slowly Bob got closer to me until his snout was resting on my knee.

"Ignore him," said the Minister. "He thinks you're a soft target."

After lunch the Minister invited me to watch as he placed a large biscuit on the end of Bob's nose. Bob focussed on it with crossed eyes but never moved. He was then given a one word command from his master: "Eat!" There was a blur; the biscuit disappeared as if by magic and Bob remained statuesque. I never heard Bob bark, even once, throughout my stay. When we parted the same padded paw was politely offered to me. I enjoyed Bob's company and behaviour almost as much as I enjoyed that of his delightful owners. He was a dog that knew his place and won the love and admiration of one who is not a 'doggy person'.

Another visit north of the border worth particular mention was to Alloa for the half-term retreat of the Scottish Scripture Union group of George Watson's College, attended by about fifty young people. Although I had accepted the invitation to be the guest speaker some months before, I was in poor shape when the time came to fulfil the engagement. I had just returned home from a particularly difficult tour and was again suffering from a very sore throat. I felt like death warmed up!

I was considering cancelling the appointment but realised it would put the organisers into a very difficult situation at the eleventh hour. As I prayed about it I was constrained at least to set off and do what I could. Perhaps I could return home early. I must emphasise that I would have given anything for that visit to be cancelled. I felt totally inadequate for the task both physically and mentally. I very reluctantly took my leave of the family (again) and pointed my car up the A1. I was not a happy bunny!

As I approached Alloa I was surprised to find my throat was easing. Doubtless it would rough up again as soon as I started using it in ministry. I put on as brave a face as I could when meeting my hosts and the assembled teenage students.

As the weekend progressed my throat slowly healed. My joy at sharing the things of God returned, and I found the whole experience a blessing. The young people were most interested in all I had to share with them, which included my testimony of God's dealings in my life thus far, the work of MAF and most importantly the exposition of God's Word.

Some fifteen years later I heard from one of the teenagers, Kevin Gruer, who was now married with two children. He told me that at that weekend in Alloa the Lord had spoken to many of the teenagers there. Several, including Kevin, had committed their lives to Christ and two had subsequently been ordained. As I write, Kevin himself is completing his final training as a Minister in the Church of Scotland, and it is my privilege to count his whole family in the circle of my dearest friends; I am so glad I did not miss out on such a blessing by cancelling that engagement! God again overruled events.

There were so many more visits undertaken during those years of deputation and ministry, but most have slipped from the memory after such a long time. A few, but only a few, stand out for the wrong reasons, such as the occasion when I arrived late in the evening at my appointed lodging, after a long and difficult journey, to be greeted with the comment "I do hope you have eaten as we're fasting today!" I muttered some reply which included the first part of verse four of Matthew's fourth chapter and, after settling into my room, took a pre-retiring constitutional to the nearest fish and chip shop!

On another occasion, supper being ended, the host brought out an impressive pile of books, topped by a large family Bible, and proceeded to read passages from each one of the tomes. On sight of the books being brought in, his wife was heard to mutter under her breath, "Oh no! Not this performance again!" It transpired that "this performance" was a ritual laid on whenever a visiting missionary stayed with them!

My itinerary included the universities at Southampton, Strathclyde and Salford, various student weekends, Royal Air Force stations including Cranwell, and lots of schools - even a week at Gordonstoun! I also had the privilege of taking the Bible studies at a student weekend when Dr. Helen Roseveare led the mission sessions. Her books are essential reading for any Christian: 'Give Me This Mountain', 'He Gave Us A Valley', and 'Living Sacrifice'. She is smaller than me (if you can believe it!) but a spiritual giant!

Although a few of my visits to churches were disappointing, nothing was as bad as the experience one MAF pilot had when he responded to an invitation to take a *MAF Weekend* at a church in London. He turned up on the Saturday evening to give his presentation and found nobody there! He set up his equipment and waited. Eventually six elderly ladies appeared but still no organiser. Bang on the advertised start time the vicar poked his head around the door and said, "Welcome David! Glad you could come. Today's my day off so I'll see you tomorrow!" and disappeared.

David duly completed his presentation to the six elderly ladies, one of whom gave him hospitality and overnight accommodation. He was about to retire for the night when he was summoned to the phone. It was the vicar.

"David, I forgot to mention when I saw you this evening that tomorrow is our harvest thanksgiving. Perhaps you could give us a harvest-flavoured sermon tomorrow morning."

David duly burned the midnight oil changing his prepared sermon to conform to the vicar's request.

Having preached at the morning and evening services, David was thanked by the vicar for coming but no offering had been taken up for MAF and no mention of expenses being paid.

The vicar's parting shot was "Help yourself to something off the harvest display - a cauliflower or something!"

My itinerant programmes would be interspersed with receiving potential pilot candidates and their wives at our home for initial assessment. MAF was indebted to Carl Wilkinson, a Christian farmer living near Malton, who allowed me to use his private aircraft for the assessment flights. Usually the candidate and his wife would spend about three days with us in Ripon.

Virtually all of the assessment was done informally as we toured the beautiful North Yorkshire countryside, walked around Ripon, and chatted over meals. I was particularly looking for spiritual maturity, adaptability, flexibility, marital solidarity, social skills, creativity, leadership, a willingness to learn, and a sense of call to mission confirmed, of course, by the candidate's home church.

In the airborne assessment I was looking for potential, not current performance. We frequently had candidates come to us who had never previously flown an aircraft. Others had thousands of hours of military or commercial flying. The profile of the assessment would vary with a candidate's experience, but overall I was looking for natural ability, environmental awareness, retention of instruction, application of the instruction received, his talking / listening ratio skills, his mental / physical co-ordination and his ability to handle an element of pressure and stress.

I also tested his sense of priorities. What a pilot is looking at generally indicates his priority at that moment. By placing my map on the rear seat behind me and, later in the flight, asking the candidate to retrieve it whilst he was in control of the aircraft, usually proved the point! Does he give his full attention to getting the map, or does he locate the map with a rearward glance, return his attention to the control of the aircraft and feel for the map with one hand? I also looked for the candidate's ability to split his attention. One method was to ask him simple questions about his grandparents whilst he was physically fulfilling another task which required some concentration. Was he able to prioritise his tasks?

Overall I was basically asking the question, "Has this guy the potential to qualify as a Commercial Pilot and, if so, would I let him fly my wife and children?"

One cannot emphasise enough the role of the wife. In addition to her domestic and family duties, she would be expected to keep radio contact with remote mission stations and the aircraft in flight. She might also be responsible for arranging schedules, dealing with customers' queries and demands, keeping accounts and performing other administrative duties, not to mention giving hospitality at the 'drop of a hat'. An MAF wife is a jewel and can never be valued too highly. She also has to have a cool head. It is not unheard of for a wife to receive her own husband's *Mayday* call!

Assessing a wife's suitability was far more difficult than assessing the pilot, but even in a short stay Elizabeth and I were able to get a reasonable picture of the lady's suitability. In order that they might have a better understanding of their husband's 'office' and the work he did in it, I offered each wife a brief flight in the pilot's seat and gave them control after the necessary demonstration and "follow me through". There were a few occasions when the wife's assessment was better than her husband's!

Once a number of candidate couples had been provisionally accepted, I organised an annual flight camp. This meant more separation from Elizabeth and the family as I drove our Volkswagen Dormobile down to Kent and pitched camp at either Lympne or Headcorn airfields.

Candidates came from all over Europe and the UK with their families and lived under canvas. They brought their own tents and equipment. The idea of the flight camp was to create a microcosm of the mission field - being thrown together with people of other nationalities and cultures and living without the western so-called 'necessities of life'. Electricity was a torch. Water was only obtainable by carrying it in buckets from a single stand pipe situated away from the site. Stores could be bought locally but had to be carried by hand. The overall question was "Could this candidate family make a functional home out of a tent?"

It only took a couple of days to identify the leaders and the followers and see the true personalities and talents emerging. In addition to the attributes observed on the initial assessment we looked for creativity, forbearance, team spirit and the ability to face circumstances as a total unit rather than just as individual families.

Although sometimes the candidate families found themselves washed out of bed by thunderstorms, having difficult relationships with each other due to their children's tantrums, illness and occasional injuries, many still parted from each other at the end of the camp with tears. They had learned so much about themselves and had become so fond of their newfound friends, that they did not want to leave! They had also learned that they could do without a lot of their western trappings.

The flying at flight camp was intensive when the weather was suitable. Otherwise it was ground school. The aim was to develop a pilot's basic skills and knowledge, directing him towards MAF's particular requirements. More experienced pilots frequently had to learn how to fly a tail-wheeled, single piston engine aircraft, as all their flying had been on jet aircraft with a nose wheel! Such phenomena as propeller torque, slipstream effect, gyroscopic effect and the *P factor* were all new to them.

Well-controlled slow speed flight was also a new skill to perfect. All were conversant with the stall but few had experienced manoeuvring the aircraft accurately just above the stall with the warning horn sounding continuously!

We also demonstrated to the pilot candidates a few requirements for the MAF pre-field orientation course which would be undertaken once they had qualified as commercial pilots. One chap described it as "MAF's Flying Circus"! Among the many new skills to be learned were various take-off and landing techniques to cope with short airstrips having dog-legs, ant-hills, humps and bumps, sandy and water-logged surfaces and tall trees at either end. Uphill, downhill and tail-wind take-offs and landings were also demonstrated together with the basic principles of mountain flying - not what your usual pilot encounters in his flying career!

In February, March and April 1976 I had responsibility for preparing a Swiss pilot for mission flying. Maurice Houriet and his delightful wife Josiane had already been accepted by MAF. Maurice had obtained all his necessary licences and had attended a flight camp. He had not yet acquired the statutory minimum hours necessary for an overseas assignment, so I had the responsibility of ensuring he gained those hours in the shortest possible time.

I managed to get the couple some rented accommodation in Ripon, and most of the flying was done in an Auster Mk V from Sherburn-in-Elmet. The airfield manager allowed us to use a small cabin as an office, but there was no furniture. I telephoned MAF headquarters in Folkestone, asking if I could purchase a small second-hand table and a couple of chairs. The reply I received from the Financial Manager was "Certainly not! We have no money! Use orange boxes!" In those days MAF was still a very small mission, and virtually all the income had to be spent on financing the limited overseas operations.

It was during their stay in Ripon that Maurice and Josiane became parents of twins: Coralie and Patrick. Josiane spoke very little English but was so calm and serene that the staff of the local hospital marvelled. They asked what relaxation classes she had attended. She had attended none! She simply rested in the knowledge that she was in the hands of her Sovereign Lord.

Some weeks later Maurice and I were in conference in my study when the telephone rang. A rather plaintive female voice said, "M'aidez! M'aidez! Feu!" ("Help me! Help me! Fire!") Whilst Maurice sped off home I telephoned the fire brigade before following him. I had to overtake the fire appliance and re-direct it as it had overshot the house. When we arrived on the scene, Josiane was sitting in the kitchen with the twins fast asleep in their carry-cots.

The fire in the lounge was soon extinguished but the damage was extensive. Having had the twins checked over by a doctor, we heard Josiane's account of the incident.

She had placed the twins in their carry-cots and positioned them on the floor of the lounge whilst she read a book in the kitchen. She became aware of a strange crackling noise. Fearing an intruder, she went outside to look through the lounge window. She saw flames. Crawling into the room she grabbed the carry-cots and dragged them to safety, having the presence of mind to close the lounge door after her. She then made the telephone call to me.

The house was rented from a local Christian farmer who usually had students in residence, but they were away on a long vacation. Many photos and posters were fixed to the walls with *Blu-Tack* and the shelves were full of books. Some nappies were drying on an airing frame standing a few feet in front of an electric fire.

Apparently one of the posters had fallen from the wall and dropped in between the fireguard and the elements, catching alight. With the sudden change of temperature, other posters followed and the nappies also caught fire. The heat was so intense that the plastic hooks on the curtains had warped and all the curtains had fallen to the floor; thus Josiane had been able to see the flames through the window. Photos curled and fell off the wall, and some of the books were scorched.

In spite of the heat and flying debris, not a speck of ash had settled upon either of the twins' carry-cots. We later discovered that the landlord had temporarily disconnected the telephone during the students' absence; yet Josiane had used it to make her "M'aidez" call. Miracle?

Maurice and Josiane came from a culture which was happy to leave sleeping children in unlocked houses. Neighbours would meet the needs of any child needing attention on behalf of the parents. On the night of the fire, Maurice had asked Josiane if she would like to accompany him on his visit to me so that she could spend some time with Elizabeth. After a moment's thought, she was constrained to remain at home. One dare not think of the consequences if she had not experienced that constraint. From whence did it come?

Josiane was to experience another traumatic event when she and Maurice eventually went to Chad. It was during the rebellion which occurred not long after my own visit.

Keith Jones had gone to N'Djamena city centre to collect mail, and Maurice was flying to Bébalem leaving Josiane and Lin Jones with the twins Patrick and Coralie and baby Fiona at the MAF compound. Suddenly machine gun bullets began coming through the walls and rockets started exploding in the courtyard.

Grabbing the children, the ladies dived under the kitchen table which afforded some protection, and there they remained for twenty four hours. They were unable to get to the radio room or the telephone to contact anyone for help.

Meanwhile, back in town, Keith heard the commotion and saw smoke rising from the direction of the MAF compound but could not make any contact with it nor reach it for the confusion on the streets. Rebels were also attacking the airport.

In all the noise and confusion, Josiane and Lin had resigned themselves never to seeing their husbands again and were praying, huddled under the table, waiting for the end.

Gradually the shooting ceased and a Red Cross ambulance was able to enter the compound, finding the occupants still alive. There was much rejoicing as Maurice and Keith were reunited with their wives and the children. What a start to three little lives - two survivors of a house fire and all survivors of an uprising! Happily all three are now married and have children of their own.

Figure 23: The MAF compound in N'Djamena where Josiane, Lin and the children were under fire for 24 hours. [Photo: courtesy of MAF]

Although serving full-time with MAF, I also had the opportunity to fly as a pilot in the Royal Air Force Volunteer Reserve. This was done in my spare time, which usually occurred on a Saturday when I was not away on a MAF deputation visit. No. 11 Air Experience Flight was based at Leeming and was tasked to give air experience to air cadets. The aircraft then in use was the faithful Chipmunk T10 which I had first flown at Celle and subsequently at the various stations where I had been the Air Cadet Liaison Officer.

A group of cadets would arrive at Leeming and be given a thorough briefing. Their officer, together with one of the ground crew, would see them safely attached to a parachute, securely strapped into the rear seat and connected up to the intercom. It was then up to me to make the cadet feel at home and at ease before giving him, or her, a twenty minute flight.

For some it was the very first time in an aircraft, so the initiation had to be gentle.

One of my cadet passengers, a young Scots lad, was obviously a bit nervous so I chatted to him over the intercom and kept him informed about all I was doing. I told him that as it was his very first flight we would simply take off and get used to being above the ground. We would find out what the world looked like and just how far we could see at a thousand feet. I told him that the flight would not last more than twenty minutes, but if he wanted to cut it shorter then we would do so. This seemed to pacify him, and he remained silent as I carried out the checks prior to the take-off and accelerated the aircraft down the runway.

No comment was forthcoming as we lifted from the ground but, as I very slowly and gently applied fifteen degrees of bank, the cadet yelled, "Will ye no stop the aerobatics!"

Needless to say this guy proved to be a bit of a challenge, but I eventually managed to get him to 'follow me through' on the controls until, towards the end of the flight, he did some banking himself. He had a huge grin on his face as he walked away from the aircraft - another satisfied customer.

Some cadets were at the other end of the experience scale, having flown many times before. With these one could carry out aerobatics as single manoeuvres and even get them to have a go themselves. I found the flying stimulating and satisfying. It kept my own flying up to scratch and kept me in touch with military procedures and disciplines, some of which I was able to introduce into MAF. I flew a total of 145 hours with No. 11 Air Experience Flight and enjoyed every minute.

Although essentially a civilian, I was subject to Air Force law, discipline and procedures as soon as I donned the uniform. This meant an annual check flight with the Examining Wing of the Central Flying School. Thus I found myself on the other side of the fence, with me the examinee and a young regular officer, Flight Lieutenant Jonathan, as my examiner.

As soon as the flight had finished he asked, "What was my examining technique like? Was it okay?"

I considered that very gracious of him and was quick to re-assure him that it was of the highest standard. I then asked him, "Did I pass?"

With a cheeky grin he said, "Just about. Not bad for a civilian!"

Occasionally I was asked to visit the MAF teams overseas with three objectives in view: first, to update my own knowledge of the operations, in order that my presentations would be firsthand and current; second, to carry out such flying and flight safety audits as necessary which included standardisation flights with some of the pilots; third, to get alongside the staff and their families in a more pastoral role. Sometimes I had the huge privilege of giving Bible ministry to a staff conference arranged for the MAF team in Kenya or in Tanzania.

Figure 24: The congregation assembling at Babaiyou in Tanzania. Some will have walked for 4 hours. Note the Pastor's house in the background.

I only had one visit to Ethiopia and Chad, but several to Kenya and Tanzania with Elizabeth occasionally accompanying me. Our nine-year-old son, Christopher, also visited East Africa with us on one occasion - a memory still very precious to him and invaluable to his character development. I only wish all children could have the same opportunity of experiencing another culture firsthand.

The visits overseas taught me some valuable lessons about myself, my Christian brothers and sisters in other cultures, and the wonderful God who we together serve. It also had its lighter moments! On one occasion a colleague of mine landed at a remote airstrip in Tanzania delivering an assortment of goods to the resident mission team (including a motor bike!) but, as he was preparing for take-off, he noticed the windsock was missing. It had certainly been in position when he landed. Then he noticed a little group of giggling local women. One of them was wearing it as a dress!

When in Chad, I invariably flew with my colleague Ernie Addicott, a very experienced MAF pilot who was a Cambridge graduate in Aeronautical Engineering and spoke French fluently. He knew just about everybody in Chad and just about everybody in Chad seemed to know him! Wherever we went he was warmly greeted by missionaries, airport officials, government representatives, air traffic controllers, refuelling staff and even rebels! On one occasion we had been warned by a government official that rebels could be in possession of hand-held anti-aircraft missiles. We were advised to fly as high as we could and spiral down rapidly over our destination. This we did. On landing we were greeted warmly by rebels!

"Why do you fly so high these days?" they asked.

"Because the government says you might shoot at us," Ernie replied.

The rebels roared with laughter. "We would never shoot at *le MAF!* " they exclaimed.

*Figure 25: Landing at a MAF airstrip typical of those
encountered in Africa.*

At another remote village we were greeted by the Chadian pastor, who invited us to lunch. This meant about three hours off our schedule! We could hear rebel gunfire in the surrounding hills as we walked away from the airstrip into the village. We passed his little church which sported many bullet holes.

"Yes," he said, "we have much rebel activity in this area. Just a few nights ago I was in bed with my family when I saw the beam of a torch being directed onto my little transistor radio (the only western possession he had!) and I heard a subdued voice say, 'Let's go get it and see what else they have.' Then another voice said, 'No! He's a poor man. Leave it.' My wife and I pray for the rebels every day, and last Sunday three came to the service. We thought they were spying on us, but they came to know the Saviour! That made over a hundred souls saved this year."

I had the privilege of meeting another Chadian pastor - Jean Ratou - who was blind, yet he carried out all his pastoral duties with his Braille Bible and study books, a Braille typewriter and a motorcycle! One of his young helpers rode pillion and directed him! Sadly this brave man was later killed in crossfire during a rebel attack on his village. My last memory of him was of him standing halfway up the airstrip with his faithful *pillion navigator* waving us goodbye as we took off for our next destination.

At that time the Chadian church was beginning to recover from dreadful persecution. I met some of the widows of pastors who had been martyred in front of their families and congregations because they refused to renounce their faith in Christ.

I had the honour of meeting a man named Joel. He had been a medical dispenser in Hyloulou, a remote clinic in the north of Chad. Rebels had raided his dispensary and stolen all the stores, taking Joel with them. He was made to treat their wounded and even perform operations! Joel was simply trained to dispense medicine and drugs as prescribed, not to do the work of a doctor. His tools were primitive to say the least. He was constantly threatened with death if he did not become a Muslim, but he refused, pointing out that his death would mean no doctor for the rebels! On one occasion he was ordered to remove a bullet from a rebel soldier's brain. He laid out his primitive instruments, offered his open hands to God's service and prayed. The bullet was removed successfully and the rebel survived.

Joel loved the rebels for Christ and prayed for them. He saved many lives. Unfortunately he contracted Malaria, becoming so ill and weak that he became dysfunctional. He expected to be put to death as had happened to another dispenser under similar circumstances. Instead his captors lifted him into a vehicle and drove him many miles to a government hospital.

As staff came running out, the rebels placed Joel on the ground and beat a hasty retreat shouting, "Look after him! He is our *Capitaine docteur!*"

The rebels thought so highly of him that they had not only spared his life and risked their own capture but had given him an honorary rank in their army!

Joel gradually recovered and eventually was transferred to the mission hospital at Maiduguri in Nigeria. Ernie, Keith Jones and I flew the hundred and fifty miles from Chad's capital, Ndjamena, in the hope that we might bring him back to his wife and children. Before visiting him in the hospital we were given a meal and it transpired that our host was a cousin of the Nigerian President. I was able to inform him that I had flown with another of the President's cousins when he was undergoing instructor training at the Central Flying School!

Although Joel was in good spirits, his arms and legs were desperately thin and he was too weak to travel, but we enjoyed fellowship and prayer with him before taking our leave. We were able to take a few things back to his wife. Although Joel eventually returned home, he later died as a result of his malnutrition and captivity. What a soldier of Christ!

It was at this time that MAF pilots were required to wear protective helmets. Ernie, Keith and I were already fitted out, and our new millinery was causing much hilarity and comment from the missionaries we visited. Word had obviously got around! When we landed at the American mission station at Doba, we were greeted by the whole Sanders family wearing helmets of various descriptions! And what a family! If anyone had a good reason for not being on a remote mission station in Africa, this lot had. One of their four children, Brad, was paraplegic, confined to bed or a wheelchair. His distorted but smiling face was half hidden by an enormous 'helmet' - a saucepan - as he was wheeled out to greet us! This family was an outstanding example of God's grace, compassion and enabling.

Their house had been self-built, incorporating everything necessary for their disabled lad including bed and toilet hoists. With the help of a modified typewriter operated by a finger pad fixed to his head, the boy was undergoing an American educational course by mail. In fact we had his next assignment of tutorial books on board. It was a blessing just to be in their company. It was the type of family that had indeed made a home out of a tent and was giving a ministry to the local people that was deeply appreciated and blessed of God.

Another mission station at Abéche was reached from N'djamena by flying over very featureless desert for about three hours on an easterly heading. The airstrip was marked with animal bones bleached in the sun. The mission belonged to the World Evangelisation Crusade staffed by three ladies responsible for an orphanage. Virtually all their stores came in via the regular flights of MAF. Imagine the consternation among all mission groups when a civil war resulted in MAF being ejected from the country, leaving many mission stations, including the orphanage, without support and without a means of emergency evacuation! Many other missions, in addition to MAF, had to leave Chad.

Years later, when the situation became calmer and MAF was able to return, we wondered what we would find at Abéche. Due to the war the orphanage had grown in numbers, but there were the three faithful female soldiers of Christ still in position and testifying to the protection, provision and presence of the living God in spite of all the afflictions and difficulties they had experienced.

Although I had spent some time overseas with the Royal Air Force, my service with Mission Aviation Fellowship in Africa showed me, close up, something of the poverty and daily hardship experienced by these people. I came back from each visit a changed man.

The affluent West owns and consumes seventy percent of the world's resources. Look at the waste! Look at the reaction when there is a brief power cut or when stand pipes have to be erected for a day or two in the streets due to a water mains problem. Why should we have the audacity to grumble about waiting an hour, or even two, to see a doctor when some invalids in Africa have to walk three hundred miles to visit a clinic?

I have experienced something of the emotions known to other mission staff on returning to their homes in the West and seeing the shelves of a supermarket. One weeps at the abundance which is so much taken for granted by our society. How generous is our giving to those mission organisations and relief agencies seeking to bring the basic necessities of life to such needy people as those in parts of Africa and other under-developed countries?

If we cannot physically go and help, and if we cannot spare much cash to support those who do, at least let us be truly thankful for all we receive in terms of water, food and medical care, rather than wasting it or grumbling about it!

During my nineteen years in Mission Aviation Fellowship, I served as Deputation Secretary, responsible for making MAF better known around the UK; as a training officer responsible for assessing pilot candidates and assisting in their pre-overseas training; and latterly as the Candidate Secretary responsible for all candidates and their families coming into MAF. The latter work brought me into a close relationship not only with individuals but also with their sending churches.

Thus my travels continued extensively, including visits to the Irish Republic, the Channel Islands, France, Sweden, Denmark, Norway, Holland, Switzerland and Germany. Sometimes the visit would be to a church supporting an MAF family; sometimes to present the work of MAF together with Bible ministry at various churches, exhibitions and conferences including those at Filey and Luzern. I also took the display to RAF Lossiemouth for a Battle of Britain weekend and to the annual air show at Fairford.

During one visit to Bangor in Northern Ireland I was asked to speak at an open-air meeting on the sea front. All went well until the PA system failed. A technician rushed up and started checking the various connections. He was standing close to the microphone when he discovered the cause. His findings were broadcast for all to hear: "No problem! The speaker had a loose screw!"

It was a particular delight to visit the main army base at Rheindahlen in Germany where sponsored parachute jumps had been organised to raise funds for a modified Land Rover to be presented to MAF. The senior chaplain who instigated all this was John Murray - one of the first to join the Christian Union at the Purley County Grammar School as a boy in the second form. He was highly esteemed and loved by all ranks and had a wonderful ministry which continued after he left the army as a Lieutenant Colonel in the Chaplains' Branch. Subsequently John became the Minister at Eastbourne Baptist Church and was active even through his terminal illness - a soldier of Christ right to the end of his life. It is a privilege to have been his friend.

My itinerant ministry led to an increasing involvement with pastoral care and counselling, not only for individuals contemplating service with MAF but also churches experiencing difficulties. I was the sympathetic ear available to church leaders who were ready to share their concerns confidentially with someone completely independent of their situation.

As a result of these experiences, and because of promptings from some friends and colleagues, I eventually left MAF and took up the post of Pastor at a small free church in Dorset. Sadly, after only sixteen months of ministry, I suffered clinical depression due to a deficiency of a chemical in the brain. Although my doctor assured me of a full recovery, he warned me it would take a couple of years. It actually took an extra six months, by which time Elizabeth and I had decided to take premature retirement and move back to Ripon. Thus I retired at the age of sixty – or so I thought!

Those were the darkest days in my whole life. It is impossible to explain how one feels - it has to be experienced. The first sign was a lack of concentration. I would read a page of a book and simply not register anything. My mind was in turmoil and my nights frequently sleepless or greatly disturbed. I felt very emotional, broken in spirit and defeated. Every task, even the simplest, was a mountain to climb. Fear (of nothing in particular) and the feeling of being totally out of control predominated. I found some relief in walking and doing a practical job about the house, but generally I was tired out and felt the weight of the world upon my shoulders with a sense of hopelessness and morbidity.

I could not pray and found the reading of my Bible as difficult as any other reading. In the end I gave up both, and thoughts of suicide began to invade my soul.

One afternoon Elizabeth had to go shopping in Poole, and she asked if I wished to go with her. I declined, with the express purpose of fading out of this life. She was on her way to the car when a compelling constraint came upon me.

"Hang on a minute. I'll come too," I said.

The constraint I experienced was similar to that which I had found on many other occasions in my life, some of which I have already mentioned.

Could it have been the same constraining force experienced by my father in his fox-hole?

In spite of my state of mind, there was one phrase that continually shone as a dim and distant light in my dark wilderness: "God is." Somehow I found myself still believing in the existence of God. The other factor which reached down into my abyss was "Remember what the Lord has done." I was faced with the uncompromising evidence of God revealing Himself not only to me as a boy but also to Elizabeth and, in turn, to all my children. Each was experiencing an ongoing new life which was evident in their everyday lives and relationships. I also had the evidence of what God had done at my school and in the Royal Air Force in bringing so many people "out of darkness into His marvellous light".

As the treatment took hold and I saw a new future back in Ripon, my condition slowly improved, especially when our house in Dorset was sold and the purchase of our new home in Ripon was finalised.

I look back in praise and thanksgiving for God's loving and gentle dealings with me in bringing me through that particular cloud. Whilst I was helpless and virtually estranged to Him, He was still there protecting and providing for me with the love and grace that only He can give.

I also thank God for giving me such a wonderful wife. Elizabeth must have suffered much torment and turmoil in her own heart as she saw the husband of her youth become withdrawn, unloving, non-communicative and morose. She had already had to see me, back in Air Force days, lying silently in a hospital bed with tubes protruding from various parts of my anatomy and later to see me suffering from Infective Hepatitis in Catterick Military Hospital for five weeks.

Often I said things on the spur of the moment, in a fit of anger, that I did not really mean. Elizabeth took it all and somehow managed to love me in spite of the hurt it must have caused. I cannot thank her enough for her sacrificial love, loyalty, faithfulness and understanding over all our married life but especially during those particularly difficult years.

Looking back on those days I am reminded of instrument flying. On dark nights, in cloud, with turbulence buffeting the aircraft, a pilot cannot fly by 'the seat of his pants' – that is, by his feelings and sensations; if he does, he is doomed. The only answer is for him to fix his eyes on his instruments and believe unfalteringly in what they are telling him. Often his feelings and sensations will be contrary to what he sees, but he must override those false indications and trust exclusively in his instruments. He has to rely upon a source of information outside himself.

This is true faith. Not feelings but facts. Not me and my opinions, but God and His Word. Recovering from my darkness was like descending through cloud at night, then breaking clear to see the lights of the runway dead ahead. Among all the lines of lights which outline a runway and lead to its threshold are two which form the shape of a cross - a fitting sight for one coming "out of darkness into His marvellous light" as they reminded me every time I saw them of the cost of my salvation and deliverance.

In that great eleventh chapter on faith recorded by the writer to the Hebrews, faith is defined as "...the substance of things hoped for, the evidence of things not seen..."

A pilot exercises faith in his instruments because he cannot see visually, but what he is doing is the substance of what he knows as fact; it is the evidence that there surely is a runway ahead, albeit at present unseen.

What faith do you have? A blind faith? A faith that is based upon your own opinions and feelings? Is it mere belief in a man-made philosophy or a set of rituals that must be observed? Or is your faith set on that which is outside yourself, trusting in the Person who died on that cross for you in AD33 and rose again three days later?

What you or I believe can make no difference to the facts as they are. When we trust ourselves to the beliefs we hold, then we find out whether or not they are facts! I never had to bail out or eject so I do not know what it is to trust myself to a parachute, but I know many who have done so, including my daughter and eldest granddaughter who did a sponsored jump on behalf of the *Caring for Life* charity working in Leeds. They believed in their instructor, believed in their parachute and believed the testimony of many others who had made similar successful jumps, but until they launched themselves out of the aircraft they did not *trust*. There is a world of difference between believing and trusting!

So many people today are rather like a parachutist who wants to trust his parachute but prefers to keep one hand on the aircraft just in case the 'chute does not work! That is not trust. That is not faith. One has to abandon the aircraft in order that the conditions are fulfilled for the parachute to open. It means no turning back. This is what becoming a Christian is about: commitment to Christ to the point that, should He fail, then one is totally lost. The wonderful thing is that, unlike a parachute, He never fails.

This book is an autobiography, but I would prefer my readers to consider it as a testimony of what the Sovereign Lord can do with, through and in spite of a human being who was a failure from the first and a fickle, faithless follower of Christ for most of his life.

Since coming to know Him as a reality I have sought to honour Him but have failed miserably. Yet, He continues to love me, to use me in His service and even occasionally to make me a blessing to others. In spite of all my failings, sin and stupidity, He has been active in my life and made it purposeful and fulfilled. I look back upon my years on this earth as I looked back on the clouds through which I had frequently climbed, bringing me into a new world of glorious blue sky, unmolested by clouds and dominated by the brilliance of the sun.

Are you looking up fearfully at clouds which are imposing, threatening and demoralising? Are you in those dark and turbulent clouds, experiencing confusion, darkness, panic and doubt? Do not trust your feelings. Do not trust yourself. Do not even trust the opinions of others. Trust only in the One who has been this earthly way and knows what it is to be despised, forsaken, misrepresented, misinterpreted, homeless, friendless, beaten up and alone – even crucified. But three days later...!

If Christ is truly risen from the dead, then He is alive now and making Himself known to any who seek Him. He is even active in our lives prior to our coming to know Him, because, if the truth be known, He seeks us rather than us seeking Him! He was active in my father's life well before Dad became a Christian. Jesus was there with him in that fox-hole in France. Jesus was there in that cockpit at Middleton-St-George. Jesus was there at the 'chop board' in Kirton Lindsey. Jesus has been, and is, working in your own life - perhaps even through reading these pages. Are you struggling with your clouds, relying on your own feelings and opinions, or do you trust in Christ and His Word?

"Trust in the Lord with all your heart and lean not on your own understanding. In all your ways acknowledge Him and He will direct your paths."

From the Publisher

Titles in the **True Stories** series:

1.	From One King to Another	*Mark Jeffery*
2.	Mountains of Joy, Valleys of Hope	*Veronica Martindale*
3.	One-way Ticket to Finland	*Carol Westerlund*
4.	Jesus Rocks – No Turning Back	*Pontus Back*
5.	Ducks Quack, Eagles Fly	*Diana Jeffery*
6.	The Real Deal	*Olanike Adebayo*
7.	The Sound of Caring	*Batya Fulcher*
8.	Losing Tom – Finding Grace	*Jackie Slough*
9.	Diamonds in the Darkness	*Pat Nickson*
10.	Building Hope	*Bryan Parr*
11.	Battling With Nazi Demons	*Werner Oder*
12.	The Little Things	*David Chapman*
11.	Running on Empty	*S. Amos*
12.	GOD and ME in THREE	*Simon Flett*
13.	Below Me, The Clouds	*Ron Collard*

These books and more can be ordered from the publisher's web site:

www.onwardsandupwards.org